BLACK MAN, WHITE HOUSE

ALSO BY D.L. HUGHLEY

I WANT YOU TO SHUT THE F#CK UP

BLACK MAN, WHITE HOUSE

An Oral History of the Obama Years

D.L. HUGHLEY

WITH MICHAEL MALICE

WILLIAM MORROW
An Imprint of HarperCollins*Publishers*

HarperCollins books may be purchased for educational, business, or sales promotional use. For information please e-mail the Special Markets Department at SPsales@ harpercollins.com.

FIRST EDITION

Designed by William Ruoto
Frontispiece design by Rodrigo Corral Design, Inc.
Frontispiece photographs: © Getty Images (Obama); © John Parrot/Stocktrek Images/ Getty Images (clothes): © seraficus/Getty Images (frame)

Library of Congress Cataloging-in-Publication Data has been applied for.

ISBN 978-0-06-239979-3

16 17 18 19 20   RRD   10 9 8 7 6 5 4 3 2 1

CONTENTS

Prologue   Democratic National Convention,
July 27, 2004   1

1   Senator Obama, 2004–2006   5

2   Becoming the Nominee, 2007–2008   25

3   Winning the White House, 2008   49

4   The Inauguration, January 20, 2009   63

5   Senate Supermajority, 2009   83

6   Making Appointments, 2009   101

7   The Beer Summit, July 2009   119

8   Health Cares, July–October 2009   139

9   Wins and Losses, October 2009–
January 2010   159

10   The Shellacking, February–November 2010   177

11   OBL & BS, November 2010–July 2011   193

12   Ready for Romney, July 2011–May 2012   215

13   Long Hot Summer, June–September 2012   237

14   Winner and Still Champion, September–
      December 2012   273

15   Second Chances, January–December 2013   293

16   Packing the Bags, 2014–2016   311

      Index   325

BLACK MAN, WHITE HOUSE

DEMOCRATIC NATIONAL CONVENTION, JULY 27, 2004

PRESIDENT BILL CLINTON: *Who the heck is this nigger?* That's the thought that kept going through my head. I'm sitting there, watching Barack Obama give his keynote speech, and I'm wondering who the heck is he? Where did he come from?

HILLARY RODHAM CLINTON: It was an honor watching that speech. It was like the culmination of Martin Luther King's dream, which so inspired me as a young girl and throughout my life, and as the proud wife of our first black president.

BILL: I've had a very long career in politics. I've seen more political speeches than I can count. And as amazing as watching that speech was for those seeing it on television—and I watched it again on tape, just to be sure I wasn't being crazy—it was that much more impressive live. It was almost as good as one of my own speeches. That's how good it was.

HILLARY: First. We were the first. Remember that. *First.*

BILL: Yes, the South is still very clearly informed by racism, both past and present. Little Rock, site of the legendary battle over desegregation, is in Arkansas. Orval Faubus was our governor only a decade before me. But I've been around black people all my life. Being the fat son of a single mother didn't exactly catapult me into the ranks of the plantation class. I've always felt more comfortable around what we called "colored" people when I was a kid. *They* were the ones who treated me fairly and equally.

HILLARY: Yeah, me too.

BILL: At the same time, I was always very consciously aware that the color of my skin allowed me certain opportunities that my friends would never have. And I felt that that was wrong. It was unfair and it was un-American. So as I went to college and then to law school, and later when I became governor and president, those inequities were always something that I worked hard to change.

HILLARY: I also did that, worked hard to change those things. I agree.

BILL: Political conventions are opportunities for the two major parties to demonstrate who they are and what they stand for. They show clearly who they consider to be important in America. Is it the wealthy CEO who simply wants more—or is it the fair-minded businessman who is comfortable making a healthy profit while paying his workers a fair wage? Nowhere is the difference between the two parties as stark as when it comes to race. Democrats have black speakers who have *earned* their speaking slots. Jesse Jackson had a few hundred delegates going into the 1984 convention and over a thousand in 1988. When Republicans have a black speaker, most of the time they are only there because of the color of their skin. It's just one congressman out of a few hundred, with nothing noteworthy except that he looks a little darker than John Boehner.

HILLARY: I was just saying the exact same thing the other day, only more so.

BILL: But let's be frank: Most of these speeches are *interesting,* but they are not really *captivating.* There's a little bit of preaching to the choir. Yet Barack Obama's speech was different. There was an enormous amount of hype leading up to it. He was being touted as a rising star of the party, even though he hadn't even been elected to the Senate yet. But it really was captivating. He hypnotized that crowd like nothing I had ever seen. My jaw was on the floor. Where did he come from? How did I not know of this amazing, singularly talented young man who would one day—I thought—follow Hillary into the White House?

HILLARY: F-o-l-l-o-w. *Follow.*

MICHELLE OBAMA: You know, I was more nervous than Barack was that night. That's not to say that he was totally calm—he wasn't, of course—but there were many times that I'd seen him more on edge. When Sasha and Malia were being born; of course, everyone's excited during those moments. Or when he spoke to my parents about us getting married. But Barack knew that keynote speech inside and out. He wrote it himself, in his own words. He was going to be introducing himself to America. Rather than nerve-racking I think he thought of it as exciting.

JOHN KERRY: I had a smile from ear to ear. I knew that I had made the right choice for keynote speaker as Barack Obama went up there, hitting line after line. It was like a baseball player just knocking out one home run after another. Maybe if I made some other choices as well as that one, then I would have been elected president. Who knows? I do hope that people remember my campaign for introducing Obama to America—and forget that I introduced John Edwards to them. I guess that's what he meant by the audacity of hope, right? Ha, ha.

JOHN EDWARDS: I don't know what everyone is so bothered about. It's not like I forced my baby momma to get an abortion.

RAHM EMANUEL: How would I rate his speech? Come on, it was a total slam dunk. That was an A+ performance.

MITCH McCONNELL: In terms of substance, I'd give it a C, C-. In terms of delivery, it was objectively an A all across the board, both in terms of Obama personally and in terms of the Democratic ticket. And politics is far more about delivery than substance. That speech made us all very nervous, because I knew he was firing up the Democratic base.

KERRY: No presidential candidate wants to be overshadowed by some other convention speaker, but everyone remembers Obama's speech and unfortunately no one really remembers mine. So he gets his A, his gold star. He earned it fair and square—as I'm reminded every single day when I go to work as his secretary of state. Literally, I remember it every day.

VICE PRESIDENT DICK CHENEY: Didn't watch it. If I wanted to hear liberal claptrap, I'd phone up Romney.

HILLARY: Eh, I'd give it a B. I've heard better. I mean, come on, it wasn't exactly the Emancipation Proclamation. It's, like, what else you got?

BILL: I might not have known who that nigger was—but I knew that he sure had something.

1

SENATOR OBAMA, 2004–2006

MICHELLE OBAMA: Getting Barack elected to the Senate was hardly a foregone conclusion. I don't know that he could have gotten elected in another state, but Illinois had a couple of things in our favor. First, it's very blue. That meant that, all things being equal, the Democratic candidate began with an advantage. Second, Carol Moseley Braun had become the first African American woman ever elected to the United States Senate. That proved that Illinois was ready to vote in another black candidate.

DAVID AXELROD: Ready and willing are very different things in politics. Just because Carol had been elected once didn't mean that Barack would be. Remember, she was also defeated for reelection. Illinois might be a blue state, but it still had a history of sometimes electing Republicans to the Senate. Most importantly, however, the fact that it was so blue meant that there was a huge primary on the Democratic side. It actually ended up being the most expensive Senate primary in history.

MICHELLE: All eyes were on Carol to see if she was going to run again against Senator Peter Fitzgerald, who had beaten her in 1998.

CAROL MOSELEY BRAUN: I've always thought that you should set your sights high and aim big. If I didn't do that, I would never have considered myself electable to the Senate as a woman—and, especially, as a woman of color. So I did consider running again. I knew it would be a tough fight, since the voters had already voted against me. Psychologically, that would have made it easy for them to vote against me again. So I thought, *You know what, Carol? If you're going to run and lose, why not run and lose for the highest office?* So I decided to run for the White House instead. And I *did* run. And I *did* lose. And I don't regret it for a minute!

MICHELLE: Barack tossed his hat into the ring as soon as Carol declined to run. And let me tell you, it was a very crowded ring. There were six other people running.

AXELROD: When there are that many candidates, it makes it that much harder to make your voice heard. It adds a sense of randomness that made me nervous as the campaign manager.

MICHELLE: I wasn't nervous. I knew that Barack had it in him. The more people got to hear him talk, the more they learned about him, the more they would end up falling in love with him. Trust me, I am speaking from personal experience here!

AXELROD: It became a huge deal when Senator Fitzgerald chose not to run for a second term. There went the power of incumbency, which is a major advantage for a race like this.

PETER FITZGERALD: Why didn't I choose to run for reelection? That's like asking why people don't go to the dentist during their vacation. When you're in the Senate, you have enormous pressure to vote with your party. That's just how the system works. There were many issues on which I butted heads with the Republican leadership. I was facing some competition in the primary, then *more* strong competition in the general, very strong. Why would I want to do that to my family? For six more years of headaches and egos? Thanks, but no thanks.

AXELROD: One by one, all the newspapers began endorsing us. Both the *Chicago Sun-Times* AND the *Tribune*. There were seven Democratic candidates, *quality* candidates. You'd think statistically they'd be more spread out. But no, they all sided with us. I'd never seen anything like it.

> MARCH 16, 2004: BARACK OBAMA WINS THE
> DEMOCRATIC SENATE PRIMARY WITH OVER 50% OF THE
> VOTE.

MICHELLE: You have a vote split seven ways, you'd expect someone to win with maybe 30 percent, something like that. No. We got as many votes as all the other candidates put together, candidates who put a lot of money into their races. Their own money, too.

AXELROD: That was one hurdle we'd overcome, and it was a big one. But the Republicans ended up nominating Jack Ryan, and I knew he wouldn't be a pushover. For one thing, he had deep pockets.

MICHELLE: But he also had skeletons, apparently. He'd been married to Jeri Ryan from *Star Trek: Voyager*. I think she played the Borg girl or something, I never watched the show. My husband is the nerd of the relationship.

AXELROD: The newspapers were suing for Ryan's divorce records to be released, and the next thing we knew they were all over the place.

JACK RYAN: It was Obama's people and their dirty tricks who made this happen. Neither Jeri nor I wanted them released, and they were anyway. How crazy is that? But that's Chicago politics for you.

MICHELLE: We did not want those records released. Absolutely not. Barack specifically and publicly said that they shouldn't be a campaign issue. We were the parents to two young girls, and we appreciated trying to have some measure of family privacy.

AXELROD: Well, the stuff that was in there was pretty bad. Jeri said he wanted her to come with him to sex clubs, things like that. I've heard of "swing voters," but I don't think that's the kind of swinging they're talking about.

PRESIDENT BILL CLINTON: Asking your wife to go to a sex club with you is a bit extreme.

JOHN EDWARDS: It's basically akin to asking her for a threesome.

BILL: A threesome is easy. She's there so she knows what's going on and everyone is a consenting adult. It's like asking her for anal.

EDWARDS: It's not hard to ask your wife for anal. She's your wife! Everything goes within the confines of the marriage bedroom. It's a sacred relationship. That's why you can't bring another party into the mix.

BILL: Mix is right. You can't ask for anal when your wife's ass looks like a cement mixer.

EDWARDS: Oh please, asking for a threesome is way harder.

BILL: Anal is harder.

EDWARDS: Threesome.

BILL: Anal!

EDWARDS: Threesome!

BILL: Fuck, now I'm all horny.

RYAN: I had to withdraw. That was it.

AXELROD: The Republicans didn't have a backup candidate. It was July of 2004, election was in November, and there was no Plan B.

EDWARDS: And there never is, not when you really need it. Story of my life! Which was also the story of my wife's death.

AXELROD: Word had it that they even asked Mike Ditka to run.

MIKE DITKA: I'd rather go to a sex club with Jack Ryan. At least there I'd only be fucked by one dude instead of ninety-nine senators.

MICHELLE: So instead, for reasons that I couldn't really fathom, the Republicans nominated Alan Keyes.

AXELROD: If I rubbed a lamp and a genie came out and granted me three wishes, and I combined all three to wish for a candidate that would be easy to defeat, even that candidate wouldn't be as easy to defeat as Alan Keyes. His biggest claim to fame was being the last

Republican presidential candidate standing in 2000—which served to make George W. Bush seem downright normal.

MICHELLE: Mr. Keyes wasn't just a conservative Republican. He was really a far-right fringe member of the Republican Party. He made Rush Limbaugh look like Lenin. Not only that, but he had never even lived in Illinois!

AXELROD: Not since Moses parted the Red Sea had a path opened forward for someone so neatly and so cleanly as Barack Obama's path to the Senate.

ALAN KEYES: It was God who parted the Red Sea for Moses. But I tell you that it was Satan who was the one paving the way for Barack Obama. He was born in Kenya, but his communist soul could only have been forged in hell.

AXELROD: Not only were we destroying Keyes on the issues, but Keyes kept saying crazy things to boot.

MICHELLE: Communism? When was the last time you heard a communist or even a typical Democrat speak highly of Ronald Reagan, which Barack did publicly and frequently?

KEYES: Like it says in the Bible, even the devil can quote scripture when it suits his purpose.

MICHELLE: That's actually a Shakespeare quote. But Mr. Keyes had a habit of getting things . . . shall we say, *confused*.

VICE PRESIDENT DICK CHENEY: The man's a fucking asshole, and that's even by my party's standards.

AXELROD: Keyes was very outspoken in his opposition to homosexuality. Not only in the abstract, but personally so.

MICHELLE: He specifically condemned Dick Cheney's lesbian daughter, Mary, by name. I was absolutely horrified. That to me was the lowest point in the Senate campaign. What did she have to do with anything?

KEYES: I was asked a question by an interviewer. What was I supposed to say? If it's wrong in principle, it's wrong when an individual practices it—no matter who that individual is. Unlike Barack Obama, I practice what I preach.

CHENEY: Alan Keyes disowned his daughter when she came out as a dyke. What kind of father is that? He should have been shouting from the rooftops: "I love my dyke daughter! I am proud of her and want her to be happy." That's what I did. When I was a kid, women came together to play softball. Now they want to play house. That's not my business. Now oil, that's my business. Times change, and we have to change with them.

MARY CHENEY: I am certain of three things: One, that my father—*both* my parents—loves me fully, completely and unconditionally. Two, that he was uncomfortable with my being a lesbian but he got used to it. And three, that he has no idea how lesbians have sex. None.

CHENEY: They use those vibration rods, right? I mean, something's gotta be going in *somewhere*. Help me out here.

MARY: Frankly, I'd expect an ambassador—as Mr. Keyes had been in the Reagan administration—to have been a bit more *diplomatic*.

MICHELLE: Look, I understand the case against gay marriage. It's not hard to understand the case. If you view marriage as some traditional union between one man and one woman, and you view homosexuality as a sin, it's not going to make sense to you. But to turn your back on your own child in the name of Christianity? If his daughter chose to be gay, as he seems to believe, what did that say about the way he raised her? Shouldn't *he* feel guilt, instead of trying to get her to feel shame?

AXELROD: Fortunately the voters of Illinois—even the rural ones who traditionally vote very Republican—were not buying what Alan Keyes was selling.

MICHELLE: As November 2004 drew closer and closer, Barack's lead grew wider and wider. Mr. Keyes grew increasingly desperate with his attacks and people were just tuning him out and turning away.

KEYES: I was free to speak my mind on the issues and on this dangerous degenerate candidate that is Barack Hussein Obama.

AXELROD: One man's freedom is another man's freak show, let me put it that way.

MICHELLE: It doesn't always happen this way, and sometimes it's easy to forget, but it's my belief that given enough time and enough information, a majority of the American public will choose hope over hate. It has to be my belief, by definition, if I uphold hope as the basis of my politics. And week after week, we saw that with the growing repudiation of Alan Keyes in the Illinois polls.

KEYES: Are we supposed to believe that it was just a coincidence that he had the same name as Saddam?

MICHELLE: Given that Barack was born before Saddam Hussein was in power, and given that he was named after his father—Barack Hussein Obama Sr.—yes, it was a coincidence. That's pretty much the definition of a coincidence.

KEYES: I had my doubts about where he was born. His father was African and his mother was Caucasian, and he's born in Hawaii. But I've been to Hawaii, and they're all sort of Chinky-looking. I'm no geneticist, but something wasn't adding up.

AXELROD: We had such a lead, and we had so much money pouring in, that we started sending cash to other states and campaigning there for embattled Democratic candidates. This is also pretty much unheard of for a nonincumbent, but Obama was exploding in popularity within the party and among independents and even some Republicans.

KEYES: I'm proud to have been the first Republican to stand up to Barack Obama.

AXELROD: He was the first Republican to *lose* to Obama, and lose big. We set all sorts of records with our election night victory. It was a total blowout even by blue-state Illinois standards. I honestly think that we even got the racist vote, because Alan Keyes is African American and Obama mixed.

MICHELLE: I was just so proud of him. The state and the country were seeing what I saw. We ran a fair, decent, honest campaign based on the issues. Barack laid out his vision and people responded to it desperately. I think after 9/11 Americans were very scared. Maybe they were right to be scared. But they also wanted to not feel fear anymore.

AXELROD: This wasn't some sort of paranoia on our part. At the time, the Sears Tower was the tallest building in America—and it's in Chicago. New York beefed up security hard after the 9/11 attacks. We would logically be the next city to attack. But you can only be so scared for so long. Yes, you can be cautious, we'll always be cautious, but you can't work and go to school and come home to your family if you're on edge all the time.

MICHELLE: We saw the country rally around President Bush in 2001. But when he was reelected—barely—in November of 2004, our nation was extremely divided. What was dividing us was this war in Iraq and the ongoing conflict in Afghanistan. It was a complete mess, and everyone was increasingly coming around to Barack's view that the Iraq invasion had been a mistake and was only getting worse.

NANCY PELOSI: I think W. believed that the Iraqis would be carrying us on their shoulders like we'd just won the big game for them. And even if that were true—and we saw that it was, in fact, anything but true—that was kind of beside the point.

MICHELLE: They were constantly talking about "shock and awe." "It's going to be so great, we'll get them with shock and awe, and they won't even know what hit them!" Well, what happens the day after shock and awe? When you've leveled their capital city and killed a bunch of people? Someone was going to have to rebuild, and that someone clearly was going to have to be us, at least in part.

JOHN KERRY: Come election night, I really thought that we had it in the bag. I have to accept responsibility for the loss. I let down my team, my family, and my party. But most important, I feel as if I let down my country.

NOVEMBER 2, 2004: GEORGE W. BUSH IS REELECTED
TO A SECOND TERM. BARACK OBAMA WINS ELECTION
TO THE UNITED STATES SENATE.

HARRY REID: It was a bad night. The Democrats lost four Senate seats, and among those was minority leader Tom Daschle. It was the first time a Senate leader had lost in fifty years. So my feelings about becoming the new leader were mixed, given the circumstances. On the one hand, my good friend was out of a job. On the other hand, I got it myself! Plus the office. I even got one of those big sweepstakes checks. It didn't come with the gig, but I had them make me up one. Who was going to stop me? No one, that's who.

KERRY: It was like, how much worse can things get? Going back to the Senate after losing to really one of the worst presidents of my lifetime was tough. My fellow Democrats had believed in me. Let me tell you, there was also more than one Republican who pulled me aside to admit that the war had been a mistake and that they wished that they could've changed their vote. Barack Obama's Senate victory was one of the few bright spots of that night. He brought a sense of hope to our side.

MICHELLE: Barack gets into the Senate, and immediately he's like a rock star. The press likes to say how the Senate is one hundred huge egos and I'm sure that's true. But some of those senators weren't acting like egomaniacs but like fans. "Let me get a picture with you for my niece," that sort of thing. "It's the first time that my grandkids think I'm important!" That one made us both laugh.

HILLARY RODHAM CLINTON: Sure, he was the future of the party. The *future*. But guess what? We weren't living in the future. There weren't any flying skateboards and cars that folded into suitcases. We were living in the *present*—and the *present* of the Democratic Party was *me*.

REID: I met with all the new Democratic senators individually to establish a rapport. Senator Obama really did stand out to me; there was something about this man that I just found . . . I want to say *compelling*. I have to be very careful in how I talk about him. I got in trouble at one point for referring to his lack of Negro dialect. Look, I was born in 1939; it's hard for me to keep up with what the latest term is to refer to colored Americans with respect. For a while it was *jive* and then it was *Ebonics*.

MICHELLE: Barack's strategy as a senator was a simple one: to be a decent, honest senator who put forth a progressive message in clear, inspirational terms.

REID: *Ooga booga*, I know has always been offensive. Seriously, what do people want from me? I'm a Mormon from Nevada. We don't have many Afro-Americans here, if that term is correct. Our minorities speak Redskin and, increasingly, they speak Mexican. And since this is America, I wouldn't have it any other way—unless I offended someone, in which case I apologize.

MICHELLE: One of the first things that Barack felt was that he had a target on his back. And not just from the Republicans, that much was known. But he made it a point to be very, very careful not to step on anybody's toes.

HILLARY: That was *my* strategy when I was elected in 2000. Not to be the former First Lady, but to be the junior senator from New York. If you look at all the articles at the time—I have them in scrapbooks—

even the Republicans were praising my work ethic. So I'm real glad Senator Obama followed in my footsteps. That's all the proof I need to see that *he* looked to *me* for leadership.

REID: Senator Obama had a lot of ideas, but the Democrats were in the minority. But even if we had the majority, it wouldn't really have mattered. The Senate is very heavily based on seniority and people waiting in line. For a new senator to put forward a lot of ideas, it would really put his colleagues off—and all ninety-nine of them have one vote just the same as he did.

MICHELLE: I remember Barack coming home one night, and something just seemed a bit off. Now, my husband is not a whiner. He doesn't complain, he doesn't raise his voice. He is calm, calm, calm. You look up "grace under pressure" in the dictionary, you'll find a picture of Barack Obama. So I asked him what was the matter and he pretended that everything was OK. But I could tell that it wasn't. He felt kind of handcuffed. There was so much support for him in the country, but he wasn't in a position to deliver on that in the Senate. His rivals wanted him to trip up or to put forward a bill that they could defeat. It was like Barack had been arrested: anything he said could and *would* be used against him in the court of public opinion.

CHENEY: If he'd really been arrested, then we wouldn't be having this mess. Just a whole other mess, all over the sidewalk, like that kid down in Florida.

JEB BUSH: Will you please stop calling me a kid? I'm a senior!

REID: Broadly speaking, there are two types of politicians. There are those who get very technical, who really sort of engineer bills and get into the numbers. For the Republicans, it would be like a Paul Ryan. For our side, it would be Al Gore. I would also certainly put Hillary Clinton in that capacity, especially with all the technical groundwork she laid down with her health care plan.

HILLARY: Finally, some acknowledgment! Thank you.

REID: Then there are politicians who have a vision, lay it out, sell it, and don't necessarily get bogged down in details. More inspirational than technical. That would be where Bill Clinton excels.

HILLARY: Wait a second, hold on.

MICHELLE: Barack fits into that second category. He inspires people; that's his great strength. So I suggested that, rather than trying to beat his head against the wall and get nowhere in a Republican Senate with a Republican president, he should work on getting his message across and speak to the American people directly. He could do that by writing another book. His first book was selling extremely well, ten years after it had first come out. But *Dreams from My Father* was more of a memoir. Why not take his speech from the convention and expound on it? That way, no one could twist his words. It's all laid out there in print.

HILLARY: I wrote a book too, you know. It came out in 2003, *Living History*. I sold one million copies in the first month. *One million*. Not too shabby!

MICHELLE: So that's what Barack did. Instead of trying to write a bill, he wrote *The Audacity of Hope*. He felt that this was his opportunity to change the national conversation. One of the insights he made, one of the things that moved him, was that there were two visions of America. These visions transcended political parties. Some people felt America's best years were behind us, like we were over the hill. A mean, divided United States. You saw that in people like Richard Nixon and Newt Gingrich and many of the Southern Democrats. Even Jimmy Carter, though he got a bad rap for it, with his "malaise" speech. Then there are the smilers. Reagan, always smiling. JFK, always smiling. Even Eisenhower. It often didn't matter what they were saying. Smiles are contagious. They're infectious. Like the title says, the book was meant to bring hope back to America. By the time it was due to come out in October 2006, we sure needed some hope again.

HILLARY: You know, we already had a "man from Hope" in the White House. His name was Bill Clinton, and that was the title of our famous campaign video from 1992. Obama just lifted it from us. That's some audacity, wouldn't you say?

REID: The fall of 2006 was a very different America than November of 2004, when George W. Bush was reelected. His approval ratings had begun falling right after he was sworn in for a second term, and they kept getting worse and worse. The American people were turning against the Republicans and this of course was to the advantage of the Democrats.

LARRY KING: There was a huge sense of resurgence and rebirth in the Democratic Party at that time, two years after Obama got into the Senate. This was an opportunity for them to reevaluate who they were and move in a new direction. America was at a crossroads, and it made me recall a similar moment in 1992. That year, Ross Perot launched his presidential campaign on my show and went on to become the most successful third-party candidate since Theodore Roosevelt eighty years prior. People forget this, but at a few points Perot was actually in the lead in the polls, ahead of both the first President Bush and then governor Bill Clinton.

H. ROSS PEROT: I'd rather go to a sex club with Jack Ryan *and* Mike Ditka than actually serve as president.

KING: I thought that maybe I could make lightning strike twice. There was already a lot of buzz about having our first female president, meaning Senator Clinton. America was ready. But if we were ready for one woman, then maybe we were ready for another. So when Oprah was on my show in September of 2006, I asked her if she preferred magenta to burgundy. Then, I asked her to rank the days of the week in her order of preference. I followed that up with a quiz about *Fat Albert*—people often get Mushmouth and Dumb Donald confused, because Donald has the cap covering his face.

PEROT: You can see why I chose to announce on his particular program. Larry has a way of making senile old white men seem downright cogent.

KING: Finally I asked Oprah if she had any interest in running for the White House.

OPRAH WINFREY: I'd been asked that question before, and of course it's tremendously flattering that people think that I'd make a good president. It's really a very tough, thankless job. I always think about what it does to the president's family. They don't have a moment's peace. I didn't need the press constantly bothering Gayle . . . um, I mean, Stedman. *Stedman.* Not Gayle. Still just friends. *Stedman.*

KING: So on my show I asked Oprah about the presidency, and she said that actually she was for Obama. This was major, major news. Oprah had always been very apolitical, and I think it was the first time that she had endorsed someone for the presidency.

OPRAH: My television show was a safe space dedicated to positivity, where people—especially women—could feel free to be themselves and be vulnerable about their issues and problems. We were like an hour-long tampon commercial, that sort of environment. Because of that, I made sure that my welcome mat was open to politicians of both parties. Obviously, as a Southern black woman who lives in Chicago, it was pretty apparent that I leaned Democrat. But I tried not to make my personal political views known. That wasn't what my show was about. I wasn't like, say, Jon Stewart.

JON STEWART: And I'm no Oprah, unfortunately. Because that seems like it would be really cool, to wake up every day and be, like, "Holy shit, I'm Oprah fucking Winfrey!" Then you have to wonder if you're, like, going to give out cars to people that day or whatever.

OPRAH: At the same time, I *was* a Southern black woman who lived in Chicago and who leaned Democrat. I knew the Obamas and I found them to be very impressive. This was a once-in-a-lifetime opportunity for the black community and for America as a whole. As much as it would have meant for young black kids to see a black president, it would have meant just as much for white America to demonstrate that we were overcoming racism together.

BILL RICHARDSON: There's other options than black and white, you know. Mexicans, for example. We're not like that swirl ice cream you get from the truck, we are our own thing with our own racial identity and heritage. Just wanted to point that out!

> **SEPTEMBER 25, 2006: OPRAH WINFREY ENDORSES BARACK OBAMA.**

KEYES: Upon further reflection, maybe Obama's from Haiti. Some place like that. So many things worked for him in the right way that it could only have been caused by voodoo. Come on, now *Oprah's* endorsing him?

OPRAH: I was in a unique position. I was a woman of color who suburban white women and rural white women viewed as one of their own. It meant something coming from me. It wasn't as if Jesse Jackson were endorsing him.

HILLARY: Well, it's clear that modesty isn't what kept her from running.

MICHELLE: We were on Oprah's show only a couple of weeks later, and once again she reiterated that she wanted Barack to run for president. Not at some point in the future, but for 2008. It was a very scary proposition.

OPRAH: As is saying no to Oprah.

MICHELLE: *The Audacity of Hope* just went huge. *Huge* sales. The lines were around the block whenever Barack went to sign books; the excitement was like for Drake. Everyone kept telling him the same thing: "I hope you run for president. We need you to run."

HILLARY: That's demonstrably false. They didn't "need" him to run. We already had a great candidate who knew where all the rooms in the White House were.

PRESIDENT GEORGE W. BUSH: Heck, that's nothing. If you get me drunk, I can tell you all the rooms where her husband stuck things up different people. *If* you get me drunk.

HILLARY: I even wrote a book about the White House! *An Invitation to the White House* it was called. That one *also* sold very well.

MICHELLE: The message we were getting wasn't that he should run *someday*. They wanted him to run *now*. These were partisan Democrats speaking. Barack was really starting to feel the pressure. He was genuinely torn.

HILLARY: Oh, poor thing! Well, some people are used to handling hard choices and some people aren't. And some of us even wrote the book on hard choices, like the title to my recent memoir.

MICHELLE: Barack felt that it was Senator Clinton's turn to get the nomination. He liked her and admired her. He didn't want to go down in history as possibly being the man who kept the first woman from the presidency.

OPRAH: I didn't think that he had that option, to wait. He was the right man in a wrong time. Everyone in America was realizing that we were on a desperately wrong track.

MICHELLE: I pointed out that it wasn't personal, that Hillary was dead wrong about the major issue of our time: the war. So let's have a campaign of ideas. If it's her turn, then she should be able to earn it. If she couldn't beat you, I told Barack, then how was she going to beat the enormous resources of the Republican Party?

HILLARY: Same way we beat them in the 1990s is how.

MICHELLE: I'll never forget this. Barack said that she was President Clinton's wife, and President Clinton showed the Democratic Party that we could win. He showed America that we could govern successfully as progressives and achieve goals that the Republicans talked about but never did: Balanced budgets. Peace across the globe. An America that was admired by our allies and respected by our enemies.

HILLARY: I remember those days pretty well. That's because I was there.

MICHELLE: So I said to him, I agree with everything that you're saying. And it *is* important that Hillary was President Clinton's wife, that she rewrote the role of the First Lady and remade it into a tough, modern political force. But I'm *your* wife, I said, and *I* am giving you permission to run against her.

HILLARY: You know, I've never really cared for Mrs. Obama.

2

BECOMING THE NOMINEE, 2007–2008

MICHELLE OBAMA: We knew that we were going up against the Washington establishment. The Clintons had many, many friends in the Democratic Party—in *both* parties—as well as in Washington and throughout the nation. Hollywood, Wall Street, you name it: They knew people at the very top who were going to be supporting them.

DAVID AXELROD: I signed on to be the campaign manager alongside my business partner David Plouffe. We'd both worked on the Obama Senate campaign. When we got the call in the very beginning of 2007, we had just finished getting Deval Patrick elected governor of Massachusetts in 2006. I thought we were going to have some time off. Boy, how wrong that was!

DEVAL PATRICK: Like Illinois, Massachusetts is a blue state, very blue. But unlike Illinois, it almost always votes for Republican governors. To put things in perspective, the previous Democratic governor had won his final election twenty years prior—and that man was Michael Dukakis.

AXELROD: The first black man to be a United States governor—and it's a great trivia question—was P. B. S. Pinchback. He'd served as governor of Louisiana for two weeks in the 1870s. In addition to Governor Pinchback, African American David Paterson became New York's governor in 2008 when Eliot Spitzer had resigned.

DAVID PATERSON: I don't see color. Actually, I don't see *anything*. I'm legally blind.

AXELROD: There had been one and *only* one black person who was ever elected as a governor in the United States: Virginia's Douglas Wilder in 1989. So Deval certainly had a challenge ahead of him. But we ended up beating the Republican nominee, Kerry Healey, by about twenty points. Total landslide. This became the model that we were going to follow with the Obama campaign, both in terms of our approach to race and in how to handle a female opponent without seeming like a bully.

MICHELLE: On paper, the 2008 Democratic presidential primary was a very crowded field. There were a total of eight candidates, in addition to Governor Tom Vilsack who withdrew only a few months after he announced.

TOM VILSACK: I've taken dumps that lasted longer than my presidential campaign, and I assure you that they felt better too.

AXELROD: Most of the other candidates didn't realistically have a shot at capturing the nomination. But there are many reasons why people run for president. They're not always expecting to win.

DENNIS KUCINICH: I wanted to change our foreign policy from "strike first, ask questions later" to having war as a last resort. Also, to show that even though I'm of leprechaun ancestry, I can bag a wife half my age, twice my height, and totally out of my league.

CHRIS DODD: I wanted to cut down on the corrupt corporate ties between Wall Street and Washington—something that I foresaw would end up hurting Wall Street, Washington, and all of America.

MIKE GRAVEL: My last elected office had been as a senator from Alaska. Why *not* run for president? Why should Palin have all the fun?

BILL RICHARDSON: I wanted to be the first Hispanic president, but I was realistic about my chances. I knew a good—albeit unsuccessful—presidential campaign would set me up to make for a great vice president.

VICE PRESIDENT JOE BIDEN: I'd run once before, and it was a hoot and a half. Besides, my grandkids like seeing me on TV.

JOHN EDWARDS: I had been John Kerry's running mate, so I knew about presidential campaigns from top to bottom. I thought that I could position myself as the alternative to Hillary Clinton, since many of the primary voters had reservations about her. I figured that Barack Obama was still too unknown and untested, still too green, which gave me an opportunity to actually win. Worst-case scenario, I could get Bill's sloppy seconds.

VICE PRESIDENT DICK CHENEY: His firsts seemed pretty sloppy to me. That Lewinsky chick looked like a shopping bag filled with mayo.

HILLARY RODHAM CLINTON: I was in it to win. Full stop.

MICHELLE: What most people don't understand is that there's what insiders call a "hidden primary." Candidates have to prove that they have what it takes, and the way they do that is by raising as much money as possible.

AXELROD: It's kind of a dick-swinging contest. At the end of each quarter, each campaign has to publicly report how much money they've raised.

HILLARY: Guess who'd raised the most money in that first quarter? Not Barack Obama. No, it was the Clinton campaign. *I* had the biggest dick.

AXELROD: But we were close behind. I'm sure that this put a scare into the Clintons, because they thought they'd be able to suck the donor class dry and basically starve out any competition.

HILLARY: Bitch, I'm not scared of anybody. I am Hillary fucking Clinton.

AXELROD: By March of 2007, it was very clear due to the monies being raised that the three realistic candidates were Hillary, John Edwards, and us. Donors and especially private citizens were showing their support for Barack. These weren't rich people either, but true-blue Democrats from all types of backgrounds.

MICHELLE: We proved that we had enough cash to go toe-to-toe with her. The argument that Senator Clinton was head and shoulders above the other candidates was disproven by the simple math of the funds we raised. I'm almost six feet tall, so I'm actually in a position to say who's heads and shoulders over everybody.

HILLARY: Careful you don't hit your head on that glass ceiling.

AXELROD: We showed that we could compete with the Clinton campaign financially. Now we needed to show that we could compete with Hillary *directly*.

MICHELLE: The Democratic presidential debates began at the end of April 2007. There were eight people on that stage, and Senator Clinton and Barack stood out simply because of the visuals.

EDWARDS: Some of the press called it "Snow White and the Seven Dwarfs," which I thought was offensive. I mean, just because Dennis is five foot seven?

KUCINICH: Hey!

AXELROD: Even if we didn't beat Hillary in the debates, we didn't have to. We just had to show that we were a viable alternative.

MICHELLE: Barack demonstrated that Democratic voters had options, and they had an option who had been right about the war in Iraq from the very beginning.

AXELROD: We couldn't afford to hand this issue to the Republicans. Democratic voters started to see that nominating Hillary might be tricky. Remember when John Kerry said that he was "for the war before he was against it"?

MICHELLE: That didn't sound quite like how he meant it to sound, but that is what voters *understood* Senator Kerry to mean. That one comment probably cost him the election, since it was so close. Surely the Republicans would paint Senator Clinton with the same brush.

AXELROD: There were seventeen debates in total throughout 2007. People tend to watch debates for two reasons. The first is to see if someone lands a particularly memorable line against their opponent, like in 1988 when Lloyd Bentsen told Dan Quayle, "Senator, I served with Jack Kennedy. I knew Jack Kennedy. Jack Kennedy was a friend of mine. Senator, you're no Jack Kennedy." The second is to watch if someone puts their foot in their mouth. I cringed that same year when Michael Dukakis was asked about his wife being raped and murdered and he gave a monotone, almost robotic response.

MICHAEL DUKAKIS: Let me set the record straight on that one. Obviously, the idea of Kitty being assaulted filled me with feelings of horror and disgust. Nothing could be more terrible than that. At the same time, is there any man alive who hasn't fantasized about murdering his wife? So the two opposing emotions kind of canceled out and I came off as flat and uncaring.

AXELROD: Having so many debates meant many opportunities for both of those types of moments—but neither of them really happened. Nobody fell on their face, but nobody hit a home run either.

MICHELLE: I knew that Barack would be a standout in the debates. Everyone knew Hillary Clinton. Everyone, especially everyone in the Democratic Party, knew John Edwards. People didn't really know Barack all that well, and that was what they were tuning in to see. People who were indifferent took a liking to him. People who liked him at first now became inspired.

AXELROD: We had the energy, but now we needed people to find us acceptable—yet also not boring and not just another politician. It was a very narrow tightrope that we were walking. Senator Obama made it seem effortless, but it was anything but.

MICHELLE: As 2007 came to a close, things stood pretty much as they had in the beginning of the year.

HILLARY: Meaning, I was still the front-runner in the polls.

MICHELLE: Yes, Senator Clinton was first in the national polls, with a very significant lead. She was also raising more money. But we were competitive financially, the only other campaign to be able to make that claim.

AXELROD: Then we rolled out the big gun: Oprah.

OPRAH: I wanted to show that my endorsement mattered. It wasn't just, "Hey, I like this guy, everyone should listen to him because he has some good ideas." I had stuck my neck out, and when I commit to a project—a film, a television series, a magazine—I follow through to make sure that it's a success. I viewed the Obama campaign the same way. I helped bring it to the national consciousness, and I was going to see this thing through.

MICHELLE: At the same time, many Democratic voters were excited at the possibility of nominating a woman. Heck, *I* was excited that women had come far enough that that was a realistic option. Not just realistic, but *likely*.

AXELROD: In that vein, it meant a lot to have Oprah and Mrs. Obama campaigning in the early states. It gave women the permission to vote for a man and not feel like they were repudiating history and betraying the cause of women's rights.

MICHELLE: So yes, Senator Clinton was still the national front-runner. But we were tied with her in the polls in Iowa, where the first votes would be taking place.

AXELROD: Our consistent rise in the polls was due to attracting new voters to the process. It wasn't that we were converting Hillary voters so much as we were converting nonvoters into Obama supporters. If we could prove that we'd be able to replicate that effect nationwide, it would strongly make the case that we should be the nominee. We weren't going to run the Karl Rove strategy of just turning out the base. Our plan was to expand the base and make it as broad as possible.

MICHELLE: How many politicians can say that they make people interested in politics? We hear so much about how the government is bad and this and that, so it's a rare thing to have a candidate who lets people think, *You know, this can actually work.*

AXELROD: Iowa is a very, very white state, over 90 percent white. We knew that any minorities in Iowa, they'd be turning out for us. That much was obvious. But the question was, could we be competitive among white midwesterners? If that answer was shown to be yes, then that would be a huge boost for the campaign.

MICHELLE: And we *were* competitive. We were more than just "competitive."

> JANUARY 3, 2008: BARACK OBAMA WINS THE IOWA CAUCUSES WITH 37.6% OF THE VOTE.

EDWARDS: I came in second, squeaking ahead of Hillary. That was no mean feat.

CHENEY: Those hips! I had an easier time getting around Chris Christie.

AXELROD: Winning Iowa changed everything. I think everyone forgets that it really seemed to be a given that Senator Clinton would be the candidate.

HILLARY: I clobbered both Obama and Edwards in New Hampshire five days later, let's also not forget *that*. My husband wasn't the only Comeback Kid in the family.

AXELROD: They raise a lot of cattle in Iowa, and that's a great metaphor for the caucuses. Between that and the New Hampshire primary those first couple of weeks in January, it was like a slaughterhouse. One by one, the other candidates started to throw in the towel. Biden, Dodd, and Richardson quickly dropped out. Kucinich and Gravel were technically in the race but they were asterisks.

MICHELLE: Just like that, we were down to three candidates: Hillary, John Edwards, and Barack. Then came Nevada, where Hillary won in terms of the *vote,* but we won in terms of the *delegates*. It was basically a draw.

EDWARDS: I knew it was over when the three of us were debating and Senator Obama made a comment, something like whether you're a person of color like him, or a woman like Hillary, or else like John. I knew then that the white male monopoly on the presidency was over. As a progressive, I was happy. This is what I'd been fighting for all my life, equality of opportunity. But as a candidate, I wasn't happy at all. Far from it. But there was nothing I could do. The writing was on the wall.

AXELROD: A week after Nevada came the first Southern primary: South Carolina.

EDWARDS: I had been a senator from North Carolina. If I couldn't win in South Carolina, I couldn't win the nomination. Now the two states obviously have our differences. We make our barbecue the correct way, with a vinegar base. South Carolina uses a mustard base, which is not barbecue. What that is is an abomination against the Lord. I don't know if that's in Leviticus but it should be.

MICHELLE: One of the unfortunate relics of slavery and the Civil War is that in the South the two parties are far more segregated by race than they are in the rest of the country. Meaning, most black voters were Democrats, and most white voters were Republicans. This was a huge advantage for us going into South Carolina.

AXELROD: I'll say it: I don't think the Clinton campaign thought things through. They looked at the primaries like an afterthought and were focused on the general election. The feeling I got was that Hillary was already measuring the drapes by the time she launched her campaign.

HILLARY: Well, that's just a load of crap. I lived in the White House already. I was perfectly familiar with all the drape measurements.

AXELROD: South Carolina came in and it wasn't even close. We just blew her out of the water, and that was the end of the line for John Edwards.

EDWARDS: Even though South Carolina ended my campaign, I still maintain that it was Bill Clinton who was the big loser that night with his comments. He was just popping off without thinking. After I heard him speak, I just muttered to myself, "Someone needs to get *laid*." That "someone" being myself.

PRESIDENT BILL CLINTON: All right, let me set some things straight. I got a lot of heat that night for pointing out that Jesse Jackson had previously won South Carolina. All I was saying was that black voters often vote for black candidates. That's not a question of race. That's simply the data. It's like me saying that when I ran for president, I would win Arkansas.

CHENEY: If you ask me, he was messing Hillary up on purpose. He didn't want her to be president. No man wants to be the First Lady, especially a former president.

BILL: Maybe I spoke prematurely. Maybe my temper got the better of me. It was just shocking to me how pro-Obama the press was being, while writing off Hillary's campaign like "stick a fork in her, she's done." And she *wasn't* done. She is a fighter. It just felt awful, seeing my wife disrespected like that.

CHENEY: Call me old-fashioned, I'll admit that I am, but maybe porking the fat little Jew intern isn't exactly the best way to show America how much respect you have for your wife.

MICHELLE: There was a vibe among voters that the Clintons expected it to be not a *nomination* but a *coronation*. Personally, I think that criticism was a bit unfair; Hillary Clinton turned out to be about as far from lazy as you can get. She fought us and fought us every step of the way. There were more debates, just her and Barack, and she was *tenacious*.

AXELROD: If America wanted a coronation, it was going to get one. When the Obama campaign got endorsements from the late Senator Kennedy and Caroline Kennedy—JFK's daughter—that really put people on notice.

CAROLINE KENNEDY: The Obama presidency is what my father fought for. This is one of the things that he died for. You've got to strike while the iron is hot, and both my uncle and I saw something of my father in Barack Obama.

AXELROD: Democratic delegates are awarded proportionally. Let's suppose we're roughly neck and neck. When Hillary won a state by a few points, that meant she'd get maybe one or two more delegates than we did. But in the states where we were beating her, states with large black populations, we were beating her by double digits. In some cases it was even two to one. Looking at the map, the race became ours to lose. She simply couldn't win, mathematically, because our victories were proportionately so much bigger than hers.

HILLARY: I *could* have won, if voters didn't get swept up in this Obama fairy tale and had started asking themselves the tough questions. What did they really know about this man, Barack Obama? He spoke well, that much was certain. But President Bush spoke terribly, and look at how effective he had been at bringing about change. It was the wrong kind of change, the worst kind of change, but no one can deny that George W. Bush drastically changed America.

BILL: They were treating Senator Obama like he was the second coming, whereas it was Hillary who was the second coming of the Clinton years. We took on the Republicans and we won. I was scared that 2008 was going to be like the Al Gore campaign all over again. He never called me to go out and work for him, and it ended up costing him the presidency. I knew what it took to win the White House, and I knew that Obama's team didn't. How could they? You could only get that from experience.

MICHELLE: I would actually agree with President Clinton on that last point. But I'd say that we *were* getting experience, in the campaign against Senator Clinton. There was a feeling in the air, especially in Democratic circles, that if there was anything like a realistic chance of electing Senator Obama, we had to take that chance. And I think having Nancy Pelosi as Speaker of the House had—unfortunately for Senator Clinton—taken away a bit of the historic feminist nature of her campaign.

AXELROD: The best experience we were getting was in handling attacks that came out of nowhere. Take the religious issue. For several decades now, it's the Republican Party who've had a problem with religion. Ever since Ronald Reagan brought the religious right into politics, the Republicans have had great difficulty presenting themselves as, shall we say, something less than zealots and extremists.

PRESIDENT GEORGE W. BUSH: If he thinks that we've got a problem with religion, I'd tell him that in my view and in the view of many millions of Americans, *his* party has a problem with God.

AXELROD: In 2008, it was the Democrats who had an issue with religion. Namely, the three reverends: Reverend Jeremiah Wright, Reverend Jesse Jackson, and Reverend Al Sharpton.

MEL GIBSON: That's practically a pack of n-words.

AL SHARPTON: Many white Americans have tended to lump me and Reverend Jackson into the same box, as if we were both different incarnations of the same phenomenon.

CHENEY: Just because bullshit comes in different shapes doesn't mean it smells any better. I know something about different types of bullshit, being from both Wyoming and Washington, D.C.

SHARPTON: I have made a conscious effort to reinvent myself. Since the beginning of my career, I've always stressed that so-called black issues aren't just issues that affect people of color. Police brutality, urban poverty, a lack of access to opportunity—these are all things that hurt black people disproportionately. But they also affect *every* community to some extent.

MITT ROMNEY: What's "poverty"? Is that some sort of rap jargon?

SHARPTON: I tried a new strategy over the years. Instead of focusing on issues from a black perspective, from discussing how they primarily affected the black community, I focused on the issue itself. Then, when people work together on that given issue, the black community would still get the help and support that we needed—and so will every other community that needs it, which is in my opinion a very fair approach. In 2009, I even teamed up with Newt Gingrich to promote education reform.

NEWT GINGRICH: To be honest I thought I was going on tour with Clarence Thomas. It took me three stops before I realized why everyone kept calling him "Reverend."

CLARENCE THOMAS: Is that why Biden keeps yelling at me about MSNBC?

BIDEN: I just like telling people about it. Their programming is top-notch and highly perceptive!

SHARPTON: The point being, I had a very different approach than Jesse Jackson did. I'll leave it to him to discuss things further.

CHENEY: If Obama became president of the United States, then he would instantly be regarded as the leader of black America. It's like how I'm universally recognized as the leader of old men who shoot their friends in the face. And if Obama is the leader of black America, who the hell needs Jesse Jackson anymore? Sharpton was clever and changed gears. But if you ask me, Jesse Jackson's biggest fear was having to find a job. It's like when Superman spots a shiny green rock. For a split second, he almost has a heart attack thinking that it's Kryptonite.

JESSE JACKSON: I'm not even going to bother addressing the blatant racism of that comment, but I will say on a personal level that I wasn't thinking like that.

SHARPTON: Listen, Jesse and I weren't the only ones. Come the inauguration of a new president, whether it would have been Barack Obama or John McCain or Alan Keyes, half of Washington was going to be out of work and looking for a new gig. This happens every election cycle.

MICHELLE: A campaign is obviously very hectic and tense. You're constantly trying to put out fires and manage things. It's the perfect preparation for the presidency. I don't remember where I even was when I heard it, but in the blink of an eye all the news was harping on the same thing: Jesse Jackson had been caught saying that he was going to cut Barack's nuts off. That was almost more confusing than it was actually upsetting.

JACKSON: I did not know that mic was on.

AXELROD: The fact that he didn't realize that he was on tape made it much, much worse. It was clearly a moment of candor rather than a calculated move.

MICHELLE: If he wanted Barack's nuts, he knew exactly where to find them. In my purse! Just kidding.

CHENEY: I guess we can add laugh riot to all the others riots the Obamas caused.

JACKSON: Though my language was coarse, and I of course regretted it, my point still stood. I felt that Senator Obama was talking down to black people in an effort to put distance between us and himself.

MICHELLE: If Barack wanted to put distance between himself and black people, he certainly wouldn't have married one. He had options; this is who he *chose*.

AXELROD: I think Jesse Jackson's comments really hurt him much more than it hurt us. It was a long way from when he was kind of this spiritual adviser to President Clinton. It sounded like a schoolyard threat and he's better than that. Frankly, it helped us a bit. Many white Americans were scared that Senator Obama was basically some sort of covert black radical, and to have Jackson come out against him by mistake really assuaged some fears.

MICHELLE: It's not like the Republicans could run with the issue anyway. What Republican can honestly go on television and complain that black people are being talked down to?

MICHELE BACHMANN: I sure as heck could.

MICHELLE: I said *honestly.*

BACHMANN: Then let's talk about things that really matter to most Americans. Did you know that vaccines can make children mentally retarded? I should know; I've raised over seventy of them.

JEREMIAH WRIGHT: I didn't say anything in my sermons that many black pastors didn't say every week to their congregations. I said that there exists an enormous animus toward people of color in this country.

SHARPTON: That is undeniably the case.

WRIGHT: I said that Israel has too much influence on the federal government.

SHARPTON: I think the reality of the situation is far more complex and nuanced than that basic statement, but I understand where he's coming from.

WRIGHT: And I said that AIDS was a CIA program originally designed to wipe out the black race.

SHARPTON: Now that's absurd. It's important to be responsible when it comes to our grievances. AIDS was never intended to hurt the black community. It was designed to wipe out the gays and it only hit our community by *accident.* Everyone knows that.

WRIGHT: Few Americans realize that the Snapple bottle had a slave ship on the label for many years, blatantly disrespecting the black community.

SHARPTON: They sure changed it quick after we started pointing that out.

WRIGHT: Procter & Gamble were satanic! White America didn't catch on to that, but we did. Their man-in-the-moon logo had two horns and an inverted 666 in the beard. Many of my parishioners went home right after my sermon and poured all their detergent down the toilet, sending that poison straight to hell.

SHARPTON: It's no wonder that Tide was the devil on stains.

WRIGHT: Last but certainly not least, that Troop line of clothing? It had the Confederate flag emblazoned on it!

SHARPTON: Actually it was the British flag.

WRIGHT: All I know is that it looked like it was the *Dukes of Hazzard* car, the General Lee. Fuck that car!

MICHELLE: Yes, I heard Reverend Wright say some very incendiary things over the years. But he's a preacher. It's his job to get people riled up and emotional about moral issues. Just like the Bible itself, you can't always take things literally and at face value.

BUSH: Maybe *you* can't.

MICHELLE: Sometimes, Reverend Wright was being ironic. Sometimes, he was being intentionally provocative. And sometimes—and you can't get this through a transcript—he was just joking. He wasn't this incendiary all the time.

WRIGHT: No, I wasn't a brimstone-and-hellfire guy. But I wasn't Cedric the Entertainer, either.

CEDRIC THE ENTERTAINER: No, he's sure not. But if you want to see the real deal, you can catch me this Saturday at Caroline's and with two shows on Sunday. We've got Jimmy Failla as the opening act and every show is guaranteed laughs. Hurry, tickets are going fast!

AXELROD: No one is going to deny that a preacher can say whatever he wants when he's addressing his congregation. And no one really cared about what Reverend Wright had to say in and of itself. But what did Senator Obama think? Obviously no one agrees with their preacher about everything. So which parts did the senator agree with, and which didn't he? Well, if you're forced to deny agreeing with certain views, at the same time you're repeating those same views in the press and acknowledging that you were privy to hearing them, the whole thing had the potential to come off very badly.

BILL: I'm from Arkansas. I was familiar with those sorts of sermons because I've been going to black churches all my life. Why wouldn't I? You get a show and you get to have a great time.

HILLARY: We didn't hear any of this sort of thing when I was growing up, and I was sure most Americans hadn't heard this sort of thing in their churches either.

MICHELLE: Neither did Barack! Did I myself hear some of Reverend Wright's more controversial sermons? Absolutely. They were appalling. But I knuckled through it. Did my husband hear those sermons? Absolutely not. How do I know that? I can prove it.

HILLARY: This I gotta hear.

MICHELLE: One of the things that the Republicans hated, feared, and maybe even envied about Barack was how he always spoke his mind. Sure, he has a very cool demeanor, but he's not one to bite his tongue. If he had heard the worst of these sermons, he wouldn't have just sat there quietly. He would have confronted Reverend Wright. At the very least, he would have gotten up and left. Since I never saw him leave, that proved that he was never there during those times to begin with.

BILL: I take back what I said during the primaries. *That,* what she said, is the biggest fairy tale I've ever seen. So Barack Obama just disappears when things he doesn't like are spoken aloud? What is he, Beetlejuice or something?

AXELROD: We knew we needed to nip this in the bud. We had nothing to hide so we decided to turn a weakness into a positive. We came up with a strategy that was a little unorthodox, but we were running an unorthodox campaign for an unorthodox politician.

MICHELLE: Usually when one of these scandals erupts, the senator or governor or whoever gets on TV, issues a statement—and then stonewalls until the media gets bored and goes onto the next thing. But this was an opportunity. This didn't need to be just about Reverend Wright. Instead of trying to squash the issue, we decided to blow it up. Let's address the elephant in the room: race. And let's do it using Barack's greatest strength: his ability to speak directly to the American people without the usual political double-talking.

AXELROD: We knew this speech would be historic. The first black presidential candidate giving his first major address on race? Even if we didn't win the election, it would immediately and indelibly become part of the national conversation.

MICHELLE: If Barack didn't get the speech right, he might not have been able to win the election in the fall anyway. Fox News, the Republicans, and all the other forces on the right were going to analyze this thing to death.

MARCH 18, 2008: BARACK OBAMA DELIVERS HIS "A MORE PERFECT UNION" SPEECH.

AXELROD: Sure enough, the speech went over. I mean, it really went over. No one else could have given this speech, because no one else was as much of a product of two communities.

MICHELLE: Barack spoke frankly and he spoke from the heart. Even though the speech was political and there's obviously a bit of an agenda behind *anything* that *any* politician does, he didn't have to pander thanks to his personal history. He wasn't, you know, the angry black man castigating white America. He wasn't the white politician wagging his finger at black America either.

GINGRICH: Is she talking about me? Why would I wag my finger at black America? I don't care about black America.

MICHELLE: Nor was he the patronizing white politician trying to cotton to black communities either.

SHARPTON: Why it gotta be "cotton"?

MICHELLE: I had to have a little bit of a laugh at it, because everyone was wanting Barack to fall flat on this issue. Race has been tripping up politicians of every political persuasion since America became a country.

BIDEN: Fun fact—the vice president's wife is known as the "Second Lady." Not-so-fun fact—Vice President Thomas Jefferson owned his Second Lady, Sally Hemings. I think that's wrong, because I am a feminist.

MICHELLE: LBJ supposedly said that he had lost the South for a generation after signing the Civil Rights Act. Richard Nixon introduced affirmative action—while making extremely racist comments about black people being subhuman. It was a dance they all did, but Barack finally closed the show. Or put a pause in it, at least. And no one really had anything to criticize him on. They tried to parse it a bit but no one could really argue with the things that he said.

> JUNE 7, 2008: HILLARY CLINTON CONCEDES THE DEMOCRATIC NOMINATION AND ENDORSES BARACK OBAMA.

HILLARY: We had won more votes, and I'm very proud of that fact. But we didn't have the delegates, and that's what mattered.

BILL: Working with my wife on her concession speech was tough. The endorsement had to be sincere and the party had to be united. We could not have John McCain as our next president. I admire the hell out of him, and I think he might be one of the funniest senators I've ever worked with.

JOHN McCAIN: This one time Cindy got her pills mixed up with Betty Ford's and . . . well, you had to be there, it was a hoot.

BILL: We liked to play keep-away with him. You just have to hold things so he can't reach them, which basically works out to eye level.

McCAIN: Fine, keep it. I didn't want it anyway.

BILL: How is he going to press the button if war broke out?

McCAIN: Well, we can assume that the nuclear button isn't on a shelf. And if it were, then there would be a chair next to it anyway.

BILL: Like I said, John's just a great guy on a personal level, but my God would he have been a catastrophe as president.

MICHELLE: It was our job to make sure that that never happened.

3

WINNING THE WHITE HOUSE, 2008

JOHN McCAIN: I knew that I had an uphill battle to fight. And I knew that it would be unfair. I was going to be painted as a typical old, white male Republican, when in fact many in my party hated me because I was atypical. I was going to be painted as another George W. Bush, when in fact I had run against him in 2000 and had a different political philosophy than him. I knew that the race card was going to be played against me every chance it could, because the Bush campaign had done it against me in South Carolina.

PRESIDENT GEORGE W. BUSH: That wasn't us.

McCAIN: In 2000, Karl Rove and his people had pollsters call voters in South Carolina and ask if they would be less likely to vote for me if they learned that I—and I quote—"had fathered an illegitimate black child." At the same time, I had been campaigning with my daughter Bridget, who is adopted and who I love very much, and who isn't even black but from Bangladesh.

DONALD TRUMP: I had people that actually have been studying it and they cannot believe what they're finding. It turns out Bangladesh is actually a country! I never heard of such a thing. Here I thought John was just parading around some sort of retarded girl he had fathered while being captured.

MICHELLE OBAMA: Well, the race card wasn't played on Senator McCain during the campaign, at all.

McCAIN: Oh please, they put Obama on the cover of every magazine every week. I've never seen anything like it.

DAVID AXELROD: We got on magazine covers because there was a market for them. People were buying those magazines in record numbers. This was just supply and demand, capitalism at work—which is something that the Republicans are supposedly for, except when it works against them

McCAIN: Something else our campaign focused on was pride in our country—something which Mrs. Obama apparently didn't share.

MICHELLE: Oh, that was bad. One of the things that the Republicans kept floating was that Barack was too much of a foreigner to be president. Some were even whispering that he hadn't been born in America.

AXELROD: Which was ironic because Senator McCain had actually been born in Panama.

McCAIN: On a naval air station, which meant it was U.S. soil.

MICHELLE: Well, that outsider perception was something that Barack was fighting. So the Republicans made a big deal out of the fact that I'd said that, for the first time in my adult life, I was proud of my country. As if that was a big gaffe.

AXELROD: Some gaffes are born and some are made. This one was a bit of a mix.

MICHELLE: Well, I did say *my* country. What I really meant was that America finally had a chance to fulfill its promise of a color-blind society where everyone has the opportunity to succeed. We cheer when, say, an African American becomes the CEO of American Express. And everyone was excited to have a black president. But how great would it be if these weren't records being broken? If these sorts of things happened every day, to the point where no one would even notice them? That is what I meant.

McCAIN: It's not the First Lady who really matters anyway.

AXELROD: Is that why you publicly referred to your wife as a "cunt"?

McCAIN: That was a mistake. I meant to call her a thundercunt.

AXELROD: The real test of how a candidate would actually govern was their choice of running mate. Historically speaking, there are several paths to the vice presidential slot on the ticket. A lot of times it's simply the runner-up from the primaries, where you reunite the party and hope that puts you over the top. It was that way when Reagan picked George H. W. Bush in 1980 and when John Kerry picked John Edwards in 2004.

HILLARY RODHAM CLINTON: Which would have meant me for VP.

MICHELLE: We knew that the country wanted change but not *radical* change. If the ticket had Barack at the top and Senator Clinton—or any female for that matter—at number two, it would have been quite the gamble, and an unnecessary one.

HILLARY: Because electing someone with no experience isn't a gamble.

PRESIDENT BILL CLINTON: There's so many fairy tales I swear that their speeches are being authored by the brothers Grimm.

AXELROD: President Clinton did something unprecedented with his 1992 campaign, where he brought on another young Southern Democrat. That played into his whole theme of being a "New Democrat" and it obviously worked for him.

MICHELLE: But we didn't have another Barack Obama.

McCAIN: Oh come on, the Senate was full of random inexperienced ultraliberals. Take your pick! It's like going into a clock shop, the cuckoos were everywhere.

AXELROD: So we went with the third running-mate idea, which was to *balance* the ticket, to bring on someone with qualities that the presidential candidate lacked. A large portion of our campaign was about America's disastrous foreign policy. And a large portion of the criticism *against* our campaign was Senator Obama's foreign policy inexperience.

MICHELLE: That part was indisputably true. Barack had a vision for America's foreign policy, a strong vision, but he hadn't had the opportunity to implement it. That was why he was running for president in the first place.

AXELROD: So we thought, who in the Democratic Party could deliver foreign policy experience? The name at the top of the list was Senator Biden. He was widely expected to be a front-runner for secretary of state even in a Clinton administration, and he came from a very blue state, so his Delaware Senate seat would be safe.

MICHELLE: Barack might be classified as a "person of color," but you couldn't deny that Joe Biden is pretty colorful himself.

AUGUST 22, 2008: BARACK OBAMA SELECTS JOE
BIDEN AS HIS RUNNING MATE.

VICE PRESIDENT JOE BIDEN: Delaware is the First State, but I was happy to be number two!

AXELROD: Joe Biden had been a senator for ages, and everyone in Washington loved him. He brought foreign policy experience but also insider Washington experience to the team. At this point in the race we had a lead that we thought would be enough to carry us through to victory. We didn't want to make any unforced errors.

MICHELLE: The McCain campaign, on the other hand, didn't have such a luxury.

McCAIN: By the time of the conventions, when most Americans first start paying attention to the presidential campaign, we had been trailing slightly but consistently. That was our biggest problem, the complete lack of momentum. We needed something that would reorient the conversation, and believe it or not in a presidential campaign that's quite hard to do. By the time you've got the nominations locked down, most of the dirty laundry has already been aired out in the primaries. That leaves the debates and the vice presidential nomination.

JOE LIEBERMAN: The McCain team reached out to me for the vice presidential slot. We hadn't had a bipartisan presidential ticket since the late 1800s. It would have been absolutely revolutionary, like eating milk and meat at the same meal. But given how modern American politics works, that also made it absolutely impossible.

McCAIN: When I mentioned having a Democratic senator on the ticket, even a conservative Democrat like Joe Lieberman, everyone pretty much spit out their coffee. It was like I was asking to run with, I don't know, Osama bin Laden.

DICK CHENEY: Well, if he could have found bin Laden, then he would have won the election.

McCAIN: So we really were in a unique fix; we wanted someone who was unexpected and still qualified, someone who would make waves. And there really aren't many people who fit that bill in politics.

AXELROD: In *Republican* politics.

McCAIN: Governor Palin's name came up and we were very intrigued. She had one of the highest approval ratings of any governor in the country, we're talking like 80 percent or more. She was a strong conservative, which would appease the religious Right. But she was also a reformer who defeated a Republican incumbent in the primary. That meant she was comfortable and successful in taking on the establishment. Finally, Alaska was literally about as far away from Washington, D.C., as you could get.

AXELROD: It was a pretty blatant attempt to peel the Hillary voters away from us, and that was smart of them. It's exactly what I would have tried to do if I was managing the McCain campaign. At first it worked. They got a spike in the polls.

MICHELLE: But then, it didn't work. Like, not at all.

SARAH PALIN: I saw how the lamestream media was basically referring to Barack Hussein Obama as the second coming of Christ. Or first coming, actually, since they all hate Christianity and Christians so much. I thought, huh, maybe I could use some of that Wasilla sense of humor to show the American people that, you know what?, the Republican Party is pretty cool, too. You don't have to be black to be cool. Sure, it helps, but it's not a necessity.

McCAIN: She kept telling these jokes that didn't seem to make much sense.

PALIN: What's the difference between a pit bull and a hockey mom? Lipstick!

McCAIN: I thought that maybe I didn't understand them because I'm from another generation, like when the kids use those Internet terms like ROTFL and SLAP or whatever. Or "whatevs," I guess they say now.

PALIN: A communist, an illegal immigrant, and a Muslim walk into a bar. The bartender says, "Hi, Barack Obama! Would you like the usual?" That's a good one, always gets a laugh. I admit it, I stole that joke from Newt Gingrich—but it's OK because Barack Hussein Obama stole his foreign policy ideas from Jimmy Carter.

McCAIN: Governor Palin had been a professional broadcaster. She'd also been a beauty queen and was still very easy on the eyes, just gorgeous. (Is that sexist or can I say that? Whatevs.) Remember, beauty queens have to respond to deep questions with answers that sound profound but don't really mean anything. In other words, how politicians speak. Both of her past careers made it seem like she'd be great on camera.

PALIN: Did you hear about the time Barack Obama went hiking? Everyone got their taxes increased!

McCAIN: Of course there was a tremendous amount of interest in the governor, and our phones were ringing nonstop with interview requests. CNN, ABC, LOL, you name it, they were calling us. After a lot of discussion, the campaign decided that Katie Couric would make for a good interview. She seemed like a fair choice and her demeanor was always friendly. But I know the governor didn't really trust the press all that much.

PALIN: Sure, I trust them. I trust them as far as I can throw them!

KATIE COURIC: As a woman in the media, I was painfully aware of the double standard that female politicians have to face. I know that many of my liberal colleagues really wanted me to grill Governor Palin but I thought that that was absolutely the wrong approach.

PALIN: What do you get when you cross Harry Reid, Nancy Pelosi, and Barack Hussein Obama? *A complete economic catastrophe.*

COURIC: Whether she would ever become vice president or not, she was still a woman who became a governor through her own merits.

There's not that many women who can say that, even in this day and age. So I kept it to the sort of questions you'd expect, no gotcha moments about obscure bills or things of that nature.

McCAIN: In terms of being a disaster, that interview on a scale of 1–10 was a 9/11.

PALIN: I felt like I was on *Jeopardy!* The questions just kept coming, one after another.

COURIC: Well, that is the nature of an interview.

McCAIN: That's the *definition* of an interview.

COURIC: At one point, Governor Palin seemed to be offended and caught off guard when I asked her what newspapers she read.

PALIN: She was implying that I didn't read.

COURIC: Seriously? By that logic asking someone their favorite food is implying that they're anorexic.

McCAIN: How do you mess up a question like that? "What newspapers do you read?" Just rattle some off, no one really cares. That's like not knowing the answer to "What's your favorite color?" There is no wrong answer, but somehow Governor Palin managed to find one.

AXELROD: She wasn't ready for prime time, but, boy, was she ready for late night. When Tina Fey started with her *Saturday Night Live* impressions of Sarah Palin, I almost felt bad for John McCain. *Almost.*

McCAIN: It was torture, and I say this as someone who has actually experienced torture.

MICHELLE: Despite all the jokes, Governor Palin didn't really end up hurting the ticket that much. President Clinton had always been the butt of jokes, and he ended up being the most popular Democratic president in thirty years.

AXELROD: Putting Palin on the ticket was a wash, a blown opportunity, but it didn't change many people's minds. There were voters who thought that the Republicans were nuts; they weren't going to vote for McCain anyway. Then there were voters who did not want to see this black progressive from Chicago in the White House, so they were against us already. It really came down to a battle of visions.

MICHELLE: We were kind of gliding to a victory. Once Americans saw that we could actually win, they really, really wanted us to win. It was like, "If there's even a slight chance that this might happen, it has to happen." Of course there was skepticism about Barack's experience. But it was very clear that he would be, at the very least, *competent*. It made sense for undecided voters to say to themselves, *Hey, maybe he won't be that great, but he'll definitely be a symbol of racial progress in America*. So there was a huge upside for many people right off the bat. The symbolism worked in our favor, no question, but that's how politics works. Many veterans voted for McCain for similar reasons, just as Christian conservatives had voted for George W. Bush.

McCAIN: Then in September the economy just imploded.

AXELROD: Senator McCain insisted that "the fundamentals of the economy are strong."

McCAIN: I said it and I meant it. Anyone who disagrees shouldn't be president, because they don't believe that America has a great base that can tackle any adversity.

MICHELLE: It was not what people needed to hear at that time. It sounded insensitive, like "don't worry, everything's fine!" Well, everything wasn't fine. Fannie Mae and Freddie Mac were going under, and regardless of the economy's fundamentals, this sort of thing can snowball into a calamity very easily.

McCAIN: I decided to suspend my campaign and rushed back to Washington to help with negotiations for the bailout. That's what leadership means to me, putting politics second or, heck, even *last* when there's a crisis.

AXELROD: With all due respect, the McCain team put politics *first* and nakedly so. John McCain was not the Senate majority leader or even the minority leader. By then, the Democrats had regained control of Congress and there was already plenty of negotiating going on between Speaker Pelosi, Majority Leader Reid, and President Bush. There was a huge bipartisan consensus on what needed to be done in principle. Partisan politics had gone out the window. Plenty of very smart people from all political persuasions came together to put together a package to try and keep us from having another Great Depression.

MICHELLE: I found it a bit ironic that the McCain campaign liked to call Barack a narcissist, but then they acted as if Senator McCain's one Senate vote out of a hundred would make or break the country. This bailout bill was not going to be a close vote.

McCAIN: That really hurt us because of how it was perceived. Letterman especially ripped into us for canceling, which I thought crossed a line. I was a presidential candidate and a longtime senator. I can't begin to tell you what a low priority being on *Late Night* should be for any politician.

PALIN: I'm willing to bet that if Barack Hussein Obama had done the same thing instead of John McCain there would be a lot more understanding from the press. Just putting it out there, that's how it works.

AXELROD: Except there didn't need to be understanding because we didn't pull a stunt like that.

MICHELLE: And Barack was supposed to be the amateur?

McCAIN: They kept pretending like I would be a third George Bush term and that was ridiculous.

MICHELLE: I can't think of a single issue where there was significant disagreement between Senator McCain and the president.

AXELROD: As election day approached, the McCain campaign got more and more desperate with the attacks—especially during the debates—but nothing was sticking. How could it? Everyone knew what Senator Obama represented. We obviously weren't going to win on experience; was *anyone* in Washington as experienced as Senator McCain?

BIDEN: Aw, come on! I mean, I was on the fricking ticket! Hello?

AXELROD: We obviously weren't trying to win on staying the course, either. So all this yelling about Senator Obama being a radical new voice who wasn't a creature of the Washington establishment—those weren't criticisms. Those were the arguments that *we* were putting forward ourselves.

> NOVEMBER 4, 2008: BARACK OBAMA DEFEATS JOHN McCAIN 365–173 IN THE ELECTORAL COLLEGE TO WIN THE PRESIDENCY.

MICHELLE: Election night was a blowout. It was the highest number of votes that any American presidential candidate had received, *ever*. It was the first time that a Democrat had captured a majority of the popular vote in over thirty years.

AXELROD: We had some major coattails at the state and congressional level, too. We ran the table against the Republicans. The Democrats won pretty much every close race. Huge Senate majority, huge House majority.

MICHELLE: Did I consider this a victory of good over evil? No. There's plenty of evil in Washington to go around. I would say that it was a victory of hope over cynicism.

CHENEY: Oh, honey. You sweet, naive kid. How long did that last, eh?

MICHELLE: It didn't feel real until Senator McCain called to concede. I think he is a great guy, and I think he was much more at peace with his 2008 loss than he had been losing the primaries to George W. Bush in 2000. He's a big patriot who is of an older generation. I don't mean that as a knock against him, just that he had a longer perspective on what Barack's win meant for America.

McCAIN: Do you know what it's like to be the first man to lose to a black guy? Let me tell you: It gets pretty awkward at the country club.

MICHELLE: Anyone looking at my face that night could see that I truly felt proud of my country that night. No ifs, ands, or buts about it. It wasn't only me, either. So did everyone else, including the rest of the world. Maybe we *could* fix this mess that we'd been handed.

CHENEY: So that's why they want to legalize all those maids!

4

THE INAUGURATION, JANUARY 20, 2009

D.L. HUGHLEY: There were two black men who immediately got a job due to Obama's victory. The first was me. CNN wanted to strike while the iron was hot, while America liked black people, so they hired me to host a news commentary show for them called *D.L. Hughley Breaks the News*. Basically they saw me as the black Jon Stewart.

JON STEWART: Is . . . is that a thing? Because I would also like to be that thing.

HUGHLEY: The other brotha was Michael Steele. The Republicans have a very touchy reputation in this country on the subject of race—usually with good reason. At the same time, it's their role to offer an opposing perspective to the Democratic Party. How to reconcile these two concepts? Well, the only way they could do that was to show us that they got themselves a black guy too. That's why they voted Steele in as chairman of the Republican National Committee.

MICHAEL STEELE: See? Republicans don't have an issue in voting for a black leader—so long as he thinks like them.

HUGHLEY: As part of my show I got to be in Washington on inauguration day. I got to see history in the making. Knowing I was there for this historic moment got me thinking about the steps that led up to it. It wasn't Martin Luther King or Malcolm X that I was recalling that cold, very cold, motherfucking cold as hell January day. It sure wasn't Jesse Jackson, either. No, I was remembering Tom Bradley.

RICK SANTORUM: Was he on the Clippers?

HUGHLEY: Tom Bradley had been mayor of Los Angeles. In 1982, he was the Democratic nominee for governor in California—the first black man to have that privilege. I was still a kid then but I remember the excitement in the air. Bradley was truly an unimpeachable man.

PRESIDENT BILL CLINTON: What's that supposed to mean?

HUGHLEY: He didn't have any sort of shadiness about him. He was a decent upright politician—or at least as decent and upright as any politician could be. That's why he was leading in the polls all the way up until election day.

JERRY BROWN: Mayor Bradley was a great man and a good friend. We all thought he would win. I voted for him proudly.

HUGHLEY: Here's the thing: sometimes your guy doesn't win. That's nature. That's life. That's tough shit. It sucks, but it's the deal. The Republicans didn't have a House majority for forty years—two generations. Say what you want about them, but they kept fighting the Democrats tooth and nail. I don't mind losing and in a sense I don't mind losing over and over, just so long as it's fair. But Tom Bradley was something else.

BROWN: When the ballots were counted, Bradley had lost. It was shocking. The press pored over the polls and asked themselves how they got it so wrong. The consensus seemed to come down to two reasons. One, that voters didn't want to confess to pollsters that they preferred the white candidate over the black one. They didn't want to come off as racist. Second, that they liked to think of themselves as someone who would vote for a black candidate—but when they got in the booth, in private, their natural inclinations came out. It became known as "the Bradley effect," when pro-minority voting preferences are overstated in polls.

KARL ROVE: We're working on "the Republican effect," when pro-minority voting preferences are eliminated in the elections.

HUGHLEY: I'm not a pollster so I don't really know the technicalities of what happened. All I know is what happened in my house. My father was a janitor. He worked a thankless menial job for decades. He didn't complain. Frankly, he didn't say much of anything. He had never gone to college, and he was resigned that this was his lot in life. It was what it was. The only real aspiration he had was that I wouldn't be such a pain in the fucking ass with him all the time. He really believed Tom Bradley would win. He really believed—he really *allowed* himself to believe—that America was changing and a black man of quality could get a fair shake. And when that vote total came in, it just broke him. It was Lucy pulling the football away from Charlie Brown. It was like, "Nigga, you didn't really think we were gonna let you have this, did you? Really? When will you stupid people ever fucking learn? This shit ain't for you. Now go sweep the floor."

BROWN: That was not unique to D.L.'s family. I had many friends in tears. This wasn't a regular loss. It wasn't even a loss that could be blamed on voter fraud or something like that, where you feel cheated. To many of us it felt like the repudiation of an entire group of people.

HUGHLEY: So that's what was on my mind that January day. Part of me, a huge part of me, was convinced that Obama's election was due to some higher-up falling asleep at the switch, and that they would soon remedy the situation. I agreed with the Obama assertion that America is a place where all things are possible. I just had a darker, more cynical interpretation of that thought.

MICHELLE OBAMA: Whenever Barack repeated that he wanted to be a transformative president like Reagan, all I could think of was John Hinckley. I did not want to be like Nancy Reagan.

NANCY REAGAN: Do you mean a size zero, dear?

MICHELLE: I didn't want to hear that some crazy person with a crush, say, on Raven-Symoné had decided to prove his love by shooting my husband. That's *besides* all the obvious racial animus that being the first black president brought with it.

HUGHLEY: I really thought that they were going to put a bullet in him. That's what was going through my mind. I'll believe this shit when I see it—and even then I'll have to make sure it's not faked like the moon landing.

AGENT ███████████████: As a member of the Secret Service, it is my duty to keep the president and the First Lady safe and secure. Inauguration day is one of the trickiest days for us.

MICHELLE: The American people have a tradition of how new presidents are sworn in. The new president walks the streets of Washington, so that the people can see him for themselves. Despite all the whispers of radicalism, Barack was not about to change this tradition. He's not a king, he's a citizen just like everybody else. Frankly, he wouldn't have missed those cheering crowds for anything. That's who he was fighting so hard for.

██████████: Having harm done to the president on your watch is every agent's worst nightmare. We're all prepared to take a bullet for the president, whoever he is and whatever our personal political persuasion happens to be. We consider our work to be an honor and a privilege. The president of the United States is a symbol of freedom and the democratic process. Each and every one of us truly feels like he is defending America when we perform our duty.

PRESIDENT GEORGE W. BUSH: I was rooting for Barack Obama— every patriot roots for his president—and hoped he could possibly do some things that I had been unable to. I first ran for president in 2000 as a uniter, and not a divider. Some dismiss my tenure, but many people consider my presidency a success.

RAHM EMANUEL: Name one.

LAURA BUSH: I sure did.

EMANUEL: I meant someone who isn't in his family.

VICE PRESIDENT DICK CHENEY: I agree as well.

EMANUEL: Jeb 2016 it is!

BUSH: Many others, admittedly, consider it a failure. Personally, I think of my tenure like Harry Truman's, someone appreciated far more in later decades than he was in his time.

CHENEY: See, if we'd only dropped a couple of nukes like I'd wanted, like Truman had, we wouldn't be having this discussion.

BUSH: I'll leave my place in history for the historians to decide. I hope *they're* as good at *their* jobs as *I* was at *mine,* heh.

CHENEY: Ha, ha! Classic W.!

BUSH: Most historians have never bombed anyone. Heck, even Laura's got one fatality to her name.

LAURA: That was an accident. I ran him over because I thought he was planning to use chemical weapons.

BUSH: Whatever you may think of me and my presidency, there is one thing that no one on either side of the aisle can dispute. That is the fact that I *did* unite America and allow for our first black president. But for me, that would never have happened.

HUGHLEY: Well, I don't think he united America in the way he intended, let's be honest. In fact, on inauguration day someone had painted up a dummy in President Bush's image, and the crowd all started throwing shoes at it like had been done to him in Iraq. I thought it was so unnecessary and disrespectful. The man was defeated and his entire ideology discredited; let him go back to Texas with his tail between his legs. If you want respect, you've got to give respect, and sometimes you have to be the bigger man about it.

DENNIS KUCINICH: I agree.

MICHELLE: All of the audience had laughed during the debates when

Barack was asked if he thought that Bill Clinton was "America's first black president." Barack made a little joke about having to see more of President Clinton's dancing abilities before he could answer that question. Well, what Barack wasn't letting on was that this had been a sort of an inside joke between him and me. Barack really doesn't have a great sense of rhythm. It's not too bad, not terrible, but he's such a smooth operator otherwise that maybe it makes it seem worse than it is. One of the most nerve-racking things for any married couple is their first dance, and for Barack that was the scariest part of our wedding. Of course it ended up fine and everyone was happy for us. Even if he missed a step here or there no one cared.

BUSH: Well, I can see which one of them knows how to give a speech.

CHENEY: Yeah, does this story even have an ending?

MICHELLE: *My point is,* as stressful and rehearsed as that first wedding dance was, that's what inauguration days are like. It is choreographed to an extreme, minute by minute. Actually it's more like a huge dance *number,* where you're sort of standing in the middle while dozens of people are spinning around you. There was always someone taking us from place to place and telling us where to stand. It was a bit of a blur. I wanted to remember every second, but at the same time it was happening so quickly and then I realized that I didn't *need* to remember everything. Every moment was being recorded for posterity. So while I forgot some things, I remember the important ones. What do I remember most? All those crying people.

JOHN BOEHNER: There's no shame in a grown man shedding a tear when he is overcome.

CHENEY: Can someone get Boehner a handkerchief? The sissy's about to spring a leak again. It's like Old Faithful with this one.

BUSH: They were crying when I was inaugurated, too.

MICHELLE: Even though inauguration day was very cold, it sure felt like spring.

HUGHLEY: To me it was like the fulfillment of the Million Man March. You had people coming from all across America, fathers with their sons, granddads holding their grandkids on their shoulders. The Million Man March was a moment in our history that, in the end, didn't ever seem to coalesce into anything. There was no payoff at the time. I think the Obama inauguration, over a decade later, was that payoff.

MICHELLE: Then came the actual swearing-in.

BUSH: Vice President Cheney couldn't stand because he was in a wheelchair.

CHENEY: I felt bad about that. I always make it a point to get up when a lady enters the room, and I'm genuinely sorry.

MICHELLE: Well, I accept the vice president's apology.

CHENEY: I meant her husband. The real "First Lady."

BUSH: See, they don't call him Dick for nothing.

HUGHLEY: I was watching with bated breath. It was like counting down the seconds at the Super Bowl. I could not believe what I was seeing—until they messed up the oath of office.

JANUARY 20, 2009: CHIEF JUSTICE JOHN ROBERTS ACCIDENTALLY MISSTATES THE PRESIDENTIAL OATH WHEN SWEARING IN BARACK OBAMA.

CHENEY: His presidency was a mistake from the beginning, from the literal very beginning.

MICHELLE: Barack knew the oath, of course. At the same time, when he didn't repeat what Justice Roberts had said, it seemed as if *Barack* was the one making a mistake. So it was this mild awkward moment.

JOHN ROBERTS: It was my first time swearing in a president. As chief justice I don't really have to appear in the public eye much, since we don't broadcast Supreme Court proceedings. I had gone over the ceremony again and again in my mind for weeks. Then I even did a few dress rehearsals to make sure that I knew the lines by heart.

CLARENCE THOMAS: I'm not sure why I was the one he chose to rehearse with, but I was glad to do whatever Chief Justice Roberts told me to. And now, back to the silence.

ROBERTS: The flub was my bad, plain and simple. Guilty as charged!

HUGHLEY: I thought Obama was the one who had messed up. It was like, *Aw, come on, man!*

ROBERTS: I didn't want anyone to sue President Obama on some sort of arcane constitutional grounds, that the swearing-in was illegitimate. Technically I think they would have to sue *me* for messing up, and then who knows what would happen. Would I have to recuse myself? Would I be on the defendant's stand? Because it would definitely go all the way up to the Supreme Court. So we redid the oath of office the following day just to make sure there was no confusion.

VICE PRESIDENT JOE BIDEN: I think that I was president for one day. It's good work, if you can get it.

HILLARY RODHAM CLINTON: You don't say?

MICHELLE: The rock star atmosphere went on into the evening. There were so many inaugural balls, parties, and galas that it made your head spin. It's like Washington's version of the Oscars, essentially. The cheers and adulation we were getting everywhere was as breathtaking as it was humbling.

NANCY PELOSI: It was a good night to be a Democrat—but it was a bad night to be a grandmother. I wanted to stay out until all hours, but I got pretty exhausted pretty early. I don't think it was just my age; I'm used to staying up if a bill is needed or something. I think that I, like so many Americans, was just so *tired* from eight years of the Bush agenda. Eight years of war, tax cuts for the rich, and social divisiveness. It just never stopped—until the night of the Obama inauguration. And then it was like, "Go get a good night's sleep. You've earned it, Nancy!"

HUGHLEY: I remember going around to all the events and everyone was having the time of their lives; it was like the entire city was enjoying prom night.

BIDEN: I like proms. They're so festive.

JOHN EDWARDS: I like after the proms.

BILL: Preach it, brother!

HUGHLEY: It was fun for me running into people that you see on television, both the good ones and the not-so-good ones. Then I went to some of the Republican events. No, nobody thought that I was a valet and I did not have to use the back entrance.

STEELE: President Hillary we were ready for. President Hillary we knew how to fight, we had a strategy, there was a plan. But with Senator and now *President* Obama, I have to admit it seemed like we were a bit out of our depth. The Clintons had thrown everything but the kitchen sink at the guy and he had brushed it off as if it were nothing.

HILLARY: Trust me, we tried whatever we could. We had brainstormed the kitchen sink but it didn't poll well.

STEELE: By inauguration day, we still had nothing. Obama's approval numbers remained at record levels. Worse, the Democrats had enormous majorities in both the House and the Senate. We really had our backs against the wall.

HILLARY: They were as powerless as they were clueless.

HUGHLEY: The looks on the Republicans' faces was as if they were in a fog. They were listening to the music at their events, generally trying to make a show of being amiable and having a good time. But all of it was insincere, transparently so. They simply didn't know what had happened. They couldn't believe it, and worse they couldn't *understand* it. They just didn't know what to do. What's the point of picking up pieces if you don't have glue to put it back together? That sort of thing.

MICHELLE: The end of the night went off without a hitch, but it didn't seem like it would be that way at first.

VALERIE JARRETT: What people need to understand is that politics is a very unfriendly, ruthless field. On the surface, everyone is all smiles and positivity. But behind the scenes, there's a lot of squabbling and backstabbing. This has been the case since the very beginning, when Thomas Jefferson and Alexander Hamilton were both in George Washington's cabinet and at each other's throats.

MICHELLE: It was important for both Barack and myself to have advisers who knew us as people, as individuals, before we became "the Obamas." One such person was Valerie Jarrett. She wasn't jumping on the Obama bandwagon, like some others. We knew that we could count on her as a true friend.

JARRETT: I'd known the Obamas for a very long time. I knew my role was to look at things from the political angle, the public angle, but also from the *personal* angle. I know that Barack hates pears and Michelle isn't fond of lilies. These sorts of matters are beneath the president, but they still need to be taken care of. If you go to eat at your friend's house, they'll ask if you, say, hate spicy food. There's no reason that the president and First Lady shouldn't have the same courtesy.

MICHELLE: Barack and I had promised that we would attend all ten official inaugural balls. It would be intense, but after the campaign, ten stops in one night didn't seem that bad. Early on, the question became what song Barack and I should first come out to. It was just like the debate about our first wedding song. There was a brief little brainstorming session and *someone* tossed out "Paint the White House Black."

BIDEN: It was my idea. See, it's a play on words. Because Barack Obama is black, and the White House is white. So if he became president, it would mean that he had painted the White House black. Not literally, though.

MICHELLE: I cringed when I heard that suggestion. But since the person who brought it up was high up in the campaign, I didn't really confront them. I just bit my tongue.

BIDEN: No one seemed to take issue with my idea. I really hit that one out of the park!

MICHELLE: I called Valerie and—I'm not going to lie—I was a little bit panicked. One immediate concern was that the song was by George *Clinton*.

BIDEN: Is he the guy with the yarn in his hair?

MICHELLE: Were we going to have jokes about the "Clinton White House"?

BIDEN: He's also a wrestler, if I'm not mistaken.

MICHELLE: There was also such a strong racial undercurrent to the song. I knew that many in America were scared that once Barack became president he would basically drop some façade and become a Black Panther or something.

ALAN KEYES: The devil can assume many forms. Panther, Kenyan—potato, po*ta*to.

MICHELLE: I've never heard of the devil becoming a potato.

HUGHLEY: Well, potatoes become vodka, and that stuff sure is the devil.

BIDEN: Wait, George Clinton's not a wrestler? So who am I thinking of, the wrestler with the yarn in his hair? Because I know I've seen a wrestler with yarn in his hair. Ric Flair, is that it? That sounds like someone who would have yarn in his hair.

MICHELLE: That's the challenge of building racial trust in this country. Many in the white community want to reach out to minorities, but they're scared of it being a trick. You sign up for Martin Luther King, but then Malcolm X shows up with a shotgun. So the whole scenario becomes like handing off a hostage. Even though everyone wants the same thing, the entire exchange is very tense.

BIDEN: I like wrestling.

JARRETT: It's important for people in politics to have their perspectives heard and validated, even if those ideas are impractical or even absurd. I told Michelle that I'd take charge of the music issue. I smiled and nodded and told Joe Biden that we would need to take a look at the song's lyrics first. That could be a potential source for embarrassment with any number.

HILLARY: Drudge once gave me grief because I came out to "Mambo

No. 5," a song about all the women that the singer had been with. That's how desperate the right is in this country to attack people.

BILL: Worst single ever.

BIDEN: The song goes "Paint the White House black, paint the White House black, something something something, paint the White House black."

JARRETT: We told Senator Biden that there was a part where they rhymed it with "crack" and that seemed to calm him down.

BIDEN: Of course if there's a reference to crack in there, it's completely unacceptable. Truthfully I couldn't understand what the rapsingers were saying half the time. I am a politician of conviction. Unlike some other people, I have always been very strong in my view that crack is dangerous and people shouldn't do it. Those are the tough stands that you have to take to succeed in politics. I'm also in favor of doing your homework and saying "thank you."

JARRETT: So the question became which song we *should* do instead.

MICHELLE: This election was an election of young people and young ideas, very future oriented. Barack was only forty-seven years old when he was inaugurated. So in that vein, we wanted a contemporary, fun song to be our first dance.

JARRETT: I thought that made perfect sense. So I got together with some of the younger staffers and had them come up with some suggestions. Personally, I don't listen to the radio anymore.

I like to listen to Ella Fitzgerald and Aretha Franklin. I got the lists from the kids but that didn't help. I recognized the names of some of the performers but I had never heard of most of the songs.

MICHELLE: Then Valerie and I realized that the lyrics actually *were* a concern.

JARRETT: We decided that there couldn't be any songs that used the n-word.

MICHELLE: No references to sex, nothing raunchy.

JARRETT: Obviously mentions of drugs and drinking were off-limits.

MICHELLE: I did not want to hear women referred to as a *b.* or a *ho.*

JARRETT: I made the staffers go through their song selections and come back to us with a shorter list of music that would be appropriate.

MICHELLE: They came back with a shorter list all right!

JARRETT: There were no songs that fit those criteria. *None.*

MICHELLE: I guess Tipper Gore was right.

JARRETT: Well, we were back to the drawing board. Or mixing board, I should say!

SARAH PALIN: That's pretty funny.

MICHELLE: I didn't want to worry Barack with this sort of stuff, so Valerie and I just sort of paced back and forth in the office before one of us had the idea that we should just go through our iPods. Surely we'd be able to find *something* on there.

JARRETT: I thought of Etta James. She was a black woman but she always had blond hair, so that might be the closest that we could come to someone of Barack's unusual mixed heritage. Her song "At Last" seemed very apt.

MICHELLE: Love the song, love Etta. It wasn't recent, but it does have a timeless quality. We could get Etta herself to perform, too, like the Clintons had Fleetwood Mac for their inauguration.

JARRETT: I put out some calls and let's just say Ms. James was not in the best of health in any sense. She was—how do I put this?—she was *cray*.

MICHELLE: I had seen Beyoncé perform the song in the movie *Cadillac Records*. I thought that maybe she could do it at the inaugural as well.

JARRETT: To say Ms. Knowles was excited was an understatement.

MICHELLE: And a relief!

JARRETT: The other balls that night didn't really matter as much; those were regional and we figured those tracks out quickly.

MICHELLE: The thing is, I'd forgotten that the following night was a *Youth* Ball. So we needed *another* young contemporary song.

JARRETT: Michelle and I just looked at each other with exhaustion. "Screw this," I said. "Let's just get Jay Z."

JAY Z: My wife is such a feminist that I gotta perform the night after her.

MICHELLE: I was meeting so many wonderful people, really kind of sharing this joyous day with strangers, and soon it was always, "We have to go, ma'am." Then we were whisked to the next thing. It was a very long, very exhausting day for everybody. I don't know what time we ended up heading back to the White House on inauguration night. Even though I had started the day fearing for the worst, by that night I had long forgotten those fears. Heck, I was so tired I had practically forgotten Barack's name and my own.

██████████: After the stress of that day, the maximum public exposure for a new president, we Secret Service agents need a break as well. That's why we always put new agents on watch in the White House living quarters during inauguration night. Then we senior agents play dumb as they listen to the new president celebrate the spoils of his new office and claim his conquest.

MICHELLE: It felt so surreal to sleep in the White House for the first time.

██████████: There wasn't much sleeping that night. There never is.

MICHELLE: We didn't even say much, we just went to bed as husband and wife.

██████████: Going all the way back to Nixon, the dialogue that night is always the same: "F me, Mr. President! F me, Mr. President!"

MICHELLE: It was a relief to finally get a load off.

██████████: He must have gotten three or four, from the sound of it. I think her last shout was something like, "I don't think I can handle another inauguration like that!"

5

SENATE SUPERMAJORITY, 2009

MICHELLE OBAMA: Let's recall the state of America when Barack was inaugurated. The economy was in shambles and could have gotten worse at any moment. Fixing that would take time and there was no way to speed up the process. But in terms of international affairs, that was something that *President* Obama could start fixing immediately.

RAHM EMANUEL: She loved saying that, saying "President Obama."

MICHELLE: Can you blame me?

EMANUEL: No, I couldn't blame her. I said it, which is why I was so tickled to be asked to serve as chief of staff. In fact, many people throughout the world were ecstatic at an Obama administration. I read quite a few letters of congratulations that came in. I've got a good nose for separating the bullshit from the real shit. Many, many world leaders were very happy to deal with a president who was ready to be a part of the international community, rather than being apart from it.

MICHELLE: A great deal of foreign leaders felt like they had been humiliated by President Bush. In a way, they were. He had gone to the United Nations to ask for approval for an invasion of Iraq. They turned him down—so he just went ahead and did it anyway. Then what had been the purpose of asking them? Clearly he was only making a pretense of caring about their perspective. At the end of the day, America the cowboy was going to do as it darn well pleased.

EMANUEL: The biggest mess on the world stage was in the Middle East. My dad's Israeli, I'm obviously pro-Israel, but the Arabs know that there's a big fucking difference between defending Israel and basically declaring a war on Islam, which is pretty much what the Bush/Cheney neocons wanted. I mean, you had Bush on TV after 9/11 saying that he's going to go after Afghanistan and then Iraq and then Iran. The other countries were like, Hold the phone, where does this shit end? Because, yeah, we hate you and death to America, yadda yadda yadda, but we're playing to our base too. We're not *actually* attacking you guys, we're not stupid.

MICHELLE: So the idea came that Senator Clinton would make a great secretary of state. If Barack's role as president was to be diplomatic and conciliatory, we still needed someone to sort of be the administration bad guy and hold our feet to the fire. It's *good* to be surrounded by smart people who will challenge your decisions. Every president gets into a bubble and becomes surrounded by yes-men. That was something we tried to stave off from the very beginning.

VICE PRESIDENT JOE BIDEN: I *choose* to agree.

EMANUEL: I thought Hillary would be killer. I only hoped that wouldn't be literal.

MICHELLE: Barack was hesitant at first. The primary fight with Senator Clinton had been very difficult. Everyone has an ego and he just thought that it wouldn't work. He couldn't see her as a team member or as a team player. Heck, I think he was so scarred by that primary that he practically viewed her as an enemy noncombatant.

HILLARY RODHAM CLINTON: I had wanted to be VP, and I had earned the right to be VP. But they'd said no. So when they asked me to run the State Department, it sure felt good to tell them no in return. I was looking forward to a long career in the Senate, where I was well respected even among Republicans (though you'd never hear them say that).

MITCH McCONNELL: I *never* said that.

JOHN CORNYN: Me neither.

McCONNELL: I bet you it was McCain.

CORNYN: It's always McCain.

MICHELLE: I think Senator Clinton felt that the offer was just a courtesy or some sort of consolation prize, which it wasn't. We were going to have to move on to someone else, given her refusal.

EMANUEL: No, we weren't, I said. We couldn't just ignore the Clintons. I know how the press works; they were going to gin up this imaginary fucking bullshit rivalry between the president and Senator Clinton. It would never stop. The moment there was the slightest disagreement or even a "Let me get back to you," that would be taken as "proof" that there's this rift between the two camps. "The Democrats are being torn apart!" No way. No fucking way. We had to bring them into our team.

MICHELLE: Rahm made a very strong case in his Rahm way, and it was hard to argue with the case that he laid out. He reminded everyone of how the Clintons had turned their backs on Carl McCall in the New York governor's race in 2002 and how it had cost McCall the election.

It had been a complete landslide against him in a very blue state. So Barack came around to viewing it as if we didn't have a choice. We either had to have her with us, or against us.

EMANUEL: Secretary of state was it, and it had to be it. She would be great at the gig, and in that capacity she was expected to keep quiet on domestic affairs. Plus, it has a lot of gravitas to it. So we asked Hillary again, and we made it clear that this wasn't something for show. We truly wanted her in the administration.

PRESIDENT BILL CLINTON: My wife would never admit to this and she's never said as much to me, but I have my own theory. I think that after being the most successful female presidential candidate in American history—by far, it wasn't even close—I think after that, it becomes hard to take a job as a secretary. Maybe I'm being silly but I suspect that on some silly visceral level it irked her.

HILLARY: That's the job they give to the one girl in every club in high school! Couldn't I at least be a czar or something?

VLADIMIR PUTIN: Some people think she came to Russia on her broom. Those people are what is known in Russia as "correct."

MICHELLE: Once it clicked that this was a sincere offer, the tone of the conversations changed. Despite all the media attempts to paint every powerful woman as some sort of "diva," Senator Clinton only had a very few reasonable preconditions.

HILLARY: I wanted to be sure this was an actual role with actual responsibilities, that I would have the ability to influence and affect America's foreign policy.

MICHELLE: This was a no-brainer. We wanted that as well.

HILLARY: I also wanted my own office with my own staff and my own server.

MICHELLE: We let the decorating and computer people handle all that. What could possibly go wrong?

BILL: Hillary was very happy to accept under those terms, and I could not be prouder of her. On a political note, I also knew that being secretary of state would be a great stepping-stone should she want to run for president again. Frankly I expected to be back in the White House, dancing like Tom Cruise in *Risky Business*. I'd be sliding down those halls in my tighty whities and having a blast.

MICHELLE: The question now became which foreign country to address first. Did we make overtures to allies that President Bush had burned, maybe France?

EMANUEL: No one thought that was a good idea. Do you know why? Because no one likes the French. I can be eating french fries while looking at the *Mona Lisa* in Paris, and I still wouldn't like them. Why? Because fuck the French, is why.

MICHELLE: So France was off the table. Maybe England? But Bush and the UK had been so closely associated with the Iraq War, and we wanted to back away from that. Israel knew we supported her, there was no point in stirring that pot. I think at one point we almost brought out a Risk board to try and do process of elimination.

EMANUEL: President Obama's first-ever interview ended up being with Al

Arabiya, which is kind of an Arab CNN. He flew over and met with the king of Jordan, and both the Israelis and the Palestinians. So for a foreign speech we wanted some moderate Muslim country that would be uncontroversial.

MICHELLE: Egypt was the obvious answer. They had a peace treaty with Israel, so the Israelis wouldn't be ticked off. At the same time, it was also a culturally Muslim country in the dead center of the Middle East—not just a nation with a large Muslim population.

HOSNI MUBARAK: I'd been president of Egypt since 1981. I have seen American presidents come and I've seen American presidents go. This man Obama impressed me very much. When I met with President Obama, yes, I was speaking to someone from another country, another culture. He was a foreigner but he was a friend. George Bush . . . What is the expression? "He has a buzz," we say in Egypt. "A screw loose," I think you say in America. Bush, he was from another planet.

MICHELLE: We knew we were going to catch heat from the Republicans, especially the neocons. I didn't blame them. Barack was basically publicly repudiating their entire philosophy on the world stage.

JOHN McCAIN: It was an apology tour, plain and simple. Bowing down before foreign leaders—sometimes literally—and telling them how sorry he was that America was the greatest nation in the world. Our campaign slogan had been "Country First." Now it had become "Apologize First, Make Requests Later." Nowhere near as pithy.

MICHELLE: It is so ironic that the Republican Party claims to be the party of taking responsibility. Yet when Barack took responsibility for America's mistakes, he was vilified. As if we'd never done anything wrong as a country abroad, let alone at home?

McCAIN: If you ask me, other countries should try to be more like America, instead of America being more like them. But hey, what do I know? It's not like I'm the president or anything.

EMANUEL: Foreign policy is a tricky issue that cuts across parties. There's hawks and doves on both sides and internationally it's rarely good guys versus bad guys anymore. But I think the American people were desperate to try something—*anything*—different on the world stage.

BIDEN: My goal for a new foreign policy? I didn't want to have to keep going to military funerals. They're boring as hell. I am not saying that to complain. I'm saying that to point out how numb you get after a while. Being numb at the death of someone's son or daughter, their husband or wife—I don't like being in that state. You say the same thing to every parent, you praise the kid . . . and then you promptly forget about it because psychologically you can't remember them all. It is politics at its absolute worst. I'd rather go to a sex club with Jack Ryan, Mike Ditka, and Ross Perot than go to one other such funeral.

EMANUEL: The domestic front was in crisis as well. We thought we had a national consensus there too. The bailouts had worked: they had stopped the bleeding, so to speak. Now we needed to get the patient back on his feet.

MICHELLE: The idea was to have a stimulus package that would get unanimous congressional support, or close to it. We knew that the Republicans would raise a huge stink about how expensive and wasteful it was, no matter what. So we thought we'd throw out a higher number and allow them to talk us down. Then they could go back to their districts as conquering heroes and we'd still get the stimulus we wanted. Everybody won—most importantly, including the economy.

EMANUEL: The stimulus was a onetime thing. This wasn't some new annual addition to the budget. It was like taking medicine: You don't keep on with it once you're better.

MICHELLE: Then the word came back from Congress: the Republicans were saying no.

McCONNELL: I didn't come to Washington to be a rubber stamp for a president who is out of control with spending. President Clinton tried the same trick when he first came to the White House. He wanted a stimulus package to pay off all the special interest groups that had snuck him into the presidency. The Republicans stuck to our guns and we said no, hell no, absolutely not. We filibustered and the Democrats pulled the bill. We won.

NANCY PELOSI: And the American people lost. That stimulus prolonged the first President Bush's recession. Some people just can't learn from history. Those people are called Republicans.

EMANUEL: No, Republicans can't learn from *anything*. They were not opposing the president out of principle; they were opposing him *on* principle.

HARRY REID: Politics is a numbers game. If we wanted to minimize Republican obstructionism, the only way to do that was to have more Democrats in Congress. The Senate was designed to promote debate. But if you have a body designed to promote debate, that comes at the expense of promoting action. It's talk, talk, talk.

CLARENCE THOMAS: It's hell on earth.

REID: Any one senator can bring the entire legislative process to a complete halt at any time. He can talk and talk and talk. Until he shuts up, nothing else can happen. This is what's known as a filibuster. The most notorious example of this was when Strom Thurmond filibustered for twenty-four hours against civil rights legislation. He talked for an entire day straight.

MICHELLE: He peed in a bucket, which I believe is currently in the Smithsonian next to an old-timey Colored water fountain. The museum is thinking of having a "fluids of race in America" exhibit. Maybe a bottle of Aunt Jemima pancake syrup will go there too.

RAND PAUL: I filibustered the NSA (National Security Agency), and I'm proud that I did. I spoke for over ten hours, and that's pretty hard to do. After a while, you forget what you said and what you haven't. Your brain starts to repeat itself. It's hard to do. So you start telling long stories that don't really have much to do with the bill at hand. Like this one time, I wanted to get a book signed by William F. Buckley. I went to see him speak for his debate series; this was in the 1990s before I was a senator. So I got my ticket and sat in the front row. Well, after Buckley did his thing, he left the stage while the other people debating, the other debaters, were signing autographs. I was there to see Buckley. So I had to go backstage, it wasn't going to be easy. It's hard to do.

REID: The only workaround to a filibuster is a cloture vote. That's when sixty senators basically assent to stop the ongoing debate and move the business of the Senate forward. We already had fifty-eight Democrats in hand. The Minnesota election was still being counted,

it was very close, but it looked like Al Franken would pull it out—
bringing us to fifty-nine.

MICHELLE: Barack becoming president left his Senate seat vacant.

REID: That Illinois senator would be the sixtieth Democrat. This
wasn't just some tossaway Senate seat. If we had sixty Democratic seats,
that meant that we had a cloture vote. That meant that Republicans
wouldn't be able to filibuster our bills. We would be doing what the
American people had voted us in to do.

MICHELLE: Most people don't realize this, but every state has a different
way of filling congressional vacancies. It could be a snap election or it could
be that the specific state legislature appoints someone. That's how it used to
be done anyway: The state legislature would elect senators directly.

McCAIN: I remember that.

MICHELLE: With Illinois it fell to the governor to appoint an acting
senator until the next scheduled election—in this case, November 2010.
That would be two years. Unfortunately the person appointing a replacement to Barack's Senate seat was Illinois's governor. And I say
unfortunately because the governor at the time was Rod Blagojevich.

ROD BLAGOJEVICH: I was the first Democrat to be elected governor
of Illinois since the 1970s.

EMANUEL: He was also . . . how do I put this delicately? *Completely
fucking retarded.* We have a lot of retarded people both in Chicago
and Washington, in both political parties. Dan Quayle was famously
retarded. Debbie Wasserman Schultz, I love her, she's a great loyal

Democrat, but the broad is learning disabled on her best day. Blagojevich? He was something special, and I don't just mean special *needs*.
You know how you could be talking to someone and they're nodding
and you think they're agreeing with you and following your train of
thought? And then when you're done speaking you realize they weren't
agreeing with you—they were falling asleep with their eyes open, and
their chin just kept hitting their chest, which made their head bounce
up and down? That's Blagojevich. Not only was he not the sharpest
knife in the drawer, he wasn't even the sharpest drawer.

MICHELLE: Politics is about reciprocity. You do something for me,
I do something for you. If not now, then in the future. People understand this but they don't like to hear about it. They pretend it isn't so.
But there has to be something in it for people to help you out. That's
not only politics, that's life.

EMANUEL: So Blagojevich had one of the greatest gifts you can give
anyone: an open Senate seat. He's like the Hobbit, he's got this special
ring that everyone wants and now it's on him to name his price.

MICHELLE: Unfortunately, he took that literally.

BLAGOJEVICH: I never tried to sell that Senate seat. Those allegations were false.

EMANUEL: I heard that he wanted to put it on fucking eBay.

BLAGOJEVICH: That's absurd. You can't sell political offices on eBay.
I discovered that personally.

EMANUEL: I myself handed the governor a list of four names that the president-elect and I had vetted. This was still in 2008, right after the election, before Obama had even been inaugurated. We wanted our ducks in a row.

JESSE JACKSON: This Senate seat had been held by Carol Moseley Braun and then by Barack Obama. For years it had been the only African American Senate seat in the whole country. I thought it would be important that the next officeholder be a person of color, to bring some diversity to the United States Senate.

PRESIDENT GEORGE H. W. BUSH: Like when I had appointed Clarence Thomas to fill Thurgood Marshall's seat in the Supreme Court.

JACKSON: Yes, like that except for the complete opposite. I thought there was no better qualified Senate candidate than my namesake: Jesse Jackson Jr.

EMANUEL: Junior had been on our short list. He had been in Congress for over a decade and was a loyal Democrat committed to Barack Obama's vision of politics.

BLAGOJEVICH: Also, he was out of his mind.

JESSE JACKSON JR.: I later made public my struggle with mental illness. It's got such a stigma in this country and that's something that has to change. The brain is a part of the human body just like any other part. No one thinks differently of you if you break your arm. No one questions your qualifications for office if you have an ulcer. But if you have psychological issues? Forget it. You're a complete pariah.

BLAGOJEVICH: I met with him and he wouldn't stop rhyming. I was looking for a senator, not a Seuss.

JACKSON JR.: We've all read those stories about some man who hasn't stopped hiccupping in thirty years. It's a silly news article that you can laugh about, and that's fine. It is what it is. But once you start to think of this man not as a minor news piece but as a person, it isn't funny at all. You are filled with empathy and horror at his condition.

BLAGOJEVICH: The first rhyme he threw out, I didn't think anything of it. Junior's father was known for how he talked. The second rhyme, fine, that's his shtick, he's putting on a show. But after a while it was just *odd*.

JACKSON JR.: The nonstop rhyming was the worst of my symptoms. It would just creep in. I would have no choice but to talk in verse. There was no other way. I'd call a doctor or a nurse. But it would last all day.

BLAGOJEVICH: There was a look of terror in his eyes, like he couldn't help himself. It was really quite unsettling.

JACKSON JR.: My rhyming speech would come and go, and when I never knew. And sometimes when they'd hear me talk, my friends would start rhyming too.

BLAGOJEVICH: I thought he was trying to get me to talk like that so I sat there and tried to figure out what rhymes with Senate. And I meant it. That was the best I could do, "Senate, meant it." Maybe I should have been listening to more rap music.

BIDEN: I like rap music.

BLAGOJEVICH: And senator? Nothing rhymes with that.

JACKSON JR.: The meeting did not go as planned. My speech was all awry. If this rhyming shit don't stop and *soon,* I really want to die.

EMANUEL: No one gave a fuck that Jesse Jackson—both of them—spoke in rhymes, just like no one gave a fuck that President Bush spoke in mumbles and incomplete sentences.

PRESIDENT GEORGE W. BUSH: Here's an incomplete sentence for you, Rahm: Go f___ yourself.

DICK CHENEY: A great man, a great president, and a great American.

EMANUEL: According to the rumors, Blagojevich was just ticked that Jesse Jackson wouldn't pay him his money for the Senate seat. So he started shopping it around.

MICHELLE: What the governor didn't realize was that a federal investigator was tapping his phone.

EMANUEL: They arrested Blago on December 9, 2008. Pretty much exactly in between the election and the inauguration.

BLAGOJEVICH: It was very embarrassing, I'm not going to lie.

McCONNELL: I'd served with Senator Obama, been up close and personal with him many times. I'd served with many, many other men and women over the years. After a while, you get to pick up certain things about them. Any politician—or any *good* one I should say—is going to have a pretty strong ability to size people up. I never bought into this whole messianic walking-on-water thing with Obama. He seemed like a decent man to me, an honest man. But you take a decent man and an honest man and you put him in Chicago politics? He'll get a bigger makeover than Michael Jackson. Then he's bad, he's bad. *Sham on.*

MICHELLE: I think the Republicans caught a whiff of scandal, and their first impulse was to try and exploit it to their advantage. It was the same thing as with Reverend Wright, this sort of guilt-by-association thing, but I knew that nothing would come of it just like nothing really came out of the Reverend Wright controversy.

McCONNELL: Something was rotten in the state of Illinois.

MICHELLE: I agree with Senator McConnell on one point: politics does have a corrupting effect on many people over the long term. I'm sure *his* thirty years in the Senate taught him that. It's a good thing that Barack rose through the ranks of Chicago politics as quickly as he did. He was a product of a political machine but not a function of it, like Harry Truman before him.

McCONNELL: I did not know Harry Truman. Harry Truman was no friend of mine. Barack Obama—he's no Truman. There's nothing true about him.

BLAGOJEVICH: So I was arrested and was being charged. But the thing is: *I was still governor.* Maybe I wouldn't be able to score political favors—which is all I actually wanted, I was innocent of the charges— but I still had the ability to appoint a senator.

EMANUEL: We had to have a special election in my district anyway, since I was leaving Congress to work in the White House. I thought that the Illinois General Assembly should just pass a bill taking the power out of the governor's hands and calling for a special election for the Obama seat, too.

BLAGOJEVICH: I wasn't going to let them take this away from me.

MICHELLE: It caught us all by surprise.

EMANUEL: So what did that dumb fucker Blagojevich do? He waited until New Year's Eve, and then he officially appointed Roland Burris to be the replacement senator.

BLAGOJEVICH: He was the right man for the job.

DICK DURBIN: I'm the other senator from Illinois. As I stated publicly at the time, there was no way that *anyone* appointed to that Senate seat under those conditions would be able to have the legitimacy to serve. I like Roland Burris, knew him for many years in Illinois politics. But even if Blagojevich had appointed the pope to that seat, it still wouldn't have passed the sniff test.

POPE FRANCIS I: Why would a Democrat appoint me to the Senate? I'm not an American, and even if I were, I'd be registered in the Rent Is Too Damn High party.

EMANUEL: I think he chose Burris to spite Jesse Jackson, to be honest.

JACKSON: Mr. Burris and I have had our history over the years. It's fair to say that we haven't seen eye to eye on a number of issues. In fact, we had a very public altercation after the 1984 presidential election.

CHENEY: Were you planning on cutting his nuts off too?

JACKSON: My campaign manager, Richard Hatcher, had been the Black Caucus's nominee for vice chairman of the Democratic National Committee. Instead the party chose Mr. Burris, which I regarded as illegitimate and said so at the time.

ROLAND BURRIS: In other words, I was used to this sort of thing. The Illinois secretary of state refused to certify my appointment. When I went to Washington in January 2009, Harry Reid and the Democrats would not grant me entrance to the Senate.

McCONNELL: Make no mistake about it: They were campaigning on hope and change, but they were simply playing politics the same way as everyone else had for decades.

REID: Of course we were playing politics. We're politicians! That's like complaining that baseball players are playing baseball. Here's the situation. I know how the Republicans operate. If there was a special election, almost certainly the seat would be retained by a Democrat. I don't know who they would find if Alan Keyes had been their best bet last time! But if the Senate sat Burris, then the GOP could say that his vote was illegitimate. And if his vote was illegitimate—say, for cloture—then they would argue that any bills passed that way, overriding a filibuster, were illegitimate as well.

EMANUEL: Then someone pointed out that maybe it's not a good idea for the Democratic Party to literally shut the door in the face of a black man who simply showed up to do his job.

REID: I realized that the Republicans were going to raise a hue and cry regardless, so after speaking with Mr. Burris, we decided to seat him as Senator Burris after all.

BURRIS: I'm just glad that they didn't assign me a desk all the way in the back, right by the kitchen.

REID: With Burris in hand and Minnesota falling our way, we had the sixty votes we needed to pass the most dynamic progressive agenda in a generation—which is what the American people had voted for, mind you.

JACKSON JR.: I wanted to be a senator. I hoped it would be me. But if it had to be someone else, then maybe . . . oh fuck, the rhyming stopped. Thank you, thank you Jesus!

6

MAKING APPOINTMENTS, 2009

MICHELLE OBAMA: One of Barack's qualities that people respond to is his self-effacing sense of humor. He can be serious when he needs to be, intensely so, but he also encourages people to be at ease and to laugh. And, boy, did we sure need some laughter after the Bush years.

VICE PRESIDENT DICK CHENEY: I'm plenty funny and you know it.

RAHM EMANUEL: As the presidency began, we were waiting for the jokes to start too. *Saturday Night Live,* Leno, Letterman—*The Daily Show,* especially—all of them had had a field day with Bush. Before that, President Clinton had been getting clocked on the jaw pretty regularly. Usually the jokes come out during the campaign, that's when the caricaturing of the person's mannerisms and speech patterns starts. But with Obama, it hadn't really been happening.

MICHELLE: That worried me. If they're not making fun of the president, then the Republicans will say that it's not fair, look how much Bush was made fun of. I think that would really be a valid point, I'm not going to lie. We should look at our leaders of all parties with a healthy hint of skepticism. Who knows? A little more doubt and a raised eyebrow might have kept us out of Iraq.

DENNIS KUCINICH: I kept trying to raise eyebrows, but I don't have any.

WHOOPI GOLDBERG: It's the worst!

EMANUEL: From day one of the Obama administration, even before day one, all the television stations, all the cable news stations were asking for interviews. This time, however, the late-night shows were calling as well. I'd imagine they'd also been calling the Bush White House but were turned down as a matter of course.

PRESIDENT GEORGE W. BUSH: On the one hand, I think it is beneath the president to appear in a venue that's so unserious. I wanted to respect the position that my father held before me. I made it a rule that people had to wear a suit and tie in the Oval Office, for example.

PRESIDENT BILL CLINTON: Now that we can agree on. You can't loosen your tie in the Oval Office if you aren't wearing one to begin with.

BUSH: On the other hand, I wasn't going to reward those people who made a punching bag out of me day in and day out.

MICHELLE: Bill Clinton had played the saxophone on *The Arsenio Hall Show* when he had been a candidate. There were a few raised eyebrows, sure, but looking back it was an iconic moment and he didn't come off poorly at all. More importantly, it didn't diminish him. It humanized him.

EMANUEL: So we started thinking that maybe a late-night appearance wouldn't be a bad idea. President Obama had this rock star vibe, and rock stars do this sort of thing all the time. There really wouldn't be a downside to doing Leno or Letterman. They would be respectful and the audience would eat it up. It would be a good way to demonstrate a break with the previous administration. There didn't seem to be a whole lot of *warmth* there.

CHENEY: Screw you, Rahm. I'm plenty warm.

EMANUEL: Nor was there much humor.

CHENEY: Are you kidding? I'm the second-funniest Republican alive! It goes Elizabeth Dole, then me, and then maybe Lamar Alexander. You get Lamar started with the Polish jokes, and he'll have you peeing your pants. I'm saying that it's happened *literally*.

MICHELLE: We chose Leno over Letterman for several reasons. First of all, he had better ratings. Second, he had more of a mainstream audience, people who had been more resistant to Barack than Letterman's edgier, more urban crowd.

JOHN BOEHNER: Third, they knew that Letterman would eat the president alive while Leno would be about as edgy as drawn butter.

JAY LENO: I've interviewed many important people over the years, but a sitting president was a whole other level entirely. We wanted the president—not to mention his eventual 2012 opponent, we were thinking ahead—we wanted them to feel comfortable coming back again. Yet we didn't want to seem like it was a cakewalk. We knew we had to play it soft but not toothless.

MICHELLE: Barack never gets nervous with stuff like this, but the Leno interview was one of the few times that he was a little . . . *concerned*. He was the president but he didn't want to be a stuffed shirt either. Nor did he want to come off as too glib. He also wanted to be himself. So there were a mess of emotions and that's when he made that infamous comment of his.

SARAH PALIN: As the mother of a special needs child I took exception to what Barack Hussein Obama had to say. It was a really low moment.

MICHELLE: Barack said that he bowled a 129. But then he added that it was "like the Special Olympics or something."

PALIN: It was crass and it was tacky and as a former beauty queen I know from tacky. Crass, not so much. That's always been more of a Democrat quality.

EMANUEL: Bowling *is* retarded. I'll say that flat out. Anyone who ever bowls belongs in the Special Olympics, or they would except for the fact that the actual Special Olympics is full of hardworking athletes who do their best. Ever see someone bowl? You have to put on strange shoes and terrible clothes—just like a person with mental disabilities does every day. Then the goal is to throw a ball and knock over as many things as possible. Isn't that what retarded people do? Give a ball to a retard and see how many things will be knocked over within a minute. I'll tell you how many: *far more than you ever thought possible.* So bowling isn't even the Special Olympics, it's like the fucking unspecial anti-Olympics, but instead of a gold medal you get cheese fries and a thing of Coke big enough for you to take a bath in.

VICE PRESIDENT JOE BIDEN: I like bowling.

MICHELLE: It was a dumb, pointless comment. Barack realized what he'd said as soon as he had said it, and he genuinely felt bad. He was on the phone with the chairman of the Special Olympics before the show even aired that night, just to demonstrate that there were no hard feelings.

LENO: We've all had bad jokes that didn't land. This was not a big deal and I didn't even register it. I was more focused on how white the president's teeth were; it was like those squares of chewing gum.

MICHELLE: Here's the thing that struck me. It was only a little over a year after Barack had joked that he needed to see if President Clinton could dance to decide if he was a brotha—and he had said *brotha*. That was a comment with a racial context, but no one got upset about it. It was understood to be lighthearted and playful. Here, with the bowling, he was making *himself* the butt of the joke. He was trying to be self-deprecating. He was trying to lower expectations a bit, because people thought he could walk on water.

HARRY REID: Well, I've never seen a colored man *swim* in it.

MICHELLE: Now, one year later, two things had changed. First, he was president now. But second, I didn't realize how many people were now interested in twisting his words. They wanted to score points off anything he said that might be remotely construed as being off-color. They were *waiting* to trip him up and blow an issue out of proportion. It hadn't been like that in the Bush years.

EMANUEL: Well, that's partially because waiting for George W. Bush to make a misstatement is like staring at a watch and waiting for the second hand to move. Bam! There it goes. Bam! There it goes again. And again. And again.

MICHELLE: It was sort of chilling. You want to keep yourself out of this bubble, you want to interact with people as much as possible to be yourself—and at the same time you have to wonder how everything is going to come off. Or worse, how it will be *made* to come off by people who have it in for you.

EMANUEL: Then we had the fly.

JOHN HARWOOD: For most reporters, a one-on-one interview with the president is a highlight of their career. That's not exactly breaking news. I'd been CNBC's chief Washington correspondent for a couple of years. Of course, CNBC takes a nonpartisan view on the issues but at the same time we don't shy away from asking tough questions. Nevertheless, it was quite a thrill to land an interview with the president.

EMANUEL: You know how JFK said that Washington is a city of Southern efficiency and Northern charm? That ain't the half of it. It's built on a fucking swamp. Literally, it's swampland. Or they call it wetlands now, because "swamp" sounds gross and "the environment" sounds nice. Whatever. The point is, you can drain it all the hell you want, that don't make it any nicer in the summer. It's still hot and humid as fuck, swamp conditions, even without the—I don't know—gators and dudes playing banjo or whatever the fuck.

MICHELLE: Do you think that mosquitoes care that I'm the First Lady? They probably go back to all their mosquito buddies and say, "Hey, you'll never believe whose blood I sucked today. Yes, she really is that tall!"

EMANUEL: So the flies are everywhere and they're even in the White House. And between you and me, that damn tomato garden

Mrs. Obama planted in the back wasn't helping with the insect situation one bit.

HARWOOD: So I'm interviewing the president and there's a fly buzzing around.

EMANUEL: Not just a housefly, this thing looked like a drone or some shit.

HARWOOD: We both tried to ignore it and I'm just hoping it wasn't being picked up on audio or on video.

MICHELLE: I think Sarah Palin thought it was a sign of the devil or something.

PALIN: You know, I spend a lot of time outdoors. And really, it isn't that complicated. Sometimes a fly is just a fly.

MICHELLE: Well, that's comforting to hear.

PALIN: And sometimes it's a sign of the devil. Who's to say?

HARWOOD: So the fly is buzzing around and then it lands on the president.

EMANUEL: I think it just wanted to touch him. Look, if your lifespan is like a month long, wouldn't "touch a president" be on your bucket list?

HARWOOD: So President Obama cups his hand really carefully and he has the thing in his sights. Now the interview comes to a halt. Everyone always talks about President Obama as if he's magic. Well, getting this fly would be proof that he's not like normal men.

EMANUEL: You remember *The Karate Kid,* and the old fucking Chinese or Japanese dude or whatever, Mr. Miyagi, he's sitting there catching flies with his chopsticks? That's what everyone watching was thinking of.

JOHN EDWARDS: I love that movie! What was that quote?

CLINTON: Slacks on, slacks off. No stains.

HARWOOD: The president got the fly. Squashed it dead, our cameras got the whole thing—even the body of the victim on the floor.

PALIN: I heard they're really skilled at killing flies in Kenya. I'm not saying there's any connection, just stating some facts.

MICHELE BACHMANN: I had a mother come up to me one evening. She told me that her little daughter got bitten by a fly and she suffered from mental retardation thereafter.

EMANUEL: I heard that Michele Bachmann was once covered in flies. You do the math.

MICHELLE: I was impressed that Barack got that sucker. Those flies can *move*. Good for him!

EMANUEL: Then PETA opened their fucking mouths.

MICHELLE: They sent out a press release and sent us some sort of a humane kind of trap to catch and release flies for the future. Which . . . I don't know what to say.

EMANUEL: You know why there's no point in humanely catching and releasing flies? *Because they can fucking fly.* They do it so well that's their whole fucking name. A fly can write an opera or solve some scientific mystery but that motherfucker is still going to be known for the fact that he can fly. You put him in the park and he smells something in the White House, guess what? He's flying back to the White House. He's flying *somewhere,* that's for sure.

MICHELLE: I wasn't really clear as to who would be releasing these flies and where. I don't think it would be very pleasant to have someone from the White House just unbottle a bunch of flies at the Lincoln Memorial.

EMANUEL: Sure, let's just put up flypaper in the Oval fucking Office, make it look like the kitchen to some shitty Mexican joint. Are you kidding me? Get the fuck out of here with that shit.

MICHELLE: PETA said that people should be compassionate to all animals. I of course agree. But this was a *fly.* Was everything Barack said or did going to be parsed and examined through a microscopic lens, even from our own side? PETA was hardly some right-wing nutjob organization.

CHENEY: Nope, they're the left-wing nutjobs. But I repeat myself.

MICHELLE: So now what? Do we address this press release? Do we ignore them? Apologize? If we ignored them, it ran the risk of them getting more upset next time. Or maybe the next group over—I don't know, the environmentalists—would now be on guard. If you apologize, it's a whole other story in and of itself too.

EMANUEL: Who is the president supposed to be apologizing to? The fly community? If you ask me, there hasn't been a fly community since Miles Davis died.

MICHELLE: It wasn't this way with George W. Bush.

LAURA BUSH: Oh, give me a freaking break. For eight years, every morning I had to wake up to see some completely skewed and twisted story about my husband. You try and keep that from getting to you, to see the father of your kids attacked like that in the press when you know it's half true at best. I was a librarian for many years. Do you know how hard it became for me to not be able to pick up the newspaper? It was bad.

MICHELLE: I agree with Mrs. Bush, and as a fellow First Lady I can really relate to what she went through. We're both tough women who had to bite our tongues many times when we saw our husbands being treated unfairly.

NANCY REAGAN: Still not a size zero, though! Either of you.

MICHELLE: Yes, President Bush was attacked. But here's the difference between Barack and President Bush. President Bush was attacked for the war. He was attacked for killing tens of thousands of people, not one fly. He was attacked for giving tax cuts to the rich—*while spending trillions on war.* He was attacked for his explicit strategy of being reelected through divisiveness, "turning out the base" and ignoring the rest of us. Then, after he was reelected, he said he wanted to partially privatize Social Security, putting our seniors' well-being at risk with the rise and fall of the stock market. That wouldn't have worked out so well in 2008, would it? The point is, he was being attacked for his ideas and for his actions.

EMANUEL: The other difference between Barack Obama and George W. Bush—and there are many, of course—is that Obama was elected in a landslide. Not just personally, but he carried in a huge Democratic majority in both houses. We had a mandate; Bush never did. So since they couldn't go after the ideas that President Obama had campaigned on and been elected on, the Republicans had to find some other way to take him down. And if they couldn't take *him* down, then they started looking for other targets. I don't blame them. It's what I would have done!

MICHELLE: We knew the Supreme Court would be a major issue at some point. It was a big reason that the Democrats rallied together after the primary. We didn't want to have a Republican president push the court further to the radical right.

RUTH BADER GINSBURG: I've been on the Supreme Court for a couple of decades now. Before that, I'd been involved with the legal system for longer than many people have been alive. So when I say that it's changed radically in my lifetime, and especially in the last several decades, I'm not speaking from a lack of perspective.

ERIC HOLDER: I can only agree with Justice Ginsburg. I received bipartisan support when I was confirmed as attorney general. But I think the feeling was that the Democrats had the votes so why fight it. It was not really amicable or deferential like it had been in the past.

EMANUEL: They didn't want to say no to another black man, not so soon after the elections. Not even the Republicans are that dumb.

HOLDER: The Supreme Court was a different matter. This had the potential to be a hellstorm, so we were planning ahead for months.

GINSBURG: There used to be a collegiality on the court. The idea was that if a major decision was being handed down, it was very helpful to have the majority supporting it be as large as possible. That way, the possibility of it being overturned wouldn't be hovering in the air and the issue could be considered settled. Chief Justice Roberts mentioned this principle in his confirmation hearings, *stare decisis*. The law should be as stable and predictable as possible.

JOHN ROBERTS: True that. Guilty as charged!

GINSBURG: *Roe v. Wade* was a 7–2 vote. *Brown v. Board of Education*, ending segregation, was unanimous, 9–0. But now major decisions were being decided by a bare majority, 5–4.

HOLDER: There are four justices who are considered progressive. The other five have a more conservative perspective. People think that Congress is divided and partisan, and that may be true. But in my opinion the Supreme Court is really the most sharply split branch of government nowadays.

ANTONIN SCALIA: There are two philosophies. The Ginsburg school says that words have no real meaning and that it is the job of the Supreme Court to legislate from the bench and rewrite duly-passed laws as they see fit. Then there's our side, which holds that the original intent of the authors of the law—especially the Founding Fathers who wrote the Constitution—should be deferred to as strongly as possible.

GINSBURG: Here's where Justice Scalia and I disagree.

SCALIA: "Here" being everywhere on earth.

GINSBURG: The law has no option, realistically, except to reinterpret statutes in a contemporary context. Let's suppose the Founding Fathers ascribed a law to "citizens." Well, what did they mean by that? Back then, you were the citizen of a state—a Georgia citizen, a New York citizen, or what have you—and not an American citizen. Not only that, but a citizen in the full, legal sense of the term was almost certainly a white male. If one of those old laws applied to "citizens" nowadays, are we supposed to say, hey, wait a moment, they *intended* this to mean only white males? Or only a "citizen of Georgia," which no longer exists as a legal category? Of course not.

DAVID SOUTER: I was appointed by the first president Bush in 1990. By the time I was ready to retire in 2009, I was regarded as a liberal. This might have been a function of the court moving right more than me moving left. In any event, nearly twenty years was plenty. In 2009, I told the president to find a replacement and I packed my bags.

MICHELLE: Barack joked that he had an attaché ready himself, in case things got dicey.

BIDEN: I told them that it would be an honor to serve as president should President Obama resign or be incapacitated. Ol' Joe is up to the job, believe me. I can even name all the presidents in order—except for the late 1800s. That's when it gets weird and you have to count Grover Cleveland twice.

MICHELLE: We thought Sonia Sotomayor would be a flawless choice and an easy confirmation. We were replacing a left-of-center judge with another left-of-center judge, so the court's ideological direction wouldn't shift. She had originally been nominated to the district court by President George H. W. Bush, so she had a bipartisan résumé. Plus, she had the sort of life story that the Republicans love. Her parents moved to New York City from Puerto Rico, she worked hard and became valedictorian in high school and then went to Princeton. Really, if you are for hardworking families and the American dream, Sonia was your gal.

EMANUEL: Except that's *not* the story Republicans really love. They don't love Ivy Leaguers from New York City making decisions for "their" country. Or maybe I should say they like the story, in the same way that you can like the *Star Wars* story. That doesn't mean you're going to buy the fucking lightsaber.

SONIA SOTOMAYOR: Getting nominated to the Supreme Court is really the ultimate of ultimates for any judge. It's called the Supreme Court for a reason, right? At the same time, being from the Bronx means that I'm not naive. I knew that my confirmation hearings would be political theater. Both the Republicans and Democrats were going to pore through my record and pick it apart. I wasn't too concerned, simply because I didn't make judgments lightly. When I did make a judgment, I explained why I'd made such a decision. If ever I didn't remember the particulars of a given case from my career, I could go back and read over my legal reasoning at the time.

MICHELLE: But Sonia wasn't really attacked for her ideas. There was one comment she made that was blown out of proportion and taken completely out of context.

SOTOMAYOR: I had used an example once: "I would hope that a wise Latina woman with the richness of her experiences would, more often than not, reach a better conclusion" than someone without them.

MITCH McCONNELL: "Than a white male," she sometimes said. Now if you ask me, the Constitution mandates that we are all equal under the law. If you want to introduce some sort of inverted Jim Crow into the legal system—well, she wasn't going to do that on my watch.

SOTOMAYOR: It was a bad choice of words that created the exact opposite impression from what I had intended. For me, the important word was *wise*. I was speaking from my own personal experience, which informs my legal perspective—just as everyone's personal experience informs their legal perspective. I meant that I could see both how the system worked for the majority, as well as for the people who are a bit on the sidelines. My family was from Puerto Rico; we weren't always treated so well even in New York. There are plenty of people, white people, in Senator McConnell's Kentucky who aren't treated so well either.

McCONNELL: Our Latinas are doing fine, wise or *other*wise.

MICHELLE: So they tried to make it out like she was saying a Hispanic woman is automatically smarter than a white male.

McCONNELL: Well, that's sure what it sounded like, and I wasn't the only person who got that impression.

SOTOMAYOR: I was glad that I got a chance to explain what I meant by that remark. Still, it seemed to me like some of these senators felt that having me on the Supreme Court was one step closer to having Spanish mandated as America's official language.

TED CRUZ: Well, technically speaking it is *one* step closer.

MICHELLE: Here's what got to me. The McCain campaign was built on him having a different perspective. He was a "maverick," someone who operated outside the way Washington usually worked. I think that's true; many of the hard-core right-wingers in the Republican Party despised Senator McCain. Governor Palin was a hockey mom from Alaska. She didn't think the way most people in Washington do.

PALIN: No, just the way most people in America do.

EMANUEL: It ain't *that* bad. Not yet.

MICHELLE: So the Republicans are capable of understanding the concept of perspective. They talk about how Democrats don't understand business because they've never run one. So of course a Puerto Rican woman from the Bronx is going to have a different perspective from a Scalia or even a Souter. That's just a fact, plain and simple. Isn't it a good thing, though, to have a variety of perspectives informing the court? Making it, you know, more representative of America?

HOLDER: Not for some people, no.

EMANUEL: They couldn't come right out and say that they're not interested in having a Hispanic perspective on the court.

HOLDER: They wanted the court to remain as it was: Jews and Catholics.

EMANUEL: And Clarence.

CLARENCE THOMAS: Hey, I'm Catholic!

SOTOMAYOR: As was I! The thing that got to me, and it did seem a bit disingenuous, was how so many of the president's political opponents were wringing their hands and speculating about my philosophy: "What did she mean by that remark?" "What is she implying?" And I explained myself pretty clearly at the confirmation hearings, I thought.

EMANUEL: After a while it became pretty clear that they didn't really want explanations. They wanted people to be worried, to see if there was a chance to derail the nomination and make a mountain, not out of a molehill, but out of a fucking dustball. It was pretty fucking low, if you ask me.

McCONNELL: None of us did ask you, which we do not regret for a moment.

MICHELLE: Well, their plan failed. Justice Sotomayor was confirmed by a 2–1 majority and has served impeccably ever since.

EMANUEL: I have to disagree with the First Lady. Their plan actually *succeeded*. Sonia was just a trial run. They were just sharpening their knives waiting for the president to misspeak. And if anything you say can and will be used against you in the field of public opinion, that kind of thing becomes inevitable.

McCONNELL: See, it's the wise Jews who really get it.

7

THE BEER SUMMIT, JULY 2009

HENRY LOUIS GATES JR.: The original incident took place on the day of July 16, 2009. I had just returned back to Cambridge, Massachusetts, from a trip to China. I was completely jet-lagged and exhausted. I asked Dave—that's my driver—to help me bring my bags up to the door.

KEVIN NOSUCHINSKY: My name is Kevin.

GATES: I travel so frequently that Dave is practically a member of the family by this point.

NOSUCHINSKY: I don't know what he thinks my name is. He just calls me "driver."

GATES: So Dave has the luggage and I'm fishing in my pocket for my keys.

NOSUCHINSKY: Apparently Professor Gates thinks that "help me with my bags" means "carry all my bags by yourself."

GATES: I get to my front door, but I can't quite seem to open it. I ask Dave to see if he can figure it out. He puts down the suitcases and he tries. *Nothing.* What's going on? I'm so frazzled that I actually wondered if I was at the wrong house. But no, it was the right address. Now

I'm really confused. I do have the right keys, I can tell from my keychain. So I check the lock. It looked like it had become damaged somehow. I got worried that my home has been burglarized in my absence.

NOSUCHINSKY: We head around to the back door and get in that way, no problem.

GATES: Finally I get inside my residence, and quickly check to see that everything is OK, which it was. Even from the inside, however, I still couldn't get the front door open.

NOSUCHINSKY: We had to push that front door open together. Something had messed it up.

GATES: I thanked Dave and proceeded to call the Harvard maintenance department to let them know that I'd had to force the door.

NOSUCHINSKY: He basically just turned his back to me. That was my cue to leave.

JAMES CROWLEY: That's when we received a 911 call from Professor Gates's neighbor.

LUCIA WHALEN: I've lived next door to Professor Gates for many years. I had noticed something suspicious while he was gone, someone I didn't recognize on his porch playing with his door. So when I heard the sound of the door being forced open, I called 911 right away.

CROWLEY: I responded to the scene immediately.

WHALEN: I believe our neighborhoods work best when neighbors look out for each other. Apparently Professor Gates disagrees. The first time we met he told me not to call him Mr. Gates but Dr. Gates. I was kind of surprised, since we lived right next door.

GATES: That was a joke!

WHALEN: "Doctor"? His job is to trace people's family tree! Please. That sounds more *Maury* than surgery.

GATES: I was kidding. I'd have been perfectly happy with her referring to me as Professor Gates if that's what she preferred.

WHALEN: That man was always complaining if we didn't mow the lawn or something. Whatever it was, he made it into a problem. Once he came over screaming, actually screaming, because we were having a children's birthday party and he felt that it had been too loud. The kids were terrified.

GATES: I've always had the best relationship with the neighbors. No complaints. It's a nice, peaceful area.

WHALEN: He's *such* an asshole. I know his job is to trace people's ancestry. But I can trace his: His father must have been an asshole, and his father before him, and his father before him. It was an entire row of assholes, like a human centipede going all the way back to the *Amistad*.

GATES: So the next thing I know, the police are at my door!

WHALEN: You know, I think he makes stuff up. Like once I think on the show he made it out that John McCain was Big Daddy Kane's uncle. That really doesn't sound right to me. But what do I know? I'm not a *doctor*. I'm no *professor*. I'm just a neighbor who *mistakenly* called the police on an asshole trying to get into his own house. Remember, it's a crime to call the police without cause. This *wasn't* me trying to get some sort of payback. It was a *mistake.*

GATES: I had no idea why the police officer was there.

CROWLEY: It's our duty to investigate a complaint of forced entry. So I asked Professor Gates some basic questions.

GATES: I identified myself: Professor Henry Louis Gates Jr., Harvard professor.

CROWLEY: It was kind of like a "don't you know who I am?"

GATES: I didn't know what else he wanted.

CROWLEY: He told me it was his home, and that something had happened to the front door so he had to force it open. People think burglaries only occur at night. That's absolutely incorrect. The thing is, *every* burglar says that it's their house. That's the first excuse they always use. The whole situation was odd. I know how to deal with black people from poor neighborhoods, not from *China*. I had experience with racial sensitivity training, and I'd never seen anything like the way Professor Gates was acting. Every time there's a situation in a poor neighborhood—especially if the person is an African American—they understand how things must look to me. Sometimes they'll have their ID locked in the house. They don't tell me that they'll be right back. Always, always, *always,* they invite me to follow them inside to get it. Their parents had "the talk" with them. They know the drill. I guess they don't teach that to them at *Harvard.*

GATES: I didn't understand why I needed to show him my identification. I didn't do anything wrong. So I asked *him* for *his* badge number instead. I didn't want the police in *my* home!

CROWLEY: I provided him my badge number, gladly. Finally Professor Gates showed me his ID, and that was that. I was ready to leave, I had what I'd come for. But Professor Gates got very agitated and kept yelling. I told him that if he needed to continue our conversation, then we could speak outside. I was done with what I had come out to do.

GATES: I explained, very courteously, that I didn't want any trouble, that I had just returned from overseas doing research regarding the world-renowned cellist Yo-Yo Ma. Sergeant Crowley hadn't heard of Yo-Yo Ma and seemed to take umbrage with what I was saying.

CROWLEY: We're on the porch and he's yelling and carrying on. He started making comments about "yo mama." It was like I was talking to some smart-aleck high schooler or someone on MTV, not a Harvard professor.

GATES: The way he was speaking to me *in my own home* with complete disrespect—he didn't view me as a man but as a black man. Yo-Yo Ma doesn't have to put up with this shit!

YO-YO MA: Are you kidding? I've been arrested three times for Driving While Black! That's what they wrote on the ticket. No, I don't get it either.

CROWLEY: Professor Gates didn't think of me as a person but as a cop. That's the way it is with these Harvard types. They talk about police like we're the Gestapo one minute, and the next they're complaining that we don't show up fast enough. Like we're beneath them.

GATES: He couldn't get past the color of my skin.

CROWLEY: He couldn't see past my badge. I told him to calm down, that he was making an incident.

GATES: Now that we were outside, surrounded by his officer buddies, he started barking orders to me like I was a dog.

CROWLEY: He was growing increasingly agitated. At that point, I made the decision to arrest him.

GATES: Now I'm in handcuffs. I kept hoping that I was being punked, that Ashton Kutcher would jump out from the bushes. But no, no such luck. I had literally been freer in China than I was in Massachusetts.

CROWLEY: We held him for a few hours, and all charges were dropped a few days later. I didn't want to make a federal case of it.

GATES: I just wanted the whole humiliating affair to go away. At the same time, I needed it made clear that I wasn't arrested for, say, drunken driving or anything like that. So the Cambridge Police Department and I issued a press release, hoping this would put the matter to bed.

CROWLEY: The mayor made a stink. Then Governor Patrick. Then both Al Sharpton and Colin Powell. It was getting very out of control very fast. The story took on a life of its own.

GATES: Then the president got involved. The *president*.

CROWLEY: I thought and still think President Obama is terrific. I'm a blue-collar guy from a blue state. Even my uniform's blue. Blue, blue,

blue. But to hear the president basically imply that I'm a racist, that really got to me. He didn't know the facts of the case.

GATES: The president said two things that were indisputable. First, that the police acted foolishly—he said "stupidly"—by arresting me in my own home after my identity had been established. Second, that men of color are stopped disproportionately by the police. Neither of these statements would be controversial by themselves. But to combine the two had the implication that Sergeant Crowley was acting purely from racist motives.

MICHELLE OBAMA: As soon as I heard Barack say those things, I audibly gasped. I knew that the Republicans were just waiting to paint this presidency as a riot about to happen. Even his mild, off-the-cuff criticism of this specific incident would sound like Chuck D to them. He said that it's unfortunate that this occurred, but they heard "F the police."

VICE PRESIDENT JOE BIDEN: I was going to suggest that song for the inauguration, but it turns out it's *not* about encouraging young women to have sex with their policeman spouses.

RAHM EMANUEL: Now we've got cops speaking out all over; this was a mess. I told the president to nip this in the bud, quick.

MICHELLE: Of all the crazy things that were said about Barack, the one claming he was out of touch really bothered me. The media liked to talk about how President Bush was someone they'd want to have a beer with, like he was a regular Joe Six-Pack, and as if Barack came from royalty. Here's the facts: Barack was raised by his grandparents. And President Bush's father was himself a president. So the plan became, hey, let's bring both these guys over here for a beer. Kind of to show America which president they would actually want to have a beer with.

EMANUEL: That was my fucking idea. My fucking *brilliant* idea.

GATES: The president called me and invited me to the White House. To say I was honored . . . I'm still speechless thinking about it, even though it had happened in the past.

CROWLEY: "Please hold for the president of the United States." That's what the operator lady said. You know I actually fixed my hair and tucked in my shirt as he came on the line. Isn't that silly? But I wanted to, y'know, be as respectful as possible.

MICHELLE: I took charge of setting up the event with Valerie, making all sorts of preparations. If we're going to have a so-called beer summit at the White House, what kind of beer were we to serve? My staff called Sergeant Crowley and Professor Gates to ask if they had any preference.

CROWLEY: I wanted to have OE8. Olde English 800 is the real name. I had a former partner, Miles, and he and I used to drink it when we were working undercover. I gotta admit, people sometimes gimme the stink eye when they see me drinking it! Not gonna lie, not gonna lie. Anyway, me and Miles drink it whenever we get back together. We reminisce about past cases and the OE8 takes us back. Since he's black and I'm white, I thought if we all drank it at the White House, then I could maybe tell that story to ease the tension.

GATES: I wanted them to serve Colt 45, because that would send a message. Just because I'm a black man, that doesn't mean I'm a thief. Just because I'm messing with a door, that doesn't mean I'm a burglar. The same goes for so many young black men in our country: just because they're drinking malt liquor doesn't mean they're criminals. One's food and drink and clothing might correlate to socioeconomic status, but crime does not. Does anyone really think that the wealthy have stolen less than poor people have? How many young men and women—disproportionately of color—have been killed in service to this country via wars of choice?

MICHELLE: I assumed that they were conspiring against me or something when they both suggested serving malt liquor. I'm still not sure if that's even considered to be beer, technically. First Sergeant Crowley said it, then Professor Gates said it when we called him. I couldn't believe it. Maybe Barack was playing a joke? But no, that's not his style. You know, I actually considered it—for about a millionth of a second. Then I was like, *There is no way on God's green earth that we are serving malt liquor at the White House.*

EMANUEL: The First Lady came into my office, wondering if I was setting her up. I wish I could say that I was—it would have been fucking hilarious, let's be real—but honestly I hadn't been. Then I asked why the fuck we were asking them what kind of fucking beer to serve. *We're* the fucking hosts, *we* choose the fucking beer, and then the two of them can either fucking drink it or they can fuck off back home to Boston.

MICHELLE: Rahm and I had a . . . let's just say "colorful" discussion about what beer to serve.

EMANUEL: Yeah, I fucking yelled. Because they were being fucking stupid.

MICHELLE: I asked Barack which beer he would prefer to serve, and he didn't really have an opinion. His drink of choice is a glass of chardonnay. So I asked him again and he kind of shrugged. "Just give me a Bud," he said. I thought that would be a great idea because Budweiser is owned by Cindy McCain's family. It could demonstrate that we were healing the country, which was so important after the divisive Busch years.

CINDY McCAIN: Give me a break. If beer healed anything, then Paul Walker would still be driving around.

MICHELLE: So we went back to Professor Gates and Sergeant Crowley, and told them that we would not be serving malt liquor at the White House.

GATES: I said I'd be fine with a Red Stripe.

CROWLEY: It would be a Blue Moon for me.

EMANUEL: What do you call a heterosexual man who drinks Blue Moon? A fag.

MICHELLE: It all worked out perfectly. Budweiser has a white label. Combined with a Red Stripe and a Blue Moon, the beer would be red, white, and blue. It was a nice patriotic message. Everything was set—until I slept on it. Beer is full of empty calories. Why do you think they call it a "beer belly"? It was an opportunity to have a teachable moment. You can watch your weight without being a health nut. Instead of candy, have raisins. And instead of beer, just have light beer. You'll still have a relaxing drink, but without drinking yourself into obesity.

EMANUEL: So now the president was going to have a Bud Light instead of a Bud. Except Red Stripe and Blue Moon didn't have light versions.

GATES: I had no problems with what the First Lady had to say, so I just went with a Sam Adams Light.

MICHELLE: I actually had an intern do some investigation to make sure that Sam Adams didn't own slaves or anything like that. We couldn't be too careful, you know? Well, it turned out he was very much against slavery. "A slave cannot live in my house," he said. "If she comes she must be free." So that was great. That just left the Blue Moon.

CROWLEY: I was not going to sit there like a sissy and sip on a light beer. I would never hear the end of it back at the precinct. I like Michelle Obama, I think she's a great lady, but there's no woman on earth who's going to tell me what kind of drink I can and can't have.

MICHELLE: I wasn't too happy about Sergeant Crowley, but I didn't push the issue. Yes, the beers were no longer red, white, and blue, but at least everyone would have what they wanted and I could move on.

EMANUEL: When it came to the snacks, her staff knew better than to ask. They just ordered some pretzels and stuff like that. If the First Lady had had her way, they'd fucking be serving carrot sticks or some shit.

CROWLEY: So the day finally comes, and I have to admit that getting a little tour of the White House wasn't all that exciting. I'd been there on a school trip when I was a kid, and knowing that I'd be meeting with the president—it was like I was waiting for Santa to finally come down the chimney.

GATES: I don't know how people say that that building isn't haunted. Whether or not there are literal ghosts, the spirits of the men and women who have been in that space are everywhere. Every inch of the building breathed with history. It was almost palpable.

CROWLEY: Finally they brought us outside, and just like that the president and Vice President Biden came out and joined us. And the first time you see him, it's, like, "Hey! I know you! You're the president. And his sidekick Joe!" It kind of doesn't seem real.

GATES: I was very excited by the whole thing.

CROWLEY: So Obama sat us all down and started talking. It was like he's giving one of his speeches but there's only three people in the audience and I was one of them.

GATES: The president laid out the conflicts we face as a nation, and what this relatively minor brouhaha meant vis-à-vis America and who we were as a country, and where we were heading.

CROWLEY: I gotta admit, it was nothing that I hadn't heard before. All this stuff about how citizens need to treat law enforcement with respect, and how police officers should strive for courtesy—they teach us that stuff in the academy.

GATES: I truly learned more in those few minutes than if I'd taken a course on the subject.

CROWLEY: Then I realized what the problem is. Obama's a professor. When he's talking in a class, it must be an educational time. The man is clearly knowledgeable and speaks precisely. When he's talking to a crowd, it's inspiring. He's bringing that entire audience together. But when it's a small group, it's kind of just *awkward*. Like when your teacher holds you and your buddies after class. Even if she's saying nice things, that she believes in you and knows you can do better, you still just want it to end and to be excused. I looked over at Gates and he's eating the stuff up. He was so into it he practically had a hard-on.

GATES: The president was everything I aspire to be as a professor. He was what every professor aspires to be. I was as interested in *what* he said as in *how* he said it.

CROWLEY: You know how in *The Nutty Professor* Sherman Clump takes that formula and turns into Buddy Love? That's what Professor Gates thought Obama was, a kind of studly Billy Dee Williams version of himself. All he needed was that OE8, man.

GATES: After he said what he had to say, the president had us all toast to America. We each tapped our bottles—we each made sure we all got everybody else—and then took a big swig.

CROWLEY: That's when it got awkward.

GATES: I could tell the president wanted Sergeant Crowley and me to apologize and clear the air. By that point, I knew that I could have acted better during the incident. But I didn't want to apologize and have Sergeant Crowley just accept my apology without acknowledging that he, you know, *didn't have to arrest me at my own home.*

CROWLEY: I knew Gates had been waiting for me to come clean since the moment that we stepped into the White House. He was just chomping at the bit for me to say something so he could act like the victim. And I got that. He *was* the victim. That much was true. But I needed to be sure that he could be fair about it, a good sport, and realize that this had gotten way out of hand. It wasn't only him I was going to have to apologize to, but everyone I'd ever meet for the rest of my life. Gates is a professor, he has a TV show, he writes books (probably). I'm just a cop and for many people now I'd practically become Mark Fuhrman.

GATES: Thankfully, the vice president entered the conversation.

BIDEN: I could tell that everyone was still uncomfortable, and I could also tell that they just needed to let their guards down. That was the elephant in the room—and I don't mean the Republican Party! Ha, ha, ha!

CROWLEY: He said that we should start talking about our backgrounds, like on Gates's show. And that it would be interesting, maybe some of us were related or something.

GATES: I tried to explain that it wasn't really possible to find hereditary links between the four of us without DNA analysis and family trees. But the vice president was quite insistent. "Come on, you're a Harvard professor!" he said. "Aren't you supposed to know this stuff?" And what am I supposed to say to that? So I nodded. "All right, Mr. Vice President. You got me, Mr. Vice President."

BIDEN: I started the discussion. Fair is fair. Even though I'm from Delaware, most people don't know that I was actually born in Pennsylvania. Hey, if anyone doesn't believe me, *I've* got the birth certificate to prove it! Ha, ha, ha!

CROWLEY: So Biden starts talking about growing up in Scranton, the town that's so boring that the show *The Office* takes place there. I look over at Obama and he was making this weird kind of face.

GATES: These were obviously tales that the president had heard before . . . more than once.

CROWLEY: How can I describe the look on Obama's face? It's kind of like he was in pain, but not really. You know how when you fart and you're not sure if you shit yourself a little bit? Like you think that maybe the underwear has like a tiny little stain? That was his face, like "Ugh, I gotta deal with *this* crap now?"

BIDEN: We Delawareans are a proud bunch. There are certain states that have reputations for their hometown pride. Texas, certainly. New York would also be on that list. But if you checked that list—checked it really closely—you'd see Delaware there too. You'd have to check closely because we're such a small state. Ha, ha, ha! That's why they say, "Delaware is a small state with a big heart."

GATES: I'm not familiar with that expression.

BIDEN: Well, maybe they don't say that but they should. *I* say it, at least. Ha, ha!

GATES: If I had to compare the speaking styles of the president and the vice president, I would say this: Both men are charismatic. Both are eloquent in their own way, the vice president being a touch more informal but no less authoritative in his speech. On the other hand the president is perhaps more attuned to his audience and therefore does a better job of holding their interest. That's not to say the vice president is any less knowledgeable. He knows everything there is to know about Delaware—and wanted to make sure that we knew it too.

BIDEN: Not that many people realize that Delaware was the first state to ratify the Constitution.

GATES: To be fair, it only took five days before Pennsylvania became the second ratifying state. Five days. That's not even a week.

BIDEN: To be fair, again, I *was* born in Pennsylvania. I'm basically the Founding Fathers.

CROWLEY: Everyone knows only two things about Delaware. One: It's the first state. Two: "Washington crossing the Delaware." Except I don't know that Washington crossed the river by the state of Delaware, because I know the Mississippi River isn't only by Mississippi. So I guess everyone knows only like one-and-a-half things about Delaware.

BIDEN: Even though we're the forty-ninth state in terms of area, we're forty-fifth in terms of population. We're definitely punching above our weight class, that's for sure. Another fun fact: Delaware is known as the Peach State. Look it up, it's true. Georgia is also known as the Peach State, but they're actually third in terms of peach production.

CROWLEY: So Biden is going on about peaches for some reason, and I'm totally zoning out. I'm looking around, sipping on my beer, enjoying the scenery. Then my eyes land on Biden's head. On his hair. Have you ever seen a doll's head? Like how it has a little bunch of hair, then some space, and then another bunch? Kind of like planting crops.

That's what his hair was like, but in the front. Behind that, he was as bald as an eagle. I'd seen comb-overs, but never comb-*backs*.

GATES: So Sergeant Crowley keeps glancing at me and jerking his head to the side, like he was trying to get my attention. I'd been in enough classrooms to know what he was doing.

CROWLEY: I finally got Gates to look at me. Then I tried to get him to notice Biden's hair without being too obvious about it.

GATES: I couldn't tell what he wanted at first. It was hard to communicate without the president or the vice president noticing.

CROWLEY: Finally I scratched my temple and then opened my eyes wide. Gates glances over at Biden and then glances back at me. He held the beer to the side of his face so Biden couldn't see. *His hair?* he mouthed. I nodded a little and quickly took a sip before I lost it.

GATES: That did give me a hearty chuckle, but I managed to be discreet.

BIDEN: I had them in stitches with my anecdotes. You don't get the privilege of representing Delaware in the United States Senate for over three decades without having a sense of humor. Ha, ha, ha!

CROWLEY: Gates and I kept trying real hard not to crack up. We tried to make sure not to look at each other, but that only made it even worse. Then I realized that I was about to laugh in the face of both the president and the vice president—which of course only made things one hundred times funnier.

GATES: Finally the president thanked the vice president for his contributions.

CROWLEY: He said, "Thank you, Joe." But you could tell he meant, "Shut the hell up, Joe." And Biden nodded and lifted his beer in salute with that big grin of his.

GATES: The president clearly was giving Sergeant Crowley and me a chance to speak. And we both started talking at the same time.

CROWLEY: I told Gates to go ahead. And he was clever about it.

GATES: I told him that I always get the last word in my classroom. And everyone laughed at that, and I think Sergeant Crowley could see that we'd reached some sort of wordless rapport.

CROWLEY: So I apologized. I said that I was sorry that I didn't treat Professor Gates with the courtesy that he deserved, and that that was wrong of me. Also I felt bad, because it must have been embarrassing and humiliating for him. I've been in handcuffs, and they don't feel too good. I don't just mean physically. Psychologically, it makes you feel like something less than human, like you're a trapped animal. And the professor didn't need that.

GATES: I accepted his apology, fully and without condition. Or rather, on one condition: that he accept mine. I should not have lost my temper. That didn't gain either of us anything. Sergeant Crowley was doing the right thing. I was breaking into my own home in broad daylight. He didn't suspect me or profile me; he was responding to a direct complaint by a witness. I *want* the police to investigate if someone is breaking into my home, no matter what his skin color. This is one time where I *don't* care if I'm distantly related to the person.

CROWLEY: Obama chimed in then, talking about how this showed what America was all about, how two guys who had an argument could have a beer and hash it out pretty quickly. Black, white, Republican, Democrat, it didn't matter. We were more alike than we were different. It was just a matter of listening to each other instead of talking past each other.

GATES: I couldn't help but point out how the president had made things better. It used to be that if someone who looked like me stood up to the police, more likely than not he would end up found in a ditch. Now, I got an invite to the White House!

CROWLEY: Obama smiled, but he didn't really like that. He said he couldn't take credit, that it was average Americans making things better every day. But if you ask me, he seemed a bit uncomfortable about the whole thing. I mean, he has a white half and a black half, and it's not like his body is fighting itself. So why should the country be that different? I dunno, he didn't say anything to that effect but as a cop you learn to read body language pretty well.

GATES: It was only after we left that Sergeant Crowley and I started wondering if the president had orchestrated that whole conversation. He'd certainly achieved his goal for the meeting. I was hoping this started a positive trajectory for the country, and perhaps our mutual bad behavior helped with that.

CROWLEY: Maybe Obama's right; maybe our meeting proved that racism is a thing that we can all move past as a country. Maybe we can live in a world where cops and people of color won't have such bad feelings about one another.

BIDEN: Ha, ha, ha!

8

HEALTH CARES, JULY–OCTOBER 2009

MICHELLE OBAMA: Having health care for all Americans has been a goal of the Democratic Party ever since the New Deal. It seems like a no-brainer to me, frankly. Everyone needs an education in order to compete and be a decent citizen, so we have a public education system to give people a base to start from. But health care? Why would we want to have a system where someone's life can be ruined, their family torn apart, through no fault of their own? That's like outlawing hurricane insurance. It makes no sense.

MITCH McCONNELL: If you want a doctor, you hire a doctor. Just like you hire a lawyer if you want one, or a florist or whatever it is. If you get extremely sick, you can go to the emergency room and no hospital can turn you away.

NANCY PELOSI: There we have the problem. Why wait until something is an emergency before treating it? Emergency health care is enormously expensive. Emergency *anything* is enormously expensive. It's the difference between mailing a letter or having it overnighted. So even from the fiscal-responsibility card that the Republicans love to play, it really makes a great deal of sense to encourage preventative care rather than wait for crises to happen.

HARRY REID: Yes, you can build many more firehouses and hire firefighters and pay their salaries and their benefits. You can buy trucks and the poles they slide down and dog food for the Dalmatians. Or, for half the money, you can buy fire extinguishers and distribute those to everyone. Really, why would anyone choose the first option when given those two choices?

McCONNELL: Because having the government make fire extinguishers is the best way to increase the incidence of fire. They'd probably be made out of kindling with a magnifying glass attached. Assembled by Democratic unions, of course.

MICHELLE: The first thing we needed to do to reform health care was to have some broad consensus on what the goals were. Even that was a very difficult proposition. Look at it this way. Let's suppose someone said, "Everyone in America should have access to decent education." That's a statement that the vast majority of Americans would agree with, right? Well, it's not that simple.

RAHM EMANUEL: It becomes, why *everyone*? What about people who would benefit more from learning on the job than from class? Sure, it would be good if they had higher education. But it wouldn't be a huge loss if they didn't. You can make the case that the government doesn't need to be involved in those cases. OK, then what do you mean by "decent"? What do you mean by "education"? High school? College, a master's? Who is going to pay for this? If it's free, that's an incentive for people to go to school instead of getting a job. I don't really think that's a big concern, but it's not an unreasonable question for people to have.

JOHN BOEHNER: The Democratic Party is not interested in getting health care to everyday Americans. They are interested in controlling as much of the economy as they can, and we Republicans are going to fight that tooth and nail. There are many ways to provide quality health care to all Americans without getting the federal government involved. At some point the GOP will reveal what those ways are, just you wait. Stay tuned . . .

MICHELLE: The thing is, as Barack repeatedly pointed out during the campaign, we weren't building the health care system from scratch. If we were, we could do a single-payer system like most countries have. But in the United States we have an odd sort of system where most people get their health care from their employer. As a result, that made things that much more complicated.

EMANUEL: As we started drawing up plans for what the bill would look like, everyone was remembering 1994. President Clinton had tried to put over single payer, but the insurance companies had raised an absolutely enormous stink over it.

PRESIDENT BILL CLINTON: They had these ads that, in my view, were really quite deceptive. They featured a married couple, Harry and Louise were their names, just sitting around the kitchen table reading the newspaper and discussing the issues of the day. It could have been any home anywhere in suburban America. What was sinister about the ads was that the two of them were pointing out parts of my plan that they didn't like, in ways designed to make people scared. My plan was still a bill at that point, not a law. All those things they didn't like, we could have changed. Heck, we would have been happy to change them, if they were that unpopular. But those ads weren't about health, but illness. They were trying to poison the bill and by and large they succeeded.

PELOSI: I was there. I wasn't in the Democratic leadership at the time, but they were really taking it on the chin. Those ads were very, very nasty and very, very effective.

REID: We all remember those days. The president and the DNC simply did not have the money to compete with the insurance companies. Not to mention this was when talk radio and those sorts of things were really coming into their own and were really hammering us.

PELOSI: The Democrats had been decimated in those 1994 midterm elections. I mean, it was brutal. It was the first time that the Republicans got control of the House of Representatives in forty years. Newt Gingrich became Speaker of the House. Think about that. That's how badly it backfired.

EMANUEL: I was a senior adviser to President Clinton at the time, and I don't think Nancy is being entirely fair. Newt Gingrich isn't *that* bad—he is far, far worse. This time around, we knew that we had to have the insurance companies on board.

MICHELLE: You know how we always say "every vote counts"? Well, that was the case here. We exactly had the sixty votes that we needed in the Senate to get something through. That meant that every single Democratic senator had a veto power over the final bill.

REID: I sent out feelers on single payer. But Senator Lieberman had several major insurance companies in his home state of Connecticut, and he wasn't interested.

JOE LIEBERMAN: Of course I was defending the interests of my constituents. That's why they sent me to the Senate to begin with. Single payer was too radical a departure from our current system anyway. The first principle of health care is "first do no harm." To destroy all these companies that make a reasonable profit for providing a service—that didn't seem quite right to me.

REID: That was the end of single payer.

MICHELLE: So right away we started getting it from the left wing of the Democratic Party. Single payer was their goal—I understand that—but that goal was not feasible.

PELOSI: The House was a different story than the Senate. There are far more very progressive Democrats in the House than over in the other chamber, since the Senate tends to have higher-profile politicians who have to somewhat moderate their views. Except, I suppose, for Senator Bernie Sanders of Vermont.

BERNIE SANDERS: I caucus with the Democrats but I am an independent by party affiliation. The Democrats and I have some fundamental differences of opinion so that helps to keep us separated. Unlike the vast majority of Democratic politicians, I consider myself a democratic socialist in the same vein as many European politicians.

VICE PRESIDENT JOE BIDEN: I like socialism.

EMANUEL: No, Mr. Vice President, you don't. You really don't.

BIDEN: Are you sure?

EMANUEL: Yes, I'm sure.

BIDEN: Do I still like wrestling?

EMANUEL: I don't know, Mr. Vice President.

BIDEN: Are you sure?

EMANUEL: Yes, I am sure that I don't know if you like wrestling.

BIDEN: I do like wrestling. That I *am* sure of!

SANDERS: In this country, no one, not even the Republican crazies, begrudges the federal government stepping in when there's a tornado or a hurricane or some other so-called act of God. Well, getting a crippling illness is an "act of God," too. It's such an "act of God" that it happens throughout the Bible. Just look at the Book of Job.

SARAH PALIN: Gee, that's the first time I've ever heard a Democrat care about a Job or the Bible!

SANDERS: I already said I'm not a Democrat.

PALIN: My apologies. You have to give Senator Sanders credit: At least *he*'s honest when he preaches socialism for America. He really isn't a Democrat.

SANDERS: My point is, no one should have to choose between, say, going to college and getting chemo. It's just nonsensical. Yet as long as the corporate interests were involved, that would be a concern.

REID: But we needed them involved.

MICHELLE: There were a lot of people pulling Barack in a lot of different directions. He saw that he had this amazing opportunity, he saw the brass ring in front of him, and he wanted to snatch that greatness. Look, people in Washington can argue all the time about taxes or spending or all this other stuff. And that's fine. But health care reform meant a chance to save lives. It meant not having to choose between paying for another blood test and your mother's life. No one should have to check their bank account while their family members are in trouble. Come on, we're better than that.

BOEHNER: Yes, we are. Which is why we were opposed to any bill that would have made things *worse*.

MICHELLE: It's funny that the Republicans called Barack an ideologue, when he just wanted a bill that could pass. It was pretty much the opposite of being an ideologue.

REID: President Obama sat down with myself and Speaker Pelosi and told us to figure out what the best deal we could get would look like.

PELOSI: We were given very broad principles by the president. He wanted as close to universal coverage as we could get, while keeping costs down. He also wanted to make sure preexisting conditions were covered. If you get sick, your life isn't ruined. People are irreplaceable, hospital bills are not.

REID: He wanted the bill to be based on reality and not just theory, on what has actually been proven to work either in the United States or in Europe or elsewhere.

PELOSI: We didn't want this to be a strictly partisan bill. We thought that once it became clear that it was going to pass, then maybe some of the more moderate Republicans would get on board. This has happened historically with major bills. Some of the more far-sighted members would read the tea leaves and didn't want their votes to be used against them in the future.

BOEHNER: That sure as hell wasn't going to happen under my watch. Hell no!

McCONNELL: I would agree with Mr. Boehner except that I would say *heck*.

PELOSI: The best model we could come up with was Governor Romney's plan in Massachusetts. In other words, a Republican plan.

PALIN: A RINO plan is more like it. RINO: Republican In Name Only. That was not a plan I would have passed in Alaska, you betcha.

MICHELLE: I don't understand this RINO business. If a Republican governor passes a bill that the conservative Heritage Foundation came up with, how can you say it's not Republican? I can't just say I'm not black when black people do things that I disagree with.

CLARENCE THOMAS: Well, you could just shut your mouth.

EMANUEL: Listening to them, John McCain, who was the 2008 Republican presidential nominee, was a RINO. Rudy Giuliani, easily the most right-wing mayor New York City had in at least a century, was a RINO. Mitt Romney, the 2012 nominee, was a RINO. You can say whatever the hell you want about their ideas but all those guys were very effective at getting their agendas across. So a RINO is someone who actually gets things done, unlike a "real" Republican who is completely fucking incompetent and puts the blame on everything and everyone else.

RICK SANTORUM: I'd rather be ineffectively right than effectively wrong.

EMANUEL: Well, then, mission accomplished, asshole.

MICHELLE: If the Democrats aren't Republicans, and if independents aren't Republicans by definition, and if you're further pushing a huge chunk of self-described Republicans out of the party—who does that leave? It sounds like you are consigning yourself to the fringe, which I suppose might be a point of pride but does not bode well for the furthering of your ideas in a democracy. "I'm know I'm right because no one agrees with me!" Is that it? I don't get it and I wish I did.

EMANUEL: I *do* get it and I wish I fucking didn't. They were opposed to everything on principle—even their own principles. They had been all for President Bush expanding Medicare. Why? Because it's cheaper to pay for someone's medicine than to pay for their fucking doctor and hospital bills. Gee, what a fucking shocker! In the same way, it's cheaper to pay for insurance than to pay for emergency room bills out of pocket. Except now it became "Oh, that's socialism! No!"

PELOSI: Romneycare was our model. It was a Republican plan in a very Democratic state. That in and of itself told me that the program wasn't based on ideology but on crunching numbers and getting people the access to health care they deserved.

BOEHNER: That should also have told her that simply because something works for the people of Massachusetts doesn't mean it will work for the people in my home state of Ohio. Nancy Pelosi can keep her San Francisco values in her home district, and we'll have our own.

MICHELLE: I'm sorry, but Mr. Boehner's point does not make sense in this context. Yes, it's true that laws for a rural district wouldn't be the same as laws in Harlem. Shirley Chisholm, the first African American woman elected to Congress, begged off being assigned to the House Agricultural Committee because it had nothing to do with her constituents. But health care is different. Illness doesn't care where you live or what you look like or what your job is. It's a universal concern.

EMANUEL: Actually, Boehner *is* right. Different states need different levels of health care because they have different levels of health. Let's look at the data. Of the ten healthiest American states, nine of them are blue. Meanwhile, eight of the ten fattest American states are deep-red Republican states. The only exceptions are Ohio, which is a classic swing state, and Delaware.

BIDEN: That must be a typo. Delaware is the second-*smallest* state, right after Rhode Island. And we'll catch up to them, just you wait!

EMANUEL: How can a state change size?

MICHELLE: With attention to diet and moderate exercise.

EMANUEL: What?

BIDEN: *Obviously.*

EMANUEL: Holy shit, Biden's gone contagious and he's infected the First Lady.

BIDEN: Kind of like when FDR gave Eleanor Roosevelt polio.

BOEHNER: Insurance is a service that *someone* has to pay for, plain and simple. So even if everyone in Massachusetts ends up insured, that doesn't mean the program works if the people aren't interested in spending their money that way. I find it curious that a party that calls itself "Democratic" has such contempt for what the people actually want. Yes, if you passed a law that required everyone to buy high-speed Internet, then everyone would buy it. That wouldn't make it a good plan or a good allocation of people's hard-earned cash.

MICHELLE: That summer of 2009 we really started getting some pushback from middle America. They were complaining about being forced to take personal responsibility for their health. It was quite odd.

EMANUEL: Can you imagine the reaction if black people took to the streets and marched under the banner of "Stop telling me to take care of my health and my family"? What would have been the ticker on Fox News? It would be the first time in American history that the terror alert level was raised to red, because O'Reilly and all the rest of them would be going nuclear.

MICHELLE: Then we hit *another* roadblock.

DEVAL PATRICK: There was no greater congressional advocate for universal health care than Ted Kennedy. He called it the cause of his life, and he fought for it constantly. He had been very ill during this whole Obamacare debate, and finally in August of 2009 he breathed his last.

MICHELLE: Like so many women of color, it's impossible for me to overestimate how much I admire Ted Kennedy and the entire Kennedy family. His brother, JFK, stuck his neck out for black Americans at great political risk.

DICK CHENEY: And then he stuck the top of his head off.

MICHELLE: Kennedy did it out of conviction, not personal expedience. As someone who came from great wealth, it would have been far easier for him to pretend that African Americans simply don't exist.

MITT ROMNEY: She makes a good point.

MICHELLE: Barack felt that we needed to see this bill through in Senator Kennedy's memory and in his honor. Frankly, I wished the senator had stayed around to see us reap the harvest of what he had planted over the decades. There was a small part of me that prayed that some Republicans would think twice about their opposition in light of working with Senator Kennedy over the years.

McCONNELL: That's hilarious. Tell us another one!

PATRICK: It was truly a sad day for Massachusetts and America, the end of the Kennedy era. My only hope was that Senator Kennedy would be remembered as the Lion of the Senate, a fierce champion of civil rights and progressive issues, and not for that one time he drunk-drove a trick off a bridge and left her there to drown, except she ended up suffocating instead because he was too scared to call anyone for help.

REID: That's when things got dicey. Listen, as Senate majority leader I've shaken hands with presidents, world leaders—you name it. But working alongside a Kennedy, that was a once-in-a-lifetime thing. So it was very hard to have such a leader pass, someone who was a great personal inspiration to me. But just as important was the fact that we lost that sixtieth Senate vote.

PATRICK: Once again, all eyes were on Massachusetts when it came to health care.

ROMNEY: And once again, the Democrats were pulling shenanigans when it came to the law. In 2004, the question had become, what happens to John Kerry's Senate seat if he is elected president? Well, it would be filled by appointment from the governor, who at that time was me. So the Democratic legislature in Massachusetts rewrote the law so that a special election would be called instead, taking the power out of the governor's hands. Now their chicanery had backfired on them, and I for one was glad to see them twist in the wind a little bit.

PATRICK: Governor Romney might have been excited but that was premature. Senator Kennedy had been ill for a while and he saw this coming. There had been a bill in the works to restore the governor's power to appoint an interim Senate candidate, and very quickly the legislature moved to make that happen.

ROMNEY: "Very quickly." "Legislature." Pick one, because you're not getting both.

MICHELLE: It was a hiccup, we felt. We knew there would be many along the way. The fearmongering had been intense from the usual suspects, so in the tradition of past presidents we thought it a great idea for Barack to address Congress on the forthcoming legislation to clear the air.

BOEHNER: He finally decided to talk to the Republicans. Or talk *at* us, rather.

EMANUEL: Kind of hard to talk to someone who keeps hanging up the phone on you and then blocks your number.

BOEHNER: The president just should have sold tickets to his speeches, that would have paid for his health care scheme.

PELOSI: A congressional address was a good idea and it was an obvious idea. Even if we were running ads against the misinformation, the right-wing noise machine would have dismissed any of our facts as "propaganda." But you can't dismiss a president's direct appeal to Congress and to the people.

MICHELLE: So I thought. So we all thought.

PELOSI: It was just a couple of weeks after Ted Kennedy had died. Both Republicans and Democrats have been complaining in recent years that Washington has been getting more and more toxic. Nowhere was that more clear than during the president's speech.

SEPTEMBER 9, 2009: BARACK OBAMA ADDRESSES A JOINT SESSION OF CONGRESS TO DISCUSS HIS HEALTH CARE PLAN.

MICHELLE: In retrospect, the speech almost becomes an afterthought. The people who got it, got it already. They agreed on broad, moderate principles. The people who didn't get it were sitting there with their fingers in their ears. They didn't want to hear it.

BOEHNER: We didn't want to hear it precisely because we *did* get it— and the American people were going to get it good and hard.

EMANUEL: Well, that's the best fucking way to get it, no?

PELOSI: The Speaker of the House sits behind the president's left shoulder whenever he addresses Congress, most notably during the State of the Union speech. It's fun to be in that seat, there's the sense of history to be sure. It's more fun some times than other times; I sure enjoyed it more during the Obama years than during the Bush years.

PRESIDENT GEORGE W. BUSH: Funny, we couldn't really tell.

CHENEY: That's because she had the exact same face for four years.

PELOSI: The thing is, it gets old really fast.

CHENEY: . . . Nope, not going there.

PELOSI: The night of the health care speech, I knew what the president was going to say. We had looked over the text in advance to make sure that there weren't any contradictions between what he was advocating and the legislation that was moving through Congress. But I'm on camera the entire time, so I have to do my best to seem focused and interested and excited. If I zone out or something, that will be the headline the next day. I'll think of my grandkids or some movie or try to recall something from college, I don't know. Something I haven't thought about in a long time. That way, it really seems like I'm focused and concentrating.

BIDEN: I try to think of types of trees and then rank them in the order that I like them.

PELOSI: Other times I'll play Fuck/Marry/Kill. That's a game where you spot three people and you choose one to have sex with, marry another, and kill the third. There's a lot more kills than fucks in Congress, believe me.

MICHELLE: I was excited simply to see my husband do what he does best. He could read the phone book and I'd smile. . . . Well, maybe not the phone book, that's a little too Strom Thurmondy.

PELOSI: So President Obama—let me repeat that, *the president of the United States*—is making a point about the health care plan, debunking some myths. And the Republicans in the audience start grumbling and complaining, which is par for the course. We did it too when George W. Bush was talking about privatizing Social Security. Then there was a little shout in the grumbling, but I couldn't really tell what it was. I looked over, but I couldn't spot who was yelling or what they were yelling. Then the entire audience quieted down, and the president went on.

MICHELLE: That's when Joe Wilson, congressman from South Carolina, got up and called Barack a liar. "You lie!" he screamed. I heard him, Vice President Biden heard him, Speaker Pelosi heard him, everyone heard him because the mics picked it up.

EMANUEL: Joe Wilson is not the name of a congressman. Joe Wilson is the name the FBI gives you when they put you in witness protection, and that's exactly what this piece-of-shit redneck was going to need. I don't think I was ever as angry at someone during my entire time in the White House—and I'm normally so wound up that I'm just one good sneeze from stroking out on my best day.

JOE WILSON: See, if it had been two days later—September 11th—then it would have been a different story. I would have kept to my seat out of respect and bitten my tongue. So it's the president's fault for having his speech on the wrong day. Hey, as long as the Confederate flag hung over the state capitol, I knew that there was no embarrassing this state.

BIDEN: I didn't even want to see who said it. I wanted to assume it was someone's guest, maybe a kid with that disease where you yell stuff out all the time. Whatever it's called. I guess they should change it to "Joe Wilson disease." Ha, ha! No, but seriously, I have been in the Senate since 1973, elected in 1972. That's a very long time. I had never seen such disrespect toward a president in my lifetime, certainly not in such a hallowed setting. It just made me very sad. I knew I was on camera, I'm there to play a role, I understand that. But all I could do was look down and shake my head.

JOHN McCAIN: SMH, the kids say.

BIDEN: How low have we come as a country that this happened? It's the Republicans who like to wave the flag around and talk about patriotism and that's fine. But really there's no one—or virtually no one—in Congress who doesn't have respect for the institutions themselves. Or so I had thought until that moment.

PELOSI: I looked as quickly as I could to see who had heckled the president. It's hard to spot something like that, of course, but I figured maybe everyone around them would be sitting with their mouths open so I could spot them that way. How did I feel? I felt angry, and I felt disrespected, and I felt so so sorry that President Obama had to go through this.

MICHELLE: It felt like a knife. Not *what* Joe Wilson said—every politician ever is accused of lying whenever they open their mouth, usually correctly—but the fact that he felt comfortable saying that. He didn't just blurt that out. We all blurt things out all the time, sure. But you don't raise your voice when you blurt something out, you say it under your breath and then are terrified that your friend heard your comment about her red suit jacket.

PELOSI: You said it was flattering and made me look youthful!

MICHELLE: I was referring to Valerie!

VALERIE JARRETT: Naw, bitch. You most certainly were *not* referring to Valerie.

MICHELLE: We know how this process works. If the president says something you think is false, then you write an editorial, you go on the radio, you make political hay out of it. What was Barack going to do, get into a shouting match from the podium, get all angry black man on national television? He kept his calm and said, "No, it's not true."

PELOSI: Those same Republicans who talk about how President Obama makes America look weak in the world's eyes have no problems with the president being screamed at in a situation where he wasn't in a position to respond.

WILSON: Once again, 9/11 would have been a whole different story. The speech was 9/9. Though it was more like a 2/10, a D-, if you ask me.

PELOSI: No one asked him. No one asked anyone anything.

MICHELLE: Barack didn't seem that phased by it when we got home. Actually, scratch that. He didn't seem to believe that it had really happened. It's already surreal enough living in the White House. Maybe you don't literally see Lincoln's ghost, but the ghosts of every important American politician definitely haunt the halls. We had strategies for dealing with all sorts of attacks, even the mudslinging—we weren't going to be Swift-boated like Senator Kerry had been. But no one saw things like this coming, because they were without historic precedent.

CHENEY: Hey, you wanted change, right? That's change for ya. How's it feel? Not all it's cracked up to be, is it?

MICHELLE: No, it didn't feel good. Not at all.

PELOSI: Senator Reid and I were making progress getting the bills moving. We were fighting a battle on two fronts. We had to keep all our ducks in a row, and at the same time manage the media. Everyone had their own little perspective on the bill, and every slight change upset someone.

REID: It was by far the most complicated legislative work that Speaker

Pelosi or I have done in our political careers. Just a massive reform, the huge change that America had voted for.

MICHELLE: We were waiting for the other shoe to drop, so to speak. I knew something could and would go wrong. It was clear that the Republicans weren't going to go along to get along. They were going to be tenacious . . . but that's when the Nobel Committee called.

9

WINS AND LOSSES, OCTOBER 2009– JANUARY 2010

MICHELLE OBAMA: Three U.S. presidents have won the Nobel Peace Prize. Teddy Roosevelt won in 1906, and Woodrow Wilson won in 1919 because of his work with World War I and the League of Nations. Jimmy Carter won it in 2002, over two decades after he left office, because of his work on human rights.

> OCTOBER 9, 2009: THE NOBEL COMMITTEE ANNOUNCES THAT BARACK OBAMA WILL BE AWARDED THE NOBEL PEACE PRIZE.

RAHM EMANUEL: I'll never forget the president's reaction. It was like, "I did? Why?"

MICHELLE: You usually get a huge honor like that at the end of some big fight, not at the beginning.

EMANUEL: We didn't really know what to do or say. One day you have the unprecedented sight of a president being heckled by a congressman. The next you get the unprecedented sight of the president being given possibly the most prestigious award on the planet. So I guess what I'm saying is that it's basically like being bipolar.

JESSE JACKSON JR.: Can you please just leave me alone? I.Need.Help.

MICHELLE: I mean, if Barack said, "Thanks but no thanks," he would seem obnoxious and pretentious. But if he accepted, he would *also* seem obnoxious and pretentious.

EMANUEL: To quote one of the president's favorite expressions, let me be clear. This was not the Nobel Peace Prize for President Barack Obama. This was the Nobel Fuck-you Prize for President George W. Bush.

PRESIDENT GEORGE W. BUSH: Heh, heh. Do I still get the check?

EMANUEL: We sat down and wondered what to do. Then we realized we didn't even know what the fuck we *could* do. I couldn't exactly call up the Nobel Committee and say, "Hypothetically speaking, what if the president were to turn down this huge honor? Can he accept it on behalf of someone else? Asking for a friend."

MICHELLE: Any such call would immediately become international front-page news. So we brought in the only living person who could realistically give us some guidance: President Carter.

PRESIDENT JIMMY CARTER: I of course was very flattered to be asked for advice. I considered it an honor to guide President Obama through this process. In fact, I'm proud to say that I've advised all my successors in office one way or another.

BUSH: I would ask him what he would do in the Middle East and then I just did the opposite. Worked every time. Should have called before Iraq, though.

PRESIDENT BILL CLINTON: He knew all the best restaurants in Atlanta.

PRESIDENT GEORGE H. W. BUSH: I think I asked him where the bathroom was at some event, maybe?

NANCY REAGAN: He kept sending us these dopey letters when Ronnie was in the White House. After a while the secretaries started recognizing his handwriting on the envelope and threw them out. I think they even did a "Return to sender: addressee unknown" once just to creep him out.

CARTER: President Obama's staff wanted to say that the award was being accepted in the name of the armed forces or innocent civilian casualties. I let them know that, certainly, President Obama could say as much in his acceptance speech. And yes, awards have been given to groups or organizations before. But the award isn't something you can pass along. It's the committee's place to decide, and that's just how it goes.

MICHELLE: We all suspected as much, but it was good to hear it from someone who knew the inside scoop.

CARTER: I was glad to help out in any way I could.

EMANUEL: Then he wouldn't fucking leave. How the hell do you get a president out of the Oval Office? Literally, that was what we were asking ourselves. Carter's in there chewing Obama's ear off with his Southern drawl slowed down even further by his old-man cadence. It was like listening to a record at the wrong speed. Mrs. Obama finally got him out of there, I don't know how.

MICHELLE: I called Roslyn, she knew what to do. I walked in right when he was offering Barack a butterscotch for what—judging by the look on my husband's face—must have been the fiftieth time.

EMANUEL: So the president gave a brief address about how receiving the Nobel Prize truly humbled him.

JOHN BOEHNER: Clearly he didn't write that one himself. I've seen pimps that were less humble.

EMANUEL: You've seen pimps? Where, pray tell, have you seen pimps?

BOEHNER: Chicago, obviously.

HARRY REID: Within one hundred hours of the Nobel announcement, we had our first good bit of legislative news on the health care bill. The Senate Finance Committee passed the bill, which was as expected. The vote was along party lines, also as expected. But we did manage to get one of the ten Republican senators on the committee to vote for the bill, Senator Snowe out of Maine.

OLYMPIA SNOWE: No one is going to deny that health care is a crucially important issue that affects all Americans. I thought this bill had enough good things in it, was enough of a good starting point, that it deserved a full and forceful debate in front of the full Senate. I wasn't voting for the bill so much as voting to continue the debate.

EMANUEL: That's just politician talk for, "All right, let's see where this is heading. I can always jump ship later."

VICE PRESIDENT DICK CHENEY: They were worried about the

cost of all the hearts they'd have to keep feeding me. It adds up, you know.

REID: Senator Snowe was no dummy. There's a reason why she never lost an election. I thought, maybe, this was a sliver of light, that some Republicans would come around. The problem is that many of the so-called moderate Republicans were wiped out in the 2006 and 2008 wave election years. That left the GOP in the hands of the absolute extremists.

MICHELLE: The legislative progress was glacial and it was excruciating. It was like we were dealing with a terminal patient: every day I'd wake up and wonder if things were getting better or worse.

REID: I had to have several very long conversations with some of my colleagues in order to get their vote. It wasn't just pulling teeth; it was like I was pulling out their skulls.

MITCH McCONNELL: He paid off Landrieu in Louisiana, and Ben Nelson from Nebraska got a permanent exemption from paying for Medicaid expansion in his state—and *only* his state. Those were only the two most blatant and transparent.

REID: They should call me Monty Hall, because it was *Let's Make a Deal* in my office every day.

McCONNELL: The polls were clear and they were resounding: the American people did not want this monstrosity passed.

MICHELLE: Except really they did. If you asked Americans about specific provisions in the bill, then they were for it, overwhelmingly so.

Coverage for preexisting conditions? Yes. Not losing your health care when you lose your job? Absolutely.

SARAH PALIN: The death panels were not as popular as some of the other features.

MICHELLE: It's hard for imaginary things to be popular.

PALIN: What about Disney movies? Those are imaginary.

MICHELLE: That's . . . true?

NANCY PELOSI: I had to deal with the same headaches in the House. The vote was going to be extremely close, and there was a bloc of pro-life Democrats who were insisting on antiabortion language being included in the bill. That really took a lot of soul-searching.

PALIN: So did you ever find yours?

PELOSI: We finally passed the bill in November. We needed every single vote and we even had I think two or three to spare. That was good in case we'd lose a couple when we went through conference.

REID: The Senate passed it on Christmas Eve. It looked like it would be smooth sailing ahead.

MICHELLE: Well, I never thought that for a moment. The attacks kept coming and they kept coming hard, but we still had the numbers going into the final stretch.

REID: Getting legislation through Congress is a logistical nightmare, and the Founding Fathers intentionally designed it to be that way. First one branch of Congress passes a bill, then the other branch passes a bill, then they have to have the language between them agreed upon, and then both branches have to pass the final draft, so to speak. So we were waiting on that and we weren't thinking about Massachusetts when we should have been.

MICHELLE: The special election to fill Senator Kennedy's seat was called for January 20, 2010. The seat had been in Democratic hands since the early 1950s. Before man walked on the moon, before *Leave It to Beaver* even—that's how long the seat has been blue. At the end of 2009, the Democratic candidate was up by something like thirty points in the polls. The Republican National Committee weren't even thinking of contesting the race.

MARTHA COAKLEY: I was Massachusetts attorney general at the time, meaning that I had proven that I could win statewide office. I ended up winning my race for that position by 73 percent to 27 percent, about three to one. So although I didn't consider myself a shoo-in for the Senate seat, I had about as good a chance as could be expected.

EMANUEL: I'll say it flat out: The Democratic Party had gotten spoiled. We were spoiled. The 2006 and 2008 elections, we wiped out the Republican Party in New England. There were no Republican congressmen from that region, *zero,* which I think was a first since the Republican Party got founded. We took out people like Chris Shays, who had twenty years in Congress. Nancy Johnson, also twenty years. These weren't crazies either. They were sane people who we could work with. But sanity had left the Republican Party.

MITT ROMNEY: The Democratic national party didn't know Massachusetts like I knew Massachusetts. I'm not saying that as a boast, I'm saying that being elected as a Republican in Massachusetts means that you really have to do your homework. I was actually leading Ted Kennedy at one point when I ran against him for the Senate in 1994. Then, my approval rating went underwater, so to speak. If I could have done that against the giant himself, I knew that meant that we had a chance against Martha Coakley.

COAKLEY: I think the idea is that I took things for granted, and I didn't. Being a senator is a huge transition from being a statewide official. I did my homework and I studied the issues. Of course I was for Obamacare, but the United State Senate's purview is enormous.

ROMNEY: This was going to be about motivation and about turnout. My money was on her opponent, Scott Brown.

SCOTT BROWN: Governor Romney meant that literally. He said that he always wanted to make it rain, so when I came to his house he started throwing all these hundred-hundred dolla bills, y'all.

ROMNEY: Then someone pointed out that we have to report all the contributions so we just got down and put the money into nice piles.

EMANUEL: Scott Brown used to be a model. He looked like every type of douchebag guy who fucks a girl and then doesn't call her the next day. Unfortunately, Massachusetts is known for having the most douchebags per capita of any state in the union.

ROMNEY: The douchebag is our state bird. I know, it doesn't make sense to me either.

COAKLEY: I thought I was prepared to answer any questions about the issues. I didn't realize that some of the questions would be about things that really didn't matter to anyone. Politicians were coming in to support Scott Brown, even Rudy Giuliani came in, so I took a little swipe at him on a radio interview, pointing out that he was a Yankee fan.

BROWN: I was proud to have Mayor Giuliani's support—even if he didn't make it rain. The more support I got, the more legitimacy my campaign got. Then I was endorsed by Curt Schilling.

COAKLEY: I didn't know who that was, so I made a comment about how he's just another Yankee fan.

BROWN: He is not.

COAKLEY: Well, it turns out he's a catcher.

BROWN: It "turns out" he's a pitcher.

COAKLEY: He played for the White Sox.

BROWN: It was the Red Sox.

COAKLEY: He apparently led them to their first World Cup in over fifty years.

BROWN: First World *Series* in over eighty years.

COAKLEY: I was a little taken aback by the reaction. I mean, does every senator need to know what goes on in basketball? Maybe Herb Kohl, because he owned the Bucks.

BROWN: Oh, so that one she knows?

COAKLEY: Well, it does say "Owner of the Bucks" on his campaign contribution checks. That's how he signs them!

EMANUEL: Baseball is a religion over there. Not following the Red Sox in Massachusetts is like me going to a synagogue with a bacon cheeseburger: No one will know what the hell is wrong with me but they sure as hell want no part of me.

COAKLEY: It was bad and my staff started freaking out. I guess I didn't realize how bad it was until it kept snowballing.

HILLARY RODHAM CLINTON: Mrs. Coakley called me to ask for help but I didn't know what to tell her. As I've said, I've *always* been a Yankee fan myself.

BROWN: I knew that once I got her in the debates that it would be all over. I mean, check out my cheekbones. There's a reason *Cosmopolitan* named me sexiest man alive. One flash of a smile and I'd have more panties dropping than at a lipo clinic.

COAKLEY: I figured the debates would prove to the voters that I was the best choice to carry on the legacy that Senator Kennedy had left behind.

BROWN: The debates got off to a rough start for both of us. I wanted to wear sunglasses onstage, because I got these really tight shades, but they said no. It all worked out anyway. The more that the voters could see my beautiful brown eyes, the better. They might not remember anything I said, but they'd remember my eye color—and vote *Brown*.

COAKLEY: At one point I referred to the Senate seat as Ted Kennedy's seat.

BROWN: It was the *people*'s seat. It didn't belong to anyone.

EMANUEL: Yeah, no shit. We're not talking about an actual chair. It's an elected office, for fuck's sake.

BROWN: The *people*'s office, for the *people*'s sake.

MICHELLE: Scott Brown pulled even with Martha Coakley and it seemed clear that he could win. More importantly, he had the momentum. The story was such a good one—"Republican captures Kennedy seat"—that the media wanted it to happen. Maybe they were tired of all the pro-Barack news they'd been reporting, I don't know.

EMANUEL: We pulled out all the stops; every Democrat flew in to campaign for Martha Coakley.

MICHELLE: The Republicans did the same. They had everyone—especially Curt Schilling.

EMANUEL: How fucked up is politics in America that access to health care for hundreds of thousands . . . hell, *millions* of people was in the hands of some baseball player. Just think about that for a moment, because that is actually what happened.

McCONNELL: What also happened is that the American people spoke loud and clear. They did not want this bill whatsoever. There were many improvements to health care that both parties could agree on. This bill wasn't it.

BROWN: We won, exactly one year to the day after President Obama was inaugurated. Obamacare was dead.

REID: Except it wasn't. When we saw that Brown was pulling within spitting distance of Martha Coakley, we started planning ahead.

McCONNELL: They didn't have the votes to pass the bill over a filibuster.

REID: And we didn't need to. The bill had already been passed by both the House and the Senate. We knew that we could use the reconciliation budgeting process—to which filibusters don't apply—to make the law final.

McCONNELL: That was a budgeting rule which was not intended to be used for things like a health care overhaul. It was intended to be used for things like tax cuts, which is what we had used it for.

REID: Here's how things usually play out. One party puts forth their plan, the other party does their best job to criticize it—which usually makes it better—and then it becomes modified and signed into law. We knew that the health care law was a huge bill that would need tweaking. How could it not?

PELOSI: I took a lot of heat for saying that we needed to pass the bill to find out what's in it. That's because it's all well and good to imagine how the reform would play out, but only once it's law would we see how it actually worked. Then we could fix the problems. Even the First Amendment, everyone's favorite part of the Constitution, was an amendment—an *edit* to the original document.

BOEHNER: We were not interested in polishing a turd. We wanted full repeal, end of story.

PELOSI: It was odd, and a touch unprecedented. There are many bills that need repealing, absolutely. The Defense of Marriage Act, which a Democratic president passed, is a good example. That's because after twenty years America moved forward as a country and we were ready for that change. But the Affordable Care Act hadn't even been law for twenty minutes. How could they know it was so terrible?

REID: There was no need for full repeal. The Republicans could have argued for changing 50 percent, 75 percent—heck, even 99 percent of the law, keeping the bits that they liked.

McCONNELL: What my dear friends in the Democratic Party forget is that this is the first time that President Obama suffered a major defeat. First, with the Massachusetts Senate election. But, more broadly, all the polls were violently against the law. We had finally found the chink in his armor, and before anyone gets offended by that expression I'll point out that my wife is of Chinese descent.

ELAINE CHAO: I've called him much worse to his face but he doesn't understand Taiwanese.

EMANUEL: You ask me, it came down to this. The American people loved the idea of having a black president. They loved it, thought it was the best shit ever. What they didn't like is the idea of having a black man actually act like president. "Wait, he's actually going to pass laws? He's going to tell us to buy insurance for ourselves?" That kind of thing, they couldn't handle. So of course the Republicans were going to exploit this. They're *Republicans*. They didn't even need to be racists themselves. All they had to do as politicians is play to the crowd. It was craven, it was wrong—and it was highly successful for them.

MICHELLE: We expected some frothing at the mouth; we'd seen it throughout the process. The vitriol was insane, but I kept telling myself that change isn't easy and if this is what it takes to save lives, then so be it. Barack, he didn't really seem to let it get to him. I don't think he could wrap his head around the antagonism over such an issue that's at base uncontroversial. How can you be against medicine for sick people? Seriously?

McCONNELL: Off-year elections are always good for the party that's not in the White House. Recruiting is what wins or loses elections. Candidates need to be charismatic, sure, and they need to be bright, but they also need to be well connected and able to raise money. After Massachusetts showed that Republicans can win *anywhere,* suddenly our recruitment efforts really picked up. We weren't looking for moderates, either.

EMANUEL: The Republican Party was the victim of the Democrats' success. By wiping out all their moderates, they only had the far-right in charge of their party. But instead of going after us, they immediately started eating their own.

MARCH 23, 2010: BARACK OBAMA SIGNS THE AFFORDABLE CARE ACT INTO LAW.

CHARLIE CRIST: I was governor of Florida at the time. In 2010, I could either run for reelection or for the open Senate seat. I wasn't sure what to do. On the one hand, it would have been easier to run for reelection. But if I won, that was it. Because of term limits I wouldn't be able to run a third time. If I was in the Senate, well, then I'd have job security for six years at least. On the other hand, I'd have to move from Florida to Washington, D.C. That's going from good-looking old people to ugly old people.

EMANUEL: Charlie Crist would have been a nightmare candidate for us. A sitting governor? Forget it, he's been there, done that with state elections. We were very worried, because Florida would be a very key race—not to mention that the state would be crucial for the president's reelection.

MICHELLE: Senator McCain had even been considering him for the ticket.

JOHN McCAIN: It's true; he was on our short list. Then we decided that two old Caucasian men with white hair would end up like those guys in the balcony on *The Muppet Show*.

EMANUEL: Crist was pro-life, a conservative—the whole nine. The Republican Party claims they like accomplished people, and he had been elected governor, which is a huge accomplishment for any man. Plus, he did it in 2006, an extremely anti-Republican year. Not only that, he was elected after two terms of Jeb Bush! To win on a Bush's coattails in 2006? Holy shit! I wouldn't be surprised if he spent time in Cuba because that motherfucker can walk on water.

MICHELLE: But there was one problem.

EMANUEL: He had hugged President Obama.

CRIST: I was trying to restrain him! It was a citizen's arrest.

MICHELLE: It reminded me of the 1980s. It was like Barack had some disease that you could catch from hugging, and that if you voted for this person, then you would catch it too. That was literally the reaction against a governor being welcoming to the president of the United States, commander in chief of the armed forces and leader of the free world.

EMANUEL: The Republican Party was treating the fucking *president* as an infection to be contained. You can't catch black from people! Not from hugging, not no how. You can't even catch black diseases. Sickle cell is not contagious. We know this because only that one girl in TLC had it. They no more caught anemia from her than she caught car crash from Left Eye.

CRIST: Marco Rubio comes out of nowhere to challenge me in the Republican Party. Good kid, nice guy, but it's like, "Wait your turn." I kept getting hammered in the press. I don't know how you go from being a vice presidential prospect to becoming a pariah.

JOHN EDWARDS: Oh really?

CRIST: I wasn't involved in any scandal. My positions hadn't changed, and they weren't really that different from Rubio's.

MARCO RUBIO: Governor Crist had supported the stimulus, which was a huge waste.

CRIST: If I didn't support that stimulus, that federal money wouldn't have come back to Florida. If it was going to be spent somewhere, it might as well be spent in *my* state. This was simply politics. And I found it odd that no Democrats got heat for supporting the Bush bailouts, but the stimulus—the second half of the plan to fix the economy—oh no, we can't have that!

EMANUEL: It looked like he was toast in the Republican primary, which would be held in August.

CRIST: Look, we all have egos in politics. I'm as guilty of that as the next guy. But I asked myself, why would I as the governor of Florida, sitting governor, why would I go through a primary to lose when I thought I had a great shot in the general election? I mean, I had universal name recognition already. I just needed to be on the ballot. The people knew who I was, knew what I stood for. I could have gotten on the ballot by running as an independent, so that's exactly what I did. I didn't care if I had a D, an R, or an I next to my name. The letter didn't matter.

EMANUEL: You know how they say something is "the new black"? Well, black was the new scarlet letter in Republican circles. You got some on you, and everyone would shun you. As 2010 moved on, we saw it time and again.

10

THE SHELLACKING, FEBRUARY–
NOVEMBER 2010

MICHELLE OBAMA: Two thousand eight had been a huge year for the Democratic Party. But what was unprecedented was the fact that Barack kept on defeating Republicans *after* he had been inaugurated, all the way into 2010!

RAHM EMANUEL: Bob Bennett of Utah was the first. Senator for twenty years, superconservative guy. Utah conservative, and that's the reddest state there is. Yet he couldn't get through his own state convention to get renominated.

ROBERT BENNETT: I came in third. There were thirty-five hundred delegates who voted on the party nominee, and because I had supported President Bush's bailout—a Republican president—I somehow wasn't conservative enough anymore. In two years that's how far the party had moved to the right. Less than two years, actually.

EMANUEL: Then came Pennsylvania.

MITCH McCONNELL: The late senator Arlen Specter had been a very loyal Republican for many, many years. He's the one, mind you, who shepherded Clarence Thomas through his confirmation hearings and onto the Supreme Court. But Arlen was a moderate. He had been a

Democrat as a young man, and then he became a Republican when he grew up and got some sense.

MICHELLE: I didn't roll out the welcome mat when Senator Specter switched to the Democratic side in 2009. Not after what he did to Anita Hill. Sadly, we will never really know what transpired between them.

CLARENCE THOMAS: I still don't know who put pubic hair on my Coke.

EMANUEL: Wow, he *can* talk!

MICHELLE: When Senator Specter lost the primary to Joe Sestak—an actual Democrat—I didn't think it really meant anything.

McCONNELL: I started to get a little nervous. I of course wanted my caucus to be as conservative as possible. But I wanted candidates who could actually get elected. As primary season went on, we were getting conservative nominees who weren't exactly ready for prime time.

EMANUEL: They weren't even ready for Saturday morning.

HARRY REID: I knew that I personally was in for it. Nevada is a classic swing state, and I would be the Republicans' biggest target.

EMANUEL: Well, other than fairness, kindness, and decency. So the fourth-biggest.

REID: To take out a sitting Senate majority leader would certainly give them a lot to crow about. The potential Republican nominee that we were most worried about was Susan Lowden. She was bright and had been chairwoman of the Nevada Republican Party. She had a great Rolodex and could raise a lot of money.

McCONNELL: She would have been a great candidate.

REID: Then there was Sharron Angle, whose views on some issues were a little . . . extreme.

SHARRON ANGLE: I'm such a Republican that I added a second R to my name.

REID: She was *my* choice for the nominee.

ANGLE: I'm a hard-core, true-blue conservative who loves my country and hates what Barack Obama and the Democratic Party are doing to it. That's why I support the Second Amendment: so we can defend ourselves if things go too far.

REID: One minute she was musing about overthrowing the government, and the next she was worried about Sharia law taking root in America.

ANGLE: I spent too much money on my hair to cover it up for my husband!

REID: That's not to mention things like abolishing the Department of Education. Then she said that she wanted to privatize Social Security.

ANGLE: Oh, so *now* Harry Reid is in favor of giving money to old white men?

REID: It would of course have been largely illegal and highly unethical for me to interfere in another party's campaign process. But I didn't really have to. All sorts of Tea Party money came pouring in because Angle was the more extreme candidate.

ANGLE: I won the nomination because of my willingness to take a stand on the issues.

EMANUEL: OK there, cuckoo lady! Remember that Wayans brothers' movie, *White Chicks*, where they dressed up in reverse blackface? That's what Sharron Angle was like, Alan Keyes starring in *White Chicks*. But, you know, without the fart jokes or any laughing whatsoever. Just a loon in a wig.

McCONNELL: It happened in my own state too. I wanted Trey Grayson, who was the Kentucky secretary of state. Instead the voters chose Rand Paul. Rand at least I knew was electable. But some of these others? If I can be blunt, I think a lot of my colleagues in the Senate saw what was happening but were too scared to say anything for fear of losing their seat in a primary. I knew "shut it all down" was neither a means of winning elections nor a possibility in terms of running the government. It's just not.

MICHELLE: That summer was a long one. The vitriol never stopped even for a minute. The weather was hot but the people were fevered. It just kept getting worse and worse, rally after rally.

EMANUEL: I had never seen so many old white people take to the streets in my lifetime. It was like the Million Man March except everyone was from *Cocoon*.

MICHELLE: Can you imagine everyone in a state marching against having to buy car insurance? Sure, people sometimes grumble about the price, that's valid. That's why we have competition, to keep prices as low as possible—and that's why states were designed to have health care exchanges, for the exact same reasons. But the idea that you'd rally about having to switch to Geico?

EMANUEL: They preferred a gecko in their car more than a man of color in their White House is the impression that many people were getting from watching all this. And if that impression were inaccurate— which I am glad to entertain and hope to God is true—they didn't really seem to try and dispel it. It was the Rove strategy on steroids: let's worry about our base and to hell with everyone else.

MICHELLE: Then we got another Supreme Court vacancy, and Barack nominated Elena Kagan. I think he was just looking for someone who had a record that couldn't be eviscerated, and someone young enough with the stamina to deal with the nonsense.

EMANUEL: She was solicitor general in the White House, and everyone liked her. Smart, upbeat, hardworking. I tried to figure out how they were going to attack her. And you know what? They went after her personally: "Gee, she hasn't been married." "Uh-oh, she enjoys playing sports!"

ELENA KAGAN: What, a gal can't play softball once in a while—or every chance she gets, depending on her schedule?

EMANUEL: This whisper campaign about her sexual orientation. It was like, come on, really? That's the best you got?

KAGAN: Sure, I listen to the Indigo Girls. I got into them in college. It's calm, fun music. Who doesn't like that? And yes, I am partial to carpeted floors. That's just having taste!

MICHELLE: I am absolutely certain that a progressive gay judge would rule the same way as a progressive straight judge when it came to LGBT issues. These are *legal* questions that they are trained to address.

KAGAN: Yes, my home is carpeted. But I fail to see how that is of any legal relevance whatsoever.

EMANUEL: If anything, the gay ones are going to err on the side of caution to make sure they're being impartial. Listen, you put a gay man in a black robe with no sparkle to it whatsoever—this guy clearly respects the law and takes it seriously. Maybe on weekends it's a different story.

KAGAN: I'm still waiting to hear why my having a short haircut made so many people uneasy.

MICHELLE: So even though Elena had no scandals to her name and there was nothing remotely objectionable to her record, she was still only confirmed on a party-line vote. And she was replacing a progressive! It's not like the court was shifting to the left.

REID: The rule used to be, defer to the president as much as you can stomach, and fight him when he puts up the real nuts for nomination. He's the president, it's his prerogative to pick his staff and his judges. It was an honorable system. But I saw it fading away right before my eyes—and once the other side started doing it, some of us felt that we had to as well. It kept escalating with no end in sight, and we're *still* getting worse.

OFFICIAL WHITE HOUSE PHOTOGRAPH/AMANDA LUCIDON

"THIS PRESIDENT EVEN MADE THE SKY TURN GAY." -RICK SANTORUM

OFFICIAL WHITE HOUSE PHOTOGRAPH/PETE SOUZA

OFFICIAL WHITE HOUSE PHOTOGRAPH/PETE SOUZA

"GREAT. NOW THE NEGRO'S STEALING MY FURNITURE." -ABRAHAM LINCOLN

OFFICIAL WHITE HOUSE PHOTOGRAPH/PETE SOUZA

"I THINK MICHELLE HAS THAT DRESS."

OFFICIAL WHITE HOUSE PHOTOGRAPH/AMANDA LUCIDON

FICIAL WHITE HOUSE PHOTOGRAPH/LAWRENCE JACKSON

OFFICIAL WHITE HOUSE PHOTOGRAPH/AMANDA LUCIDON

YOU KNOW IT'S LOVE WHEN YOU'RE MAD
BUT STILL HOLD HANDS.

MICHELLE: Then Glenn Beck had his huge "Restoring Honor" rally in Washington. What honor had been lost by this presidency?

EMANUEL: The Tea Party just kept plowing forward. In Alaska, at the end of August, Lisa Murkowski lost her primary to a nobody named Joe Miller. It was like the Republicans were fighting a zombie invasion, and anyone who had ever served in Washington was suspected of being a carrier.

McCONNELL: Governor Palin made it a point to insinuate herself in these primaries. Now, here's the thing about the Republican Party, and the Democratic Party as well. We'll huff and puff and say all sorts of nasty things, but at the end of the day we'll get things done. At least, that's how it used to be. I'm all for ideology, but did these people think they were going to come to Washington, turn off the lights in their offices, and shut the door?

EMANUEL: Palin kept picking these absolute losers who had no résumés and no shot of winning. If there were that many right-wing ideologues in America, Obama would never have been elected. Hell, even Bush probably wouldn't have been fucking elected.

MICHELLE: The Republican Party is very crafty. You have to credit them with that, they are smart operators. But those smart operators were standing by, and it was getting out of hand even for them.

EMANUEL: The center of the country is at the center. Rocket science, right? Let's accept the Republican argument that we have more conservatives than liberals in this country, let's even make it 60/40. That would be your sweet spot for winning. But the Republicans who were 60 percent conservative were precisely the ones who were getting kicked out on their asses. They wanted 100 percent or nothing.

SARAH PALIN: It was time for America to take a stand and return to her principles.

EMANUEL: You can't negotiate with someone who's at 100 percent ideologically. By definition, they're not budging. We had that at one time in this country, and you know what happened? The Civil fucking War. The South were like spoiled kids throwing a tantrum, losing the game, so then they took their ball and went home. Only in that case the ball was shackled around the ankle of some poor slave.

MICHELLE: Then it was the vice president's turn. The Republicans had three scalps they were looking for in November of 2010. The first was Harry Reid, the Senate majority leader. The second was for President Obama's Illinois Senate seat, since Roland Burris was only a temporary appointment. The third was the vice president's former Senate seat in Delaware.

McCONNELL: If we got all three, we would have a compelling case that the American people were admitting that they'd made a huge error in electing President Obama. They had buyers' remorse, and this was them saying so loud and clear.

VICE PRESIDENT JOE BIDEN: I was hoping that my late son Beau Biden would run, following in the old man's footsteps. Wouldn't that have been nice?

JILL BIDEN: Beau also liked wrestling.

BIDEN: He wasn't interested, no matter how much I tried.

JILL: The vice president presides over the Senate. Beau didn't want to go to a job where his *dad* was the boss.

BIDEN: Then things got very dicey. Even though Delaware is a blue state, there was one Republican there who was very, very popular: Mike Castle.

EMANUEL: Yeah, we were freaking out about that one. I mean, the guy's name is Mike fucking Castle! He sounds like he's solving crimes on weekends and slaying pussy the rest of the week. Who doesn't want to be friends with "Mike Castle"? I was ready to go work on the campaign myself just based on his name.

MICHAEL CASTLE: I had been elected governor of Delaware after being lieutenant governor. I also served as the congressman for the state for eighteen years—Delaware only gets one congressman but two senators, because of its small size. I figured being senator would be like closing that inside straight.

REID: Every sitting politician always has these minor fringe challengers in the primaries. Usually they're either crazy people with money on their hands, single-issue zealots, or else people not expecting to win and just trying to raise their profile. Castle had such a challenger named Christine O'Donnell. We didn't think anything about her until she started getting Tea Party support.

CASTLE: It was pretty dumbfounding. Some of these primary voters seemed to be put off by the message that I was actually electable. And here I thought the Republican Party was supposed to be the party for society's winners!

DONALD TRUMP: Losers and total clowns!

EMANUEL: We literally couldn't believe it. This broad was just an activist with a loud mouth, and I say this as a proud member of the Democrats—official home for activist broads with loud mouths.

REID: I can't remember a time when an activist ran a successful Senate campaign. At the very least they'd need to be self-funding, which Ms. O'Donnell was not. Sure, many in politics cut their teeth in activism. But at least they were elected *somewhere* first. President Obama was an activist of sorts, but he spent close to a decade as a state senator.

EMANUEL: The Tea Party nuts were making arguments that made no fucking sense. They said that the voters didn't like Obamacare—when those same voters didn't know what Obamacare was. Then they said that they needed more nominees that represented America. Well, if these fucking looney toons really were representative of America, where were all the *representatives*? Where were the Delaware state officials? If there's so many of you assholes, you should have gotten someone into office *somewhere*, no?

CASTLE: I'm as right wing as it's possible to be in Delaware and still be elected. But even I couldn't beat a nobody in the primary, because she said extreme things and that was the vibe in the air that summer. If that's what the primary voters wanted, let her have it.

REID: That seat went from a certain Republican pickup to a sure Democrat hold.

BIDEN: I like Christine O'Donnell. When she won the primary in September 2010, that made sure my seat wouldn't be held by a Republican.

EMANUEL: Who the fuck votes against "Mike Castle"?

REID: The young lady had quite an unusual backstory. Apparently in high school or college she had dabbled in witchcraft or something like that. I could relate. When I was young, I was a bit of a rebel myself—which is pretty easy to do when you're a Mormon. I'd slip the girls a Coke and they'd act like I was a pimp.

MITT ROMNEY: I used Pepsi. I was basically Bill Cosby at that point, more animal than man. And who would believe them?

CHRISTINE O'DONNELL: We wanted to combat these allegations about my past. I was and am a Christian woman and a strong conservative. My team wanted to create an ad that the voters could really relate to.

EMANUEL: It went down in history as the worst ad of 2010. She went from unelectable to laughingstock. You didn't have to take the Democrats' word for it that the Tea Party was nuts; you could just watch their fucking commercials for yourself.

O'DONNELL: Originally the ad had me with, like, construction workers, saying "I'm just like him." Then it went too long, we needed to introduce me as a person to the voters, so we shortened it to "I'm him." Well, that got confusing because I wasn't a guy. So then we shot it with me talking about a group of voters, and I said, "I'm them." That didn't make any more sense to anyone.

MICHELLE: For the record, this was never our process for making political advertisements. And let me just say, it does not seem to be an *effective* one either.

O'DONNELL: Then we were all really tired and loopy so we got into kind of a Tea Party prayer circle, where we alternated reading the Bible with the parts of the Constitution that we liked. Well, that went on for a while because there's a lot to like in the Constitution.

RICK SANTORUM: Is this bitch for serious?

O'DONNELL: After that the brainstorming got really weird, we tried all sorts of combinations like "She's him" or "They is us," none of it really putting forth the message we wanted.

MICHELLE: What language is she speaking?

EMANUEL: Fuck that, what pipe is she smoking?

O'DONNELL: Finally we settled on an ad with just my face, explaining that I'm a regular person, and the tagline was "I'm you."

MICHELLE: Wow. Just . . . wow. OK. That is something else. Wow.

EMANUEL: If your entire fucking campaign is based on far-right principles, which is fine if that's your view, and you got the nomination because the other guy is too fucking moderate, why are you running ads that literally have no political content whatsoever? What the fuck, what the fuck, *what the fuck*.

MICHELLE: She was not me.

EMANUEL: The voters in Delaware agreed. She didn't win the election and neither did she have any chance of winning it either.

O'DONNELL: I guess I wasn't you after all.

MICHELLE: It was cold comfort. We knew there was going to be a tidal wave that hit us, we expected it and we braced for it. We heard those attack ads just like everybody else; we saw the people behind the scenes getting folks riled up. But even if you brace for a tidal wave, it sure doesn't feel very nice when it smacks you upside your head, picks you up, and then slams you on the beach on your behind.

REID: Election night 2010 was bad. Very, very bad.

NANCY PELOSI: We lost the House. The Republicans picked up over sixty seats. *Sixty.* The last time a party lost over sixty seats in the House was in 1948.

VICE PRESIDENT DICK CHENEY: I wanted to call Nancy Pelosi and congratulate her on being the first woman to be fired as Speaker of the House, but they convinced me that it wasn't a good idea. Shame, really. Couldn't have happened to a nicer gal! He, he, he.

MICHELLE: Governors' races, same thing. We lost six seats, and some were very bad signs. Michigan and New Mexico went Republican, and those are bluish states. Pennsylvania too. But Ohio was the classic swing state, and they took it with one of Newt Gingrich's right-hand men, John Kasich. This was not going to bode well for reelection, when the Republicans were in charge of the electoral machinery in those crucial states.

EMANUEL: The one bright spot was the fucking Senate.

REID: I should have lost my role as majority leader. The Republicans picked up six Senate seats and needed nine to tie. They could have had those nine very easily, if only they had nominated people who could have been elected. And if you couldn't win as a Republican in 2010, you couldn't win as a Republican in the Union under Lincoln.

McCONNELL: Delaware, Nevada, and Colorado were all golden opportunities. Delaware especially would have been great to have a Republican incumbent in; that sort of opportunity happens once every forty years or so.

O'DONNELL: I'm then?

JOHN BOEHNER: It was great knowing that I would be Speaker of the House. That had been a lifelong goal of mine, because they would finally stop calling me John Boner.

JOHN EDWARDS: Someday . . .

BOEHNER: My short-term goal was to stop the Obama agenda in its tracks.

McCONNELL: We were going to do everything in our power to make him a one-term president. Jimmy Carter was a great lesson in how *not* to govern. I felt that President Obama would be the same example. Let him go and make speeches—and leave Washington to the people who really care about this country.

MICHELLE: Election night was awful. I don't mean for America and for the Democratic Party, though the second of those is indisputable. I just meant *personally* awful. My husband is not an emotional man. What people perceive as him being aloof is actually him just being even-keeled. He's always the adult in the room, so to speak.

EMANUEL: By that point, I had had enough. Actually, way before that point.

MICHELLE: We all did.

RICHARD DALEY: I had been mayor of Chicago for twenty-two years. Six terms! That was enough for any man. I just wanted to outserve my dad, who had been mayor for twenty-*one* years. Ha, ha! Fuck you, Dad!

EMANUEL: I love Chicago. It's my home, and I missed it terribly.

MICHELLE: Tell me about it!

EMANUEL: When Mayor Daley announced he wasn't going to run again, this was a golden opportunity. I knew that with the president's backing I could win and serve my city.

MICHELLE: Rahm tendered his resignation and Barack joked about hiding in the suitcase and going back with him.

EMANUEL: He kind of looked me in the eye and I almost changed my mind. He was my friend, and someone I really looked up to. I didn't want to leave him behind but I didn't really have any choice. I wanted to be mayor.

MICHELLE: After Rahm left in late 2010, there was a big difference in the air. All the Republicans were waiting to be sworn in, and they were *hungry*. I knew what that was like; I had seen it just two years prior on our side.

EMANUEL: I knew he'd be OK without me.

MICHELLE: Washington is a very lonely place, and Rahm was really a close friend. Yes, I'm Barack's friend as well—but I'm also his wife.

A man needs to have friends of his own, people he can blow off steam with. So Barack just started spending more time with Reggie Love. It was quite a transition from Rahm, that was for sure.

REGGIE LOVE: I was there to have Mr. Barack President's back. After all: Who doesn't love Love?

11

OBL & BS, NOVEMBER 2010–JULY 2011

MICHELLE OBAMA: We weren't even out of 2010 when things came to a head. The Bush tax cuts were so extreme that the Republicans had only been able to pass them with an expiration date. Now that date was coming to pass, and they wanted the cuts extended—cuts Barack had specifically campaigned against.

REGGIE LOVE: Mr. Barack President was a cool cat, and he knew how to change his step when a new song came on the radio. He had said that elections have consequences, and in 2010 the Republicans had won.

MICHELLE: Barack had tried reaching out to the GOP on the Democratic issue of health care and had been rebuffed. The thinking went, maybe if he gave them what they wanted this time, then they would work together better in the future.

LOVE: Politics is like making love to a beautiful woman. You can't always tell her how beautiful she is. Nor can you think about it, or you will blow your load. You gotta play it . . . *smooth*.

MICHELLE: So rather than making the expiring taxes into a confrontation, it suddenly became a discussion. What if we *did* give in on the tax cuts? What would you give us in return?

LOVE: It's, like, yeah, I'll buy you dinner—but you're coming back to my place, baby.

JOHN BOEHNER: It was good to see the president coming to his senses before the new Congress had even been sworn in yet.

MICHELLE: I thought it was a complete mistake, that the Republicans would smell blood in the water and see this was a surrender.

LOVE: See, Miss Michelle and I had a very different perspective. I encouraged Mr. Barack President to think of the Republicans like a lady on her period. Let her flip her shit. Hell, she can knock over a table if she wants to! But after she's spent, you sit her down and you talk it out. If you play your cards right, she'll be crying and apologizing within the hour.

MICHELLE: The Democrats were of course totally against extending the tax cuts. But when the idea came to pair it with extending unemployment insurance, things got interesting. *That* turned the Tea Party off, which kind of made me realize this was the right kind of compromise.

BOEHNER: More Republicans than Democrats ended up voting for the bill. We worked together and both sides got what they wanted. The tax cuts were continued, and there was unemployment relief.

LOVE: Sweet, sweet love leaves everybody with a smile on their face. There's plenty of happy to go around, yeah.

MICHELLE: I had never wanted to be more wrong in my life. But Barack knew what he was doing; you don't become president by luck.

VICE PRESIDENT DICK CHENEY: Well, except LBJ. Although I guess that's making your own luck, if you catch me.

MICHELLE: We got another huge victory at the end of the year with the repeal of "Don't Ask, Don't Tell."

JOHN McCAIN: I didn't ask for it, so I wish you'd stop telling me about it.

MICHELLE: Then we had to deal with John Boehner becoming Speaker of the House. It's a great accomplishment, good for him . . . But tell me: Have you ever seen a grown man cry so much on national television?

HILLARY RODHAM CLINTON: What a sniveling little pussy.

NANCY PELOSI: We already had a woman as Speaker, and it was me. I sure didn't cry when I lost, but I understood why Speaker Boehner cried—the *first* time. After that, it was like he was menopausal or something.

BOEHNER: I was not going through menopause at the time, or at any time previously or subsequently. These allegations are *false*.

PRESIDENT BILL CLINTON: I said that too, remember?

HILLARY: Yes, Bill. We all remember.

CHRISTINE O'DONNELL: I'm him?

MICHELLE: It had only been one week into the new Congress—*one week*—when tragedy struck.

LOVE: I was with Mr. Barack President when we got the news. There was nineteen people shot in Arizona by a crazy man. That look on the president's face, ooh boy! It was a mix of concern and anger, like when your dad is staying up all night to beat the crap out of you the minute you walk *safely* back in the door.

MICHELLE: It goes without saying that Arizona is the most pro-gun state in the United States. I don't think it's too hard to make the leap that when you have so many weapons around—especially ones that can discharge a lot of ammo—someone is going to get hurt.

BOEHNER: If you thought I was crying before, well, I sure cried that day. Gabby Giffords is a sweetheart, and my prayers immediately went out to her and her family, as well as all the other families affected by this senseless violence. Awful, just horrible.

MICHELLE: It was touch-and-go with her for a while. Of course, Barack said that he wanted to be told of any change in her condition immediately. He also scheduled a memorial service for the victims.

BOEHNER: It was a time to grieve and a time to reflect on why.

MICHELLE: It was a miracle that Congresswoman Giffords not only survived, but regained most of her faculties.

GABBY GIFFORDS: The doctors were worried that I would end up as a complete vegetable, but the biggest change was the fact that I like Delaware now. I mean, I really, really, *really* like it for some reason.

VICE PRESIDENT JOE BIDEN: I know, right?

GIFFORDS: Did you know that Delaware is the Peach State?

BIDEN: I *did* know that, but I would *still* like to hear more about it!

GIFFORDS: Georgia is also known as the Peach State, but they're actually third in terms of peach production.

BIDEN: That is a true fact!

CHENEY: Delaware: First in brain damage.

MICHELLE: The whole thing just left me very depressed, I'm not going to lie. I know the shooter was a very disturbed young man, this was not some assassination per se, I get that. But right away it became a political issue. *Right away.* A congresswoman gets shot in the head, literally, and no one takes a step back and does soul-searching. There is just so much vitriol in America sometimes that it feels like you can cut it with a knife.

BIDEN: This is why I talk about Delaware so much. It's a lot easier than talking about some of the other stuff.

LOVE: I went with Mr. Barack President to Arizona, to see Miss Gabby and all the brothas and sistas who got hurt by this maniac psychopath. And we were on the plane and Mr. Barack President turned to me and he was going to say something, and then he looked away, and then he kind of just patted my knee. That sort of thing will rattle any man, and I think he was wondering if this could happen to him or, God forbid, someone in his family.

MICHELLE: We were all thinking it. But life had to go on.

GIFFORDS: Delaware's capital is Dover.

BIDEN: Atta girl!

MICHELLE: One of the things that took the most getting used to as First Lady was how many news stories got things wrong. I'd read reports about supposed arguments, articles written vividly and in great detail—only I'd been in the room and had witnessed the exchanges described. It was shocking. I could get that; people love drama. What I didn't get were the conspiracy theories, like this whole idea that Barack hadn't been born in the United States.

DONALD TRUMP: Listen, I'm a big shot and I know everybody and I mean *everybody,* all right? Since *I* had no idea who Barack Obama was, OK, that meant that he was nada, zip, zero, a nobody. In other words, not an American.

MICHELLE: The certificate of live birth—which is a functional birth certificate—was publicly available. There had been birth announcements in *two* Hawaiian newspapers at the time when Barack was born.

TRUMP: I've placed ads all over the world. That's because the Trump brand is famous internationally. Anywhere you go on earth, you go to a Trump property and you will find a dedication to the tackiest accommodations at the highest possible price. Do you love the look of too much gold decor? Trick question, there's no such thing.

MICHELLE: We had ignored the story because it was such an absurdity. But now Donald Trump started making the accusations, so the media took the ball and ran with it.

TRUMP: I was just asking questions—just like I did on my smash TV show *The Apprentice* before NBC fired me.

MICHELLE: Literally, how could you prove something again? What more did they want?

LOVE: I told Mr. Barack President that he should take one of them CIA time-travel devices to go back and film his birth. I said it as a joke. But he looked at me all serious and was all, "Who told you about that? You weren't supposed to know!" I thought he was playing so I went along and was like, hold up, let's go back and meet Abraham Lincoln, because that beard of his was on fleek. Mr. Barack President said we couldn't do that, so I said no worries, maybe we can just go talk to Kunta Kinte. He told me that he wasn't real, and I said, what do you mean, I seen it on TV, he's real. Then he had LeVar Burton call me Toby when I eventually met him. I guess you had to be there. I mean, meeting LeVar, not going back in time to see Lincoln.

MICHELLE: The Tea Party members—or the most out-there ones at least—literally could not believe that Barack was president. It was something they psychologically didn't seem equipped to handle. They just wanted to wish it all away.

PELOSI: They didn't ask for my birth certificate to be sworn in as Speaker of the House. Granted, you don't have to be a native-born citizen for that. Well, I was also the first female Speaker. No one asked me for, you know, an ob-gyn exam.

RON PAUL: She kept asking *me* for a free one, and I explained to her in no uncertain terms why they call me "Dr. No." Although in this case

I believe it was "Dr. No Fucking Way on God's Green Earth." I've been a practicing ob-gyn for many years, but I'm also a religious man. Her in the stirrups, that's the gateway to hell right there.

CHENEY: That's because no one would want to see that. I'd rather look at Medusa.

LOVE: Mr. Barack President wasn't sure that he wanted to release his long-form certificate. He thought it was just giving the crazies red meat, that they'd be hungry for more. So I told him about the time when I was with this fly honey, name of Jackie, lovely girl. Well, I had been texting my sick sister all weekend. Jackie didn't know none of that, all she knew is me texting in secret so as not to be rude. So she flips out, hooting and hollering, "Who is this broad you're texting?"—that sort of thing. Usually, in a situation like that, it's "bye bitch bye!" But I liked her and I showed her the phone and explained what had happened. She felt humiliated and never distrusted me again. In retrospect that was a mistake on her part, but that's a whole other story.

MICHELLE: No, I did *not* think Reggie was a good influence on Barack. When did you ever hear of a guy by the name of "Reggie Love" who wasn't selling weed?

LOVE: My point was, yeah, giving in goes against everything you believe in as a man. You don't want to reward bad behavior. You don't want to say it's all cool that someone is openly questioning you and distrusting you. But sometimes you gotta give a little to get more.

TRUMP: My investigators were in Hawaii and they couldn't believe what they were discovering. It was remarkable, OK?

MICHELLE: The reaction to releasing the birth certificate wasn't exactly what I expected. The real nuts still didn't believe it was real, they didn't change their tune. But right-thinking people were kind of embarrassed and wanted to look away. No one wants to see a grown man humiliated for no reason. I remember once in my office—this is way back before I was First Lady—someone I worked with got fired. Security escorted him out of the building with all his stuff in a box. It was shameful for everyone involved. So very quickly the media circus over this birther nonsense was silenced.

PELOSI: Including the ringleader, Donald Trump.

TRUMP: It turned out that my investigators found that Hawaii is a wonderful travel destination for singles, couples, and families alike—and there's no better place to stay than at the Trump Hotel Waikiki Beach Walk. Now I could focus on getting birth certificates for every Mexican in America.

MICHELLE: No shame, no apologies, from anyone. "We need to take personal responsibility" in this country is the mantra.

HILLARY: I'm surprised President Obama got off so easy. My husband and I have been accused of literally everything, including rape and murder.

MICHELLE: It wasn't but a week after the birth certificate nonsense that Barack got to demonstrate who the real adults in the conversation were, and who were the children.

HILLARY: It was a huge privilege of my life to have served as secretary of state. I've had many proud moments during my tenure, all of which were described in excruciating detail in my bestselling memoir *Hard Choices*.

CHENEY: It is easier for a camel to go through the eye of a needle than for a human to get through that crapbook.

HILLARY: Undoubtedly, the proudest moments as secretary were during those first few days of May 2011.

BOEHNER: So it *wasn't* Benghazi? Gee, she sure spoiled that twist ending.

HILLARY: We got the call that *everyone* in America was desperately waiting for.

BIDEN: Rush Limbaugh is retiring.

HILLARY: They had found Osama bin Laden.

MICHELLE: Barack didn't even tell me, that's how secretive it was. I honestly think the 9/11 bombers were less circumspect about their actions than the CIA was during all this.

HILLARY: I had never been more anxious in my life. I just thought it was a completely amazing miracle that, thanks to modern technology, we'd be able to hear updates about the raid in real time.

BIDEN: We all gathered in the situation room and stared at the screen. It was simply surreal, and I don't like surreal.

HILLARY: Everything about it felt like a video game, except that the graphics weren't as good. We heard the yelling, we heard them moving. Gunshots, that sort of thing. I obviously can't get into too many details, but I still get chills thinking about it.

BIDEN: For one second, I took my eyes off the screen and glanced back at President Obama to see how he was reacting to the whole thing. He had his jaw set tight, all business.

HILLARY: I'm surprised that we didn't all die in that room, because I will swear on a stack of Bibles that no one was breathing. I doubt anyone blinked, either, it was that intense.

BIDEN: We were told "EKIA," which stands for "Enemy Killed in Action." All I could do was repeat *Holy shit* under my breath.

HILLARY: None of us knew what to do. What do you do when America's biggest enemy, a murderer thousands of times over, is finally put down? Do you applaud? Do you cheer, do you cry?

BIDEN: When it was over it was like we had all just watched some sort of corporate presentation. Our heads were spinning. We patted one another on the back and smiled but the feeling was a huge sense of relief. Thank God this finally happened.

HILLARY: Did you know he had a huge stash of pornography? It was only Israeli porn and he kept track of the ones he'd seen and the ones he hadn't.

BIDEN: He apparently called it Schindler's List and vowed to pleasure himself six million times.

MICHELLE: I joked with Barack later, pointing out that the live announcement interrupted Donald Trump's show *The Celebrity Apprentice*.

TRUMP: I didn't find it to be particularly funny, and I'm not an unfunny guy. Ask anyone who works for Trump, they'll tell you what a great sense of humor I have.

MICHELLE: I think it weighed heavily on Barack that he had to order the deaths of other people, even men who are as evil as Osama bin Laden. That's why he kept doing it, thousands of times, until it didn't bother him anymore. It takes a lot of effort to become strong enough to order the deaths of children you haven't seen—heck, it's hard enough to order the deaths of children you *have* seen.

HILLARY: Pussy.

MICHELLE: I asked him if he wasn't excited by what happened, and he kind of shook his head. "It's not that bin Laden is dead that I'm glad about, so much as all those families can have some closure" is how he put it. Boy, there were a lot of tears in America that night, of that much I am certain.

BOEHNER: It really does calm the nerves.

HILLARY: I didn't cry, but that's because I'm not a little bitch.

BOEHNER: Don't be too sure about that.

MICHELLE: What began as the death of one terrorist continued a revolution throughout the entire Middle East.

HILLARY: It started in Tunisia. A young man by the name of Mohamed Bouazizi set himself on fire. At first I was confused; I assumed it was some sort of Fourth of July fireworks thing. Then I realized that of course they don't celebrate the Fourth of July in the Middle East because they don't always hold the United States in high esteem. *Then* I realized that they don't celebrate the Fourth of July because that commemorates the Declaration of Independence, it's not an international thing like Christmas or what have you. That's when I got some coffee. I was not really with it that morning. Hey, we all have our bad days, right?

BILL: Right!

HILLARY: Well, after that there were huge protests throughout the entire country, which then spread to neighboring Algeria. *All right,* I thought, *no big deal. Let's keep an eye on it and see what transpires. This could be the spark to something huge, but nine times out of ten these protests flame out without any consequences whatsoever.*

MICHELLE: We quickly saw that this really was something, and that was thanks to social media. Barack used social media to tremendous gain in the campaign, of course, but it was fascinating to watch how it played out in other countries. If, say, the Egyptian government didn't want Egyptians to know what was happening in Tunisia, they really couldn't keep it quiet. Facebook and Twitter were bypassing the official media and keeping young people informed in real time. It was exhilarating!

HILLARY: The protests began exploding throughout the region. Yet we wanted there to be as few explosions as possible, if you get me.

MICHELLE: There was something ironic about the fact that both Barack and President Bush tried to bring democracy to the Middle East. President Bush did it via war, a war we didn't need to fight. Barack did it by example, and demonstrated how technology can liberate all of us.

CHENEY: Enough with this hippie talk. It wasn't as simple as that.

HILLARY: Vice President Cheney is right. Democracy is very many things but simple is not one of them. Messy, certainly. And admirable. But not simple.

BIDEN: During the cold war, there was something called the domino theory. It was the idea that if one country fell to communism, then they would start falling one after another just like dominoes. It was certainly plausible, the commies were really on a tear there for a while. But what they began to call the "Arab spring" showed the same sort of domino effect, only in a democratic direction.

HILLARY: One month after it all started, the Tunisian president left office after twenty-three years in power. Next, Hosni Mubarak—a longtime U.S. ally—resigned the Egyptian presidency in February 2011. The Tunisians then, in March 2011, had their first full democratic elections since the 1950s.

HOSNI MUBARAK: I was in my eighties. Every man who lives that long has earned one very important right: the right to always be able to offer complaints but to never have to entertain them. The kids in Tahrir Square, screaming their heads off. What did I need that stress for? I'm cold and I'm pretty sure my assistants are taking money from my wallet when I'm not looking.

HARRY REID: They do love to do that.

MITCH McCONNELL: I agree with Harry, you have to watch them like a hawk.

REID: Or like a dove, depending on where you sit politically.

McCONNELL: Well, doves aren't really known for watching things.

REID: I doubt Mr. Mubarak was going to dive-bomb his nurse and cut her open with his claws.

MUBARAK: Well, not *literally*.

HILLARY: Then Libya, too, was freed.

CHENEY: What could possibly go wrong?

MICHELLE: All this gave us cover to bring the troops home from Iraq.

MICHELE BACHMANN: While Barack Obama was worrying about the terrorists overseas, those of us in the Tea Party were bust coming up with the next steps to implement *our* goals. Between my biological children and my many foster children, sometimes our house felt more like a zoo than a household! Let me tell you, managing the finances was tricky no matter how successful my husband and I were—and we sure were successful. Since we were one of the few groups who had discovered the cure for homosexuality, we were making decent money from our program.

LOVE: I have known the warm, soft touch of many a fine female. But some dudes ain't wired like that, and that's cool for them. Love is love, and Love is *for* love. The only way to get gay men to stop thinking about gay sex is for them to actually *have* some. Then they're all clear for around half an hour or so.

BACHMANN: Actually, homosexuality can be cured very easily. We just showed the men naked pictures of Harry Reid, and they never had sexual thoughts of any kind again.

BOEHNER: The views expressed by Congresswoman Bachmann are hers and do not necessarily represent or reflect the views of the Republican Party.

BACHMANN: My point was, I knew a little something about how to manage a budget. You can't keep spending and spending willy-nilly. Eventually your bills will come due and you'll have to pay the piper. The debt ceiling increase was coming up in April, and we from the Tea Party thought this would be the perfect God-given opportunity to force Barack Obama to do the right thing and cut down on spending.

PELOSI: The debt ceiling increase had historically not been used as a political weapon. The repercussions of messing with America's credit would be felt worldwide; it was a very dangerous thing to even bring up.

LOVE: It's like when your broad is mad at you and tells you that maybe you should break up. Don't put that out there unless you feeling it for certain, or else Reggie Love might get ideas. Even if she cries a bit and makes nice, it still permanently poisons the relationship. I said to Mr. Barack President that messing with the debt was like that, like a fart that would never go away. He . . . um . . . he didn't care for my choice of words.

BOEHNER: The Tea Party members of the House were quite insistent. As their leader, it was my job to follow their commands.

PELOSI: I almost couldn't believe they were playing that game.

BOEHNER: The Democratic hypocrisy in this issue was astonishing. They fought tooth and nail against raising the debt ceiling under President Bush.

PELOSI: That is true, that did happen. That's because we were in the minority and we were grandstanding. Not tooth and nail . . . more like, I don't know, gums and fingertips? Regardless, that's how politics *works*. You can talk and raise a fuss but you keep the country on track. We didn't have the votes at that time, but now the Republicans did. We had been scoring political points, but they were actually going to do it!

REID: If the spending and the debt was as bad as the Republicans claimed, then they wouldn't have to engineer a budget crisis of their own making. It would have come of its own accord when we ran out of money. That wasn't on anyone's horizon, so they chose to force the issue.

LOVE: I know a little something about bad credit. It's like a demon woman sucking all the juice out of you—and not in a good way. It ruins your days and nights, you can't sleep! But I know something else about it: The way to fix your credit ain't to just stop paying your bill and shut off your phone. They *will* track you down.

MICHELLE: Barack was ready to make a deal. He was negotiating in good faith, just like with the extension of the Bush tax cuts, which he so despised. A lot was on the table. But any offers we got were only rebuffed by ultimatums.

BACHMANN: We were voted in to fight tax increases, and by gosh we were not going to raise one tax one single penny.

PELOSI: Any government spending has to be paid for by taxes. If you don't pay for it now and make it part of the deficit, you pay for it out of taxes *in addition* to the interest, which is *also* paid for by taxes. Speaker Boehner never had control of his caucus. When he went in front of the cameras, he was repeating what he was told and not what he believed. You don't become Speaker of the House as an ideologue.

NEWT GINGRICH: Speak for yourself.

PELOSI: I stand corrected. You don't *remain* as Speaker of the House while acting as an ideologue. Newt and the 1994 Republicans cut deals with President Clinton. But Boehner's Republicans were a whole other animal.

MICHELLE: It seemed like they wanted us to default on the debt so that Barack would get the blame.

BACHMANN: This is what the American people voted for.

PELOSI: No one voted for defaulting on our debt, that is absurd.

MICHELLE: Eventually we had to figure out a system that gave every politician what they wanted: complete credit and an utter lack of responsibility.

REID: No one really wanted to cut spending. The Republicans wanted to keep military spending, we Democrats want social spending. But someone had the great idea: What if the cuts weren't cuts at all? What if we had a program that triggered the cuts automatically so everyone would have clean hands?

McCONNELL: Someone used the metaphor of it being like a script that runs on your computer. Well, I don't know from computers.

REID: In my day we had computers, only they call them accountants now.

McCONNELL: So we had to sit there and listen to how a script works.

REID: Let me tell you, if you've never been on the Internet, understanding what a script is is quite tricky. It's *not* written in cursive, for one. Don't make that mistake, like some senators I don't want to mention!

McCONNELL: That was you!

REID: Yes, and I didn't want to mention it.

McCONNELL: Then someone used the example of Java, and since I'm hep I knew that's what the barristers at Starbuck refer to coffee as. Except it has nothing to do with coffee.

REID: Then why is the little picture of a coffee cup?

McCONNELL: Yeah, that little coffee picture was another good fifteen minutes of confusion.

REID: Finally we got to how the script "self-executes," and I did not see why that could possibly be considered a good thing. What is that, a more humane way to administer capital punishment after lethal injection is banned?

McCONNELL: It sounded an awful lot like committing suicide and that was not a political position that I could endorse, as I am proudly pro-life.

REID: As am I. But even if I were pro-choice, I still would not be advocating suicide.

McCONNELL: I suggested we change it to an "executing" script instead of "self-executing."

REID: Well, I think we should be restricting the death penalty and not encouraging its use.

McCONNELL: That is the typical liberal nonsense, coddling criminals while allowing families to live in fear that these murderers can escape or else be paroled and then strike again.

REID: It turned out that "executing" was just an expression, too. Why would you call it that? Couldn't you call it something nice, like, I don't know, *servicing*? *Helping*?

McCONNELL: It was confusing to everyone.

PAUL RYAN: Everyone over seventy, maybe. Thank God no one told them about "slave drives" on their computers, we would have had another Civil War on our hands.

REID: Well, it turned out that this "self-executing script" is just another way of saying that you put a process into place that runs automatically without anyone's involvement or supervision. No involvement meant no guilt.

McCONNELL: No supervision meant no responsibility.

REID: It was the solution we were looking for all along.

MICHELLE: How it worked was that a certain amount of money was going to be "sequestered." Later in the year there would be a supercommittee composed of equal numbers of Republicans and Democrats. If the committee members couldn't reach a compromise on spending and taxation, cuts would be automatically applied to both military and social services in equal measure.

BOEHNER: The bill had bipartisan support and bipartisan opposition. This was how Washington *was* supposed to work.

REID: As we say in the Senate, with great power comes complete irresponsibility.

12

READY FOR ROMNEY, JULY 2011–MAY 2012

MICHELLE OBAMA: Two thousand eleven shuddered to an end for us. About a year after Rahm returned to Chicago, Reggie left the White House as well in order to get his MBA.

REGGIE LOVE: I figured it was the perfect complement to my Ph.D.—my pimp & ho degree, which I hadn't used in a minute. It was hard to leave the Obama administration. I sat down with the president and I told him what I was thinking. I said, "Mr. Barack President, I've been by your side through ups and downs. We've been thick as thieves. You're a beautiful man, both inside and outdoors. But this is not the life for me."

MICHELLE: Barack was bummed out. Washington seemed like a bait-and-switch: you come being promised a seafood dinner—only to get cans of cat food. But we didn't have the option of leaving. Barack had no choice but to run for reelection.

HILLARY RODHAM CLINTON: Well, "no choice" is a strong way to put it.

MICHELLE: The economy was still nowhere near where we wanted it to be. The idea of passing a jobs program through a Tea Party–controlled House was a nonstarter.

MITT ROMNEY: As well it should have been. A jobs bill? Who the heck do you think is going to be creating jobs? The Obamaphone lady?

MICHELLE DOWERY: *Haaaay!* Can you hear me now?

MICHELLE: The Obamaphone lady's name is Michelle? Really? Stop playing.

ROMNEY: My point is this: The government can't create jobs. The Post Office, the IRS, whichever it is, those jobs are funded by taxpayers—and if you're paying taxes, that means you have a job to begin with. So where *do* jobs come from? Easy: It is small businesses that create them, driving our economy in the process. Two things then happen to those small businesses. They either fail, and everyone loses their jobs, or they succeed and get bought by Bain, and only half of the people lose their jobs. Then, after a certain expansion point, you go public because that company needs that cash influx to take their business to the next level. Corporations are just small businesses that have grown due to their popularity with the public.

MICHELLE: In the main, I would agree with Governor Romney. That's not all that controversial of a perspective. The big difference between us and the Republicans is that we see what happens when these corporations get *too* big. Suddenly the law, which in this country is supposed to treat the little guy and the big guy fairly, becomes manipulated in favor of the wealthy and powerful.

ROMNEY: What I take exception to is this idea that the Republicans are Wall Street puppets. Just because I might be wooden sometimes doesn't mean that someone is pulling my strings.

VICE PRESIDENT DICK CHENEY: Did Romney just make a joke?

VICE PRESIDENT JOE BIDEN: Ha, ha, ha!

ROMNEY: Frankly, if the First Lady is looking for collusion between Wall Street and Washington, Mrs. Obama would do well to look in her own backyard.

MICHELLE: The tomato garden?

ROMNEY: I'm just saying that plenty of Democratic politicians try to have it both ways on this issue, denigrating corporate America one minute and then raising corporate funds the next. I don't just mean minor officials either; this goes all the way to the top Democratic leadership.

HILLARY: Bill, I think he means you.

PRESIDENT BILL CLINTON: That's complete nonsense. I am not and never have been in the pocket of corporate interests. My access is based on whoever has the biggest contributions, regardless of whether they've gone public. Wealthy individuals, prominent heads of state, foreign governments—I'm independent because I listen to *all* of them.

MICHELLE: At some point we got news that there was a protest going on in New York in Zuccotti Park, I think the name was. I know even Barack was a little confused because he'd gone to Columbia and he'd never heard of that park. Central Park, Union Square, Madison Square—those were known. But he had to ask where Zuccotti was.

MICHAEL BLOOMBERG: My job as mayor was to keep the proud American and, especially, the proud *New York* tradition of allowing people to peacefully protest. Citizens get their voices heard and blow off steam, which keeps things from escalating and getting ugly later. It's good for democracy and it's good for everyone.

MICHELLE: The group was calling itself Occupy Wall Street, and that kind of left me a little confused because Wall Street seemed plenty occupied already. Then it also turned out that Zuccotti Park wasn't even really near Wall Street but across from where the Twin Towers had stood. It's not even an actual park! There are fewer than fifty trees and no grass to sit on, just granite benches.

BLOOMBERG: I've got homes that are far bigger than Zuccotti Park.

ROMNEY: I know, right?

BLOOMBERG: There were two other sites where the group had wanted to hold protests, and we denied them. Yes, you have a right to assemble peacefully—but the key word is *peacefully*. You can't just go anywhere you want and start yelling at people.

JOE WILSON: I know, right?

MICHELLE: We didn't really know what to make of the whole thing. Frankly, it seemed like they themselves didn't either.

BLOOMBERG: A bunch of kids basically set up a shantytown in the park. If they wanted to stay there, I thought, let them stay. This was New York City in the fall, rapidly becoming winter. The only thing colder than New York City in the winter is Dick Cheney's heart in New York City in the winter.

MICHELLE: The media described Occupy as a sort of liberal counterpart to the Tea Party. I was glad to see that our 2008 voters hadn't permanently gone away! These young men and women defined themselves as the 99 percent, as opposed to the 1 percent who have too much influence in America. I could not agree more with them. As Barack would say, "Let me be clear." To begin with the obvious, clearly as First Lady I am part of the 1 percent.

HILLARY: Well, let's not be hasty here.

MICHELLE: One of Barack's biggest accomplishments had been broadening the electorate and allowing more people to have their voices heard. So I agreed with that goal of theirs as well. The Occupy people complained about income inequality, how it's bad morally and dangerous economically for wealth to be concentrated in such a small segment of the population.

ROMNEY: Come on, 1 percent is still thirty million people!

MICHELLE: The broader the amount of people with money, the more they tend to spent it, and the more jobs are created. A human can only use so much. Once you get ultrarich, you horde it and can't spread the wealth around even if you wanted to. There's only so many $1,000 hamburgers a human can consume, you know?

ROMNEY: I *do* know. I managed to pop down five, but that was it for me.

BLOOMBERG: I could only handle three. I'm not a burger type of guy.

BILL: Ha, ha, ha! See, this is why I was president and they weren't. *Ten*, motherfuckers! I ate *ten* of those burgers. Sure, I threw them up right away, but those bad boys tasted as good coming up as they did going down.

MICHELLE: So this was the backdrop for the imminent Republican presidential nomination race. It was quite odd that Governor Romney was the clear front-runner at the very moment that people were taking to the streets to protest corporations.

ROMNEY: *Some* people. After all—say it with me—"corporations are people, too."

MICHELLE: In a sense, his nomination seemed inevitable. Since 1980 the Republicans have made it a point to nominate the guy who came in second place the prior time.

RICK SANTORUM: Don't count Santorum out in 2016! And don't Google it either.

ROMNEY: I had two big reasons for running. First, to be in office when the recovery happened so that I could take credit for it. Politics is about being in the right place at the right time. Second, to make sure that the healthcare plan that I had successfully implemented in Massachusetts wouldn't be adopted nationwide. That's because I love my home state a lot and want it to do better than the others.

SARAH PALIN: It was not going to be his nomination for the taking, that much was for sure. The Republican Party needed strong, positive leadership that I was too busy making money from TV shows and books to provide myself.

MICHELLE: The Republican field was a huge one, kind of like the Democratic one had been back in 2008. But unlike the Democrats then, this grouping was a bit . . . *different*.

DAVID AXELROD: I came back on board the campaign team to finish what we had started in 2008. I was glad to do it. I thought the president's record was superb and he was really the right man for the job. The Republicans, of course, disagreed, which was their role in politics.

MICHELE BACHMANN: The Tea Party had captured Congress and we were marching all the way to the White House!

HARRY REID: I think Mrs. Bachmann forgot that I was still the majority leader of the Senate, but she was so excited I didn't have the heart to break it to her otherwise.

MICHELLE: The Republican slate had been devastated by their losses in 2006 and 2008. As a result, they didn't really have that many experienced people to run for president.

NEWT GINGRICH: That sure hadn't stopped President Obama.

AXELROD: After the 2010 midterms, I could see why so many people smelled blood in the water, I really did. Politics is like sports: You're only as good as your last victory—or, in this case, as bad as your previous loss. Yeah, I know the Republicans thought that if Barack Obama could be elected president, then *anyone* could be elected. But I didn't think they meant *literally* anyone.

MICHELLE: Some of the people who threw their names into the ring—I didn't really know what they were thinking.

BACHMANN: I don't really know what I'm thinking either.

AXELROD: In fact, the first person to drop out of the campaign had one of the strongest records: Governor Tim Pawlenty of Minnesota. It's a bluish state, and even though he wasn't particularly exciting, that might have made for a contrast with our flashier campaign style.

MICHELLE: I liked Tim Pawlenty. I didn't agree with him, but that's OK. He was a decent person who would have made a decent Republican president. There was only one problem . . .

TIM PAWLENTY: Yes, I'm boring. OK? Is everyone fucking happy now? I admit it! I'm fucking boring! Jesus fucking Christ, do you have any idea what it feels like to be told day in and day out how fucking *boring* you are? It sucks. I was running for president, not ringmaster. What the fuck, was I supposed to be doing backflips and juggling chain saws? Is that what you fuckers wanted? Is it? Well, fuck that noise and fuck you all. I am not fucking boring. I am a man with a vision on how to make America great, is that so fucking bad?

AXELROD: Wow, even his cursing is boring.

MICHELLE: Maybe Rahm could coach him or something, poor guy.

PAWLENTY: Sorry, I'm sorry. I lost my head there for a second. It's just that hearing it over and over from the press was bad enough. They couldn't have known that my wife had somehow managed to work a reference to how boring I am into our wedding vows.

AXELROD: If only he had ranted more during those first debates, he might have made it to the primaries.

MICHELLE: The other candidate that we were really nervous about was Jon Huntsman. He had been governor of Utah, squeaky clean guy. He was also our ambassador to China, where he did a job that earned bipartisan praise. Huntsman wasn't just the ambassador, either; he actually spoke Chinese.

AXELROD: From my understanding, that is a difficult language to master. I'm pretty sure that there are Chinese people out there, in China, who haven't gotten it down.

JON HUNTSMAN: I was proud to serve my country even if it was in the administration of the opposing party. A good diplomatic relationship with China is essential for American interests. My argument was, wouldn't it be better to have the ambassador to China be a conservative Republican with conservative Republican values representing us to the PRC? It's not like the slot would have gone vacant if I hadn't filled it.

AXELROD: That rationale would have made sense if this had been a different Republican Party.

MICHELLE: No, I think that rationale would have made sense if this had been a different president. It was Charlie Crist all over again. There was this guilt-by-association thing that doomed Ambassador Huntsman before he had even started.

HUNTSMAN: I didn't realize how much the party had changed, and how I effectively had no chance simply due to my serving under the president. We didn't contest Iowa, because that really wasn't the wing of the Republican Party that I belonged to. Then New Hampshire was off the table, because Governor Romney was so strong there. Then we didn't really focus on South Carolina, since there are so many evangelicals there. And then there was Florida, which I knew I wouldn't be strong in . . . Dammit, I knew I shouldn't have hired Giuliani's advisers from 2008! No wonder they were so cheap.

AXELROD: There were other candidates, sure, but I think the Republican establishment was more concerned about them than we were. They'd tank so hard in the general that their defeat would probably even revert the House to the Democrats.

RON PAUL: I ran because I believe in liberty, like so many of my fellow Americans do. That's why I advocated returning to the gold standard and legalizing all drugs, like so many of my fellow Americans do. Also, ending all foreign aid, cutting the federal government in half, and eliminating the income tax. I had to moderate my views a bit since the 2008 campaign; everyone thought I had been a little too out there.

RICK PERRY: The way I figured it, 50 percent of the last two presidents had been Texas governors. That gave me a coin's-toss odds of making it to the White House. Many Americans wanted to go back to the Bush years, and I was the governor who thought like him, worked like him, and talked as real good like him.

SANTORUM: It seemed to me as if America had been making progress since at least the 1960s—but progress in the wrong direction. The American family was falling apart, and with it I feared would come the unraveling of our very nation itself. Running for president would be the best way to arrest this process, since so many Americans make their wedding and family decisions based on the views of the president.

GINGRICH: I felt as if many of the successes of the 1994 Republican revolution were in danger of being rolled back by a president who owed more to European socialism and Keynesian economics than he did to the Founding Fathers. I was the only Republican in the race who, as Speaker of the House, had actually succeeded in rolling back entitlements and balancing the federal budget.

MICHELLE: And then there was Herman Cain.

AXELROD: As campaign manager you pretty much prepare for any eventuality. Presidential campaigns don't have much wiggle room; one mistake and you can lose a state, and with it its electoral votes—and thereby the presidency. In addition, you also have to do some rough preliminary looks at all the potential vice presidential nominees. VPs don't really make that much of a difference, but sometimes they'll have a bad quote somewhere along the line that you can use to make the other guy's campaign squirm. Obviously it goes both ways; I'm sure the Republicans did everything they could to dig up dirt on all the Democrat candidates.

HILLARY: Fortunately there wasn't any dirt for them to dig up.

GINGRICH: No dirt, just some dirty dresses.

AXELROD: I've been around politics for a long time. I've seen it all, and if I haven't seen it, I know someone who has. So I can say with good authority that Herman Cain is the first person to ever be in the lead for a nomination without a file on him. That never happens, *ever.* Because candidates like Herman Cain don't get traction, *ever.*

HERMAN CAIN: My background as CEO of Godfather's Pizza is all the qualification I needed to run the federal government. I already had my cabinet planned out, too. The guy who runs Taco Bell is obviously good at international affairs, so he would be secretary of state. McDonald's CEO becomes ambassador to Ireland. I was going to put Willy Wonka as secretary of education because he was good at teaching kids valuable lessons.

AXELROD: Look, conservatives are always late to the party when it comes to the latest trends. Electing a black president was cool in 2008, but in 2012 the novelty would be gone.

CAIN: I called my tax plan "9-9-9." I would grossly simplify the tax code and replace it with a 9 percent income tax, a 9 percent national sales tax, and a 9 percent business tax. Order now and I'll size up your order free of charge. In the Cain administration, all audits come with complimentary breadsticks and your choice of dipping sauces— *conservative* dipping sauces, none of that sissy honey mustard stuff.

MICHELLE: It was pretty hard to imagine going from taking out bin Laden to taking out a fast-food deliveryman.

CAIN: It's true that they were unprepared for me, because America had never seen a candidate like Herman Cain before. My ideas for how to fix our country were just like our toppings: unlimited. Police brutality? OK, why don't we replace tear gas with marinara sauce? No one gets hurt, and everyone will run home to scrub the stuff out of their hair and clothes. I had commonsense solutions to all the problems that regular politicians refused to touch—most of which involved food. And who the heck doesn't like food?

CHRIS CHRISTIE: He sure had my vote.

ROMNEY: Since the Iowa caucuses were the first step in the nomination process, our campaign was in a bit of a pickle.

CAIN: Pickles and pizza? Terrible together. Pickles by themselves? *Terrific.* Pizza by itself? Spectacular! See, this was the perspective we needed more of in the race.

ROMNEY: OK, fair enough. We were in a bit of a jam, you could say.

CAIN: Jam? And *pizza*? How was this man ever taken seriously as a presidential candidate?

ROMNEY: The Iowa Republican Party is very socially conservative. Now, I'm pro-life and as socially conservative as anyone—except for the Iowa Republican Party. I'm a Mormon, and I think half of them don't regard Mormons as Christians.

SANTORUM: The other half just haven't heard of Mormonism, then. Did you know that until like the 1970s, Mormons thought black people couldn't get into heaven?

HILLARY: That's not Mormonism. That's Republicanism.

SANTORUM: To get in, a white person had to vouch for them.

AL SHARPTON: It was like buying a house in certain neighborhoods. You were basically driving Miss Daisy for all eternity.

ROMNEY: I knew it would be tricky. I could never really be conservative enough for these people, that's not who I am. At the same time, there really isn't much of a disconnect between economic conservatism and social conservatism. The more successful people are, the less likely they are to have that next child instead of having an abortion, and the less likely they are to engage in immoral behavior in general.

BILL: Amen, brother.

GINGRICH: Governor Romney was a good man, a decent man with decent ideas. The problem was that he didn't really know how to take on the Democratic machine. He didn't know how to fight dirty.

ROMNEY: I have this image as a Goody Two-shoes, but it's simply untrue. Several times in high school a few of my buddies went out and drank lattes. We were pretty messed up after those. I could only handle about one of them, maybe one and a half, but that's because I was the designated driver. Does that sound like a Goody Two-shoes? Speed limit? *What* speed limit? I regularly went five, even ten miles over. When you're that young and you're racing down the highway at sometimes *fifteen* miles over the limit, that caffeine pulsing through your veins—I felt like I was racing Joseph Smith himself.

PERRY: Governor Romney was the front-runner because he had the entire liberal establishment wing of the Republican Party behind him, while the rest of us had to split the conservative part of the pie that was left. That meant that Romney had a big target on his back—and we Texans sure like our targets like we like everything else.

ROMNEY: Wait, I know this one. Big. They like it big in Texas.

PERRY: That's exactly right.

ROMNEY: Well it was too bad that Governor Perry couldn't make it big in Iowa.

PERRY: Oh, yeah? Well, what do you get when you cross a Texan with someone from Massachusetts?

ROMNEY: I don't know, what?

PERRY: You get . . . Hold on. Hmm. Wait, I had this. Oh, yeah! You get . . . Nope, it's gone again. What was it? Something about Austin and Boston?

ROMNEY: Sounds fascinating.

PERRY: It'll come to me. I'm sure of it.

BACHMANN: Anyway, if there was one thing that the Republican Party and the Tea Party were sure of, it's that we wanted someone other than Governor Romney at the head of the ticket.

SANTORUM: During the debates, before the votes were cast, the anti-Romney people bounced around quite a bit. At one point it was Michele, then Governor Perry, and then even Herman Cain for a little bit.

CAIN: I was going to cut through the BS like a pizza cutter cuts through . . . well, you know.

SANTORUM: My team had the longer view. We knew that if we timed it right, that roulette wheel was going to land on us. Wait, roulette is a form of gambling. Maybe Bingo is what I should have said. Yeah, let's go with Bingo.

CAIN: B9!

SANTORUM: That was a metaphor, of course.

CAIN: OK!

ROMNEY: The Iowa votes came in, and it was actually quite inconclusive. Our campaign had come in first, but it was by something like a dozen votes.

MICHELLE: The networks later went over the numbers and called it for Rick Santorum. But it was like the mirror image of Barack in Iowa in 2008. Barack had to show that he was palatable to the white mainstream of the Democrats, which he did resoundingly.

AXELROD: Romney, on the other hand, had to show that he was palatable to the ultrawhite fringe of the Republican Party—which he did barely.

BACHMANN: Again: If there was *one* thing that the Republican Party and the Tea Party were sure of, it's that we wanted someone other than Governor Romney at the head of the ticket. But if there was *another* thing that the Republican Party and the Tea Party were sure of, it's that that person wasn't going to be me. My campaign came in last in Iowa and I officially called it a day.

ROMNEY: After the Iowa squeaker we were on to New Hampshire.

HUNTSMAN: No one doubted that Governor Romney was going to take New Hampshire. The state shares the same media market as Massachusetts, and from what I understand he even has a residence there.

ROMNEY: Actually I maintain residences in forty-nine states. The one exception is New Jersey, and now that I'm not running for anything I can make plain the reason why: because New Jersey is a sewer and, I might add, its governor is full of poo-poo.

AXELROD: New Hampshire and Iowa between them had a well-earned reputation for cleaning the decks, if you will. Just like with the Democrats in 2008, most of the candidates folded after New Hampshire.

PERRY: I didn't lose New Hampshire, I won an excuse to go back home to Texas—and I took it.

HUNTSMAN: Well, I did lose New Hampshire so that was that. Couldn't even place second!

GINGRICH: By South Carolina it was down to Governor Romney, Senator Santorum, and myself. And Ron Paul, technically.

PAUL: Well, I wasn't really campaigning to win; I just wanted tweaks to the government like abolishing the Federal Reserve System.

ROMNEY: It was pretty clear that we were going to win, but I still wanted to lock up that nomination as quickly as possible so I could prepare to take on President Obama.

AXELROD: While this sideshow was occurring, there was still a lot going on on other fronts in America.

MICHELLE: February 2012 ended with news that was really upsetting to me personally. A young black man in Florida named Trayvon Martin had been shot and killed by one George Zimmerman. Coming from Chicago, I know far too many parents who had to bury their children. No one should ever get that phone call; it is literally the worst thing a parent could hear. I can't even imagine what that must feel like. The pain must be both indescribable and incomprehensible.

ERIC HOLDER: Normally someone getting killed—even murdered in cold blood—doesn't warrant the attention of the federal government. That's more the purview of local law enforcement. This case was something different. A young man was dead, and there hadn't even been an arrest or what looked like a thorough investigation.

MICHELLE: I first heard about it because the family wasn't going to take this lying down. They got a lawyer who agreed to represent them for free. But that can only get you so far. One smart thing that they did was to have a publicist take on the case. Now you had the scrutiny of the national and then *international* media on the case.

HOLDER: Charges were filed, and all any of us could do was watch as the case played itself out.

GINGRICH: My focus wasn't on some young hooligan. No, I was actually getting traction in the campaign. The primary voters were kicking or screaming for anyone but Romney. One of the most beautiful things about American democracy is our principle of equality under the law. Every American citizen has a vote, everyone gets to have their say.

AXELROD: It sure helped Newt Gingrich that he had billionaire Sheldon Adelson's vote. That man had so much money that he made Mitt Romney look like he was on EBT.

ROMNEY: I'm actually not familiar with that stock symbol. Does he mean "Earnings Before Taxes"? I'm not on that, I pay my fair share!

MICHELLE: Adelson was pretty much singlehandedly bankrolling Speaker Gingrich's campaign.

GINGRICH: We took South Carolina on January twenty-first. Governor Romney was going to have to earn the Republican nomination fair and square.

MICHELLE: It was baffling to me that social conservatives, whose very ideology revolves around moral behavior, would rally around Newt Gingrich. He's admitted to some behavior that can only be described as dubious, at best. I know that Christians preach forgiveness and really do practice it, too. But those same people never seem to be able to forgive President Clinton for his ethical lapses.

SANTORUM: We will as soon as he stops making them. Between the sins and the apologies, it's like trying to bail water out of a sinking canoe. Reminded me of my 2006 Senate reelection campaign.

AXELROD: It soon came down to Santorum and Gingrich as the Romney alternatives.

PAUL: Have I just been talking to myself this whole time? Can anyone hear what I'm saying? Hello? Rand?

AXELROD: Strategically speaking, Newt Gingrich was a far better debater and much more articulate at spreading the conservative message. Santorum, on the other hand, was a loser—he lost his last Senate election by close to twenty points, and he had a bad habit of sticking his foot in his mouth. Unlike the vice president, who had a good habit of sticking his foot in his mouth. See, it's funny when our side does it.

BIDEN: I missed Rick. We had some good times in the Senate and often worked together since Delaware and Pennsylvania share a border. That's in addition to the borders that Delaware shares with Maryland and New Jersey.

SANTORUM: The voters were sick and tired of the Washington establishment, which I stood firmly against even when I was third in the Senate leadership. That's bronze, which doesn't even really count as a medal.

AXELROD: Oklahoma, North Dakota, Tennessee—many of the really red Republican states, Romney couldn't even carry in the primary. This we took as a good sign for the general election.

MICHELLE: On the other hand, it could have been a very *bad* sign. If the fringe didn't want Governor Romney, that implied that he would be that much more appealing to the more moderate, swing voters.

AXELROD: We kept hoping that Romney would slip up when he tried to pander to the Tea Party but credit where due, the man had discipline.

ROMNEY: If you think competing in the Olympics is hard, you try running them.

AXELROD: By the end of April, the Republican nomination fight was all over, and Romney was going to be our opponent.

ROMNEY: Sure, I would've liked to have had it locked in earlier. But President Obama had taken until June in 2008 to secure his nomination, so I still felt pretty good about our prospects for the general election—especially after those midterms.

AXELROD: That really was the question we were all facing: Which electorate would turn out? Would it be the younger, more diverse crowd that gave President Obama a landslide in 2008? The older, whiter voters that took to the polls in 2010? Was it always going to alternate between presidential years and midterms—or were the midterms the start of a longer-term right-wing trend? Could the country have changed that dramatically in two years?

MICHELLE: I don't know that electing someone like Governor Romney would really be all that much of a change, given American history.

AXELROD: We were constantly asking ourselves such questions at campaign headquarters. It's very, very hard to know the answers when you're in the center of it all. As the presidential campaign began in full earnest, all we knew was that the Republicans had a real shot at winning. The last election had been theirs and theirs decisively.

PERRY: Oh, *now* I remember! "What do you get when you cross a Texan with someone from Massachusetts?" You get someone from Massachusetts with a black eye! Ha, ha, ha. See you in 2016!

13

LONG HOT SUMMER, JUNE–SEPTEMBER 2012

DAVID AXELROD: Obviously the economy was going to be the biggest issue going into the general election. It *should* have been the biggest issue! There is nothing more important than for hardworking, capable adults to be able to work a full day and earn enough money to feed their kids and have a roof over their heads.

MITT ROMNEY: The more roofs the better, I say. My dog, he loves roofs. That's why he always rides on ours whenever we drive somewhere.

AXELROD: There were a couple of other issues coming up that we were quite nervous about. The first was the Supreme Court deciding on health care.

MICHELLE OBAMA: Justice Roberts sort of fast-tracked the case because this one was a doozy. We kept trying to read the tea leaves to know if that meant that they wanted the controversy to be over faster, or if they wanted to strike it down as unconstitutional faster.

JOHN ROBERTS: I just wanted to stop hearing about it when I was trying to eat lunch.

AXELROD: The other issue was gay marriage.

MICHELLE: Barack and I have grappled with this issue for years, believe me. It goes without saying that when you are at the top ranks of Democratic politics in Chicago and then in Washington, you're going to have many gays and lesbians as supporters. Not just as supporters, but as friends.

BARNEY FRANK: I talked to President and Mrs. Obama about this issue a couple of times. They knew my then partner Jim, knew that Jim and I were planning to get married later in the year. It just didn't make sense that Jim and I could get married simply because we happened to live in Massachusetts.

MICHELLE: Originally Barack was for civil unions. But the more he thought about it, the more he realized that a civil union really was legally the same thing as marriage. If the church wouldn't recognize gays as married, that would be the church's business. It's like the Bible says: "Render unto Caesar the things that are Caesar's, and unto God the things that are God's." Meaning, the church can have its own criteria different from the government's. After I put it like that, Barack was convinced.

AXELROD: Let's be honest about how politics works. When the president, any president—I don't care who—when the president of the United States decides to take a bold stance on the issue of the day, you want to milk it for all it's worth. Supporting gay marriage was supposed to be a huge rollout, the first time a president really stuck his neck out for gays and lesbians since Bill Clinton overturned the ban on homosexuals in the military.

MICHELLE: I was very proud of Barack, both for standing up for our friends and for kind of laying down the gauntlet against the religious

Right. He was going to show that he wasn't scared to take them on and say what he believed.

AXELROD: This was all in the works. Except there was *someone* in the meetings who maybe didn't get what the plan was.

MICHELLE: *Sigh.*

VICE PRESIDENT JOE BIDEN: It was an innocent interview that got all blown out of proportion. I was on *Meet the Press* and they asked me about gay marriage. The country was ready. This wasn't a political issue anymore as much as it was a generational one. Older Americans were against gay marriage, younger ones were for it. Except for me. You might say I was the president of old people on this one.

JOHN McCAIN: So tell me, at the wedding, who leads during the first dance? It just doesn't make any sense. I've been married twice, I know about these things.

NEWT GINGRICH: For me, as for most Americans, the definition of marriage is a lifelong commitment that a man makes to a woman . . . or, in my case, a series of three women.

MITCH McCONNELL: Neither of my wives were men, so I don't think anyone else's wife should be a man either. Unless it's a woman marrying a man, but then he's the husband and not the wife. Trick question.

BIDEN: All I said was that I was comfortable with gay marriage. But I also made it quite clear that I'm just the vice president. I explicitly said that the president sets the policy.

AXELROD: This fucked us bad. Like, really bad. I almost said that this "fucked us in the ass" but I'm not homophobic and that does not have the negative connotation that it used to.

MICHELLE: It was embarrassing, no ifs, ands or buts about it. Part of Barack's appeal was his sincere appreciation of progressive, urban culture. That forms a major part of his personality, his worldview, and that demographic is almost universally in his corner. Then here you have Vice President Biden, who is almost twenty years older than Barack, an entire generation apart, coming out as being more progressive on an issue upon which almost all progressives agreed—not to mention increasing numbers of moderates and even conservatives!

BIDEN: Boy, did my staff hear about it when that interview was over.

AXELROD: I think he ducked our calls for about a day. Which is no mean feat.

BIDEN: I was scared, all right?

MICHELLE: I talked it over with Barack and he had to come out, there was just no other way.

VICE PRESIDENT DICK CHENEY: I knew it! My daughter has a stronger handshake than that pansy.

MICHELLE: That's actually factual.

AXELROD: It was so clear that *someone* had forced our hand that we had to scrap our plans to make a big deal of it.

BIDEN: That's *my* whole point: No one should be making a big deal about gay marriage.

MICHELLE: It was a hiccup but we just soldiered on. The really big deal on the table was health care.

BIDEN: Now *that's* a big deal. A big fucking deal.

ERIC HOLDER: The Supreme Court was as politicized as every other aspect of contemporary Washington. Frankly, it was politicized against us. Here was the nightmare scenario: If you have the Supreme Court start striking down one social program—even if it was a new one— that logic led to some pretty nefarious consequences down the road. You'd see programs that even the Republicans wouldn't dare to touch in trouble, and then it's deuces wild.

HARRY REID: See, I'm from Nevada. Gambling slang I understand. But you start talking about "spades" and everyone's down your throat.

MICHELLE: There were lawsuits against Obamacare filed in over half the states. You only needed to have a Republican governor *or* a Republican attorney general and they'd file suit. As the issue worked its way through the legal system, it kept being in a sort of limbo. Some judges found it unconstitutional, others said it could go forward.

HOLDER: The arguments went on for several days, and it was extremely difficult to determine what the justices were thinking. It's not like in Congress, where so-called debates are really just excuses to score political points and to grandstand.

JOHN BOEHNER: Nonsense. The public has a right to know!

McCONNELL: The American people demand answers, again. And *still.*

HOLDER: The justices' questioning was pretty specific. They were clearly intent on doing a good job and really finding the truth of the matter. But then they mused aloud about what would happen to the bill if they struck down the individual mandate.

REID: That bit did make us a little worried. It showed that they were considering it, and that was very dangerous territory. If you didn't have young and healthy people paying into the insurance pools, the system simply wouldn't work.

BOEHNER: In other words, they were forcing people who didn't need insurance to buy it anyway.

REID: No one "needs" insurance—until they do. That's the whole point of insurance.

HOLDER: The justices also asked about the Medicare expansion and whether that was severable from the broader bill. These were really very nuanced and sophisticated issues and it could have gone in any direction. Whenever you try something new in politics, there comes the fair question as to whether it fits into the broader constitutional framework that the Founding Fathers established. We hadn't tried an individual mandate before on a federal level, only the state and local one as with driving insurance.

MICHELLE: Our best-case scenario was that everything would be given a green light. Our middle version would be losing Medicare but keeping the bulk of the program; we could work around that fairly easily. There was enormous debate in the White House as to whether it would be worse, strategically, to have the whole thing struck down or to just have the mandate struck down.

REID: If the whole thing was struck down, that would be terrible and would hurt many people. We would have to start from scratch. But if *only* the mandate went down, we'd be left with this huge outlay and no funding. The entire system we constructed would implode very quickly, and good luck explaining to the American people why. We would be eviscerated, and with the Republicans controlling the House we wouldn't be able to fix it.

MICHELE BACHMANN: You couldn't fix Obamacare if it were a house and Jesus was your carpenter. Of course we weren't interested in propping up a disastrous program that the American people never wanted in the first place.

HOLDER: The arguments had been delivered at the end of March. Then there was nothing to do but wait.

RUTH BADER GINSBURG: It got pretty annoying. The Supreme Court doesn't exist in some parallel universe. All nine of us live in the Washington, D.C., area. We don't, you know, pop out of some legal textbook or something. We go to the movies, the dry cleaners, all the normal things.

MICHELLE: I was as guilty as anyone else when it came to trying to figure out clues. Oh, I was bad. Like if I saw Justice Sotomayor at an event, I'd make eye contact with her and look for signals. I'd kind of do a slight nod and then a brief shake of the head to let her know I was watching but she just stared at me.

SONIA SOTOMAYOR: Seeing the First Lady out on the town reminded me how crucial health care was for all Americans. She had developed some sort of a tic where her head would twitch up and down, and then left to right. I tried to be polite and ignore it, but it seemed like she was making a point to look over at me. Listen, I'm from the Bronx. You stare someone down back home, it is not exactly an expression of warmth.

MICHELLE: She wouldn't tell me *anything,* not one clue.

SOTOMAYOR: As a judge it's not my role to judge whether a health care bill is good or bad. My role, all of our roles, is to judge whether it stands the test of legality within the common-law framework we've been building up for over two centuries in this country. Just because health care is important doesn't make any given health care bill constitutional, not by a long shot.

ROBERTS: Those months were like when America was obsessed with "Who shot J.R.?" Part of me wanted to call Larry Hagman and find out how he managed to deal with everyone prying, but I was worried people would twist that to mean we were going to "shoot down" the legislation. That's how paranoid we were getting.

GINSBURG: At the restaurants the hosts would say that they were "upholding" a table for me. Or they'd deliver a bottle of wine and tell me that they were "striking it down" from the bill. Then they would watch me for any reaction. Let me tell you something: When I go out to enjoy some fine dining, the law is the last thing on my mind. Ruth is there to get her grape juice, and they just had to keep that happy sauce flowing.

MICHELLE: It was brutal waiting for that decision to come down. Not just for us in the administration, but for so many whose lives had already been impacted by it for the better.

AXELROD: But also for us in the administration and the campaign. Politics doesn't like a loser, and I could see the Republican ads now: "Obama passed a bill that you hated and that he knew was unconstitutional!" Those ads would have been very, very effective, especially since President Obama had been a constitutional scholar. He wasn't really in a position to play dumb.

PRESIDENT GEORGE W. BUSH: You don't say.

MICHELLE: Finally at the end of June we had our answer.

AXELROD: News crews aren't allowed in the courtroom, of course. So as soon as the decision was released, all these various interns took the information and ran it back to their various organizations. It's my understanding that a lot of West African interns had just been hired for this specific purpose. I didn't want to look into it to find out if it was true, because really why wouldn't they do that?

MICHELLE: At first, CNN said that they struck down the individual mandate. I couldn't believe it. Then I looked at Fox, and they said the same thing. That made me feel a bit better, because given the source, the odds were high that they'd gotten something wrong.

HOLDER: It was a misreading of the decision, but I don't blame the reporters. Basically the court upheld the law but "struck down" our legal reasoning in its defense, substituting their own and grounding it elsewhere in the Constitution.

JUNE 28, 2012: THE SUPREME COURT UPHOLDS THE INDIVIDUAL MANDATE, THE CENTRAL ELEMENT OF OBAMACARE.

McCONNELL: Any big win for this administration was a big loss for the American people. After that preposterous, tortured decision, I was more determined than ever to make sure Barack Obama was a one-term president.

BACHMANN: Tortured is exactly right. Barack Obama was literally waterboarding America with Obamacare, and John Roberts was the towel. Or maybe the bucket.

MICHELLE: We had the wind at our sails heading into the election, at least with regard to the health care law. This had been a major roadblock and we navigated it with just a flat tire, I'd say. We were all very curious to see how Governor Romney was going to attack a law that he basically inspired and put into practice.

AXELROD: June 2012 had a very mixed message for us. While we had been waiting for the Supreme Court decision on health care, we also had our eyes set on the recall election in Wisconsin.

MICHELLE: Wisconsin is a state with a very interesting role in American political history. Several states have "punched above their weight" when it came to moving the needle in the United States. During the early days of America, it was Virginia that had an enormous amount of sway. Virginia was Gladys Knight and the other states were the Pips.

ROMNEY: Massachusetts set off the American Revolution. Woodrow Wilson's League of Nations proposal was defeated by our senator Henry Cabot Lodge, and of course the Kennedy family had an enormous effect on the nation—both good and bad.

BIDEN: And let's not forget Delaware!

MICHELLE: We couldn't forget it even if we wanted to, not in this administration. Anyway, Wisconsin is a state in that vein. Robert La-Follette, one of the absolute founders of American progressivism and a *Republican,* was a senator from Wisconsin for many years and even ran for president. LaFollette's son succeeded him in the same Senate seat, until he lost his primary to . . . Joe McCarthy. Yes, McCarthyism got its start in progressive headquarters.

CHENEY: Well, of course it did, that's where the commies were. You don't go hunting pheasants underwater, do you?

MICHELLE: Wisconsin had always been sort of a bellwether for coming political trends. Well, in 2010 Scott Walker had been elected governor along with a Republican-majority state legislature.

SCOTT WALKER: It was the first time since 1998 that the Republicans had control of both state houses and the governor's office. Because Wisconsin swings so wildly, this could have been a once-in-a-generation opportunity to effect real conservative change that would make our state more economically competitive.

MICHELLE: And that, of course, meant going after people's pensions.

WALKER: We weren't going to wait. We got right to work taking the

power out of the hands of the public employee unions while simultaneously cutting taxes for businesses.

MICHELLE: I suppose we all have our priorities. Some of us simply
have different priorities than the others.

WALKER: It was the bold fiscal plan that Wisconsin needed. It was
why I ran for governor and why I had been elected.

MICHELLE: Oh, it was bold all right! So bold that the Democrats had
a thing or two to say about it. Obviously if you don't have the votes,
you don't have the votes. As Barack said, elections have consequences.
But in general it makes sense for big bills to have the largest public
hearing possible. The Obamacare bill went through public scrutiny
for *months*. Governor Walker's plans were to be voted on within *days*.
It sure seemed like the more people learned about the plans, the more
they opposed it.

WALKER: So the losers up and left. That's why they call them left
wing; they leave whenever the going gets too hard.

MICHELLE: I couldn't really believe it myself. I got the call and I was
like, "I do not want to know!" Ha, ha.

WALKER: I'm in my office and one of my aides came back and told
me that the Democrat politicians had left. I literally didn't know what
she meant. Were they out to lunch? Taking a long break? No, she didn't
know where they were. But there were over a dozen of them missing
and that couldn't be a coincidence.

JON ERPENBACH: The Walker team wasn't interested in discussing *anything.* They were going to just ram their bill through. So we in the minority did a little research and learned that they needed at least one of us there in order to have enough people for a vote on budgetary issues. I don't remember who had the idea to flee the state, but we all thought it would at least force a conversation and give what was happening greater public visibility—and scrutiny.

WALKER: I'm from the Republican Party. Yes, we're the party of Reagan and Lincoln, inspiring, strong, positive leaders. But we're also the party of Richard Nixon. If they wanted dirty tricks, we had them in spades. First I tried to go the straight-and-narrow approach, of course.

ERPENBACH: He tried to get us arrested and brought back by force across state lines.

WALKER: That wasn't regarded as particularly legal or practical. We didn't know where they even were!

ERPENBACH: He could have emailed us. That still works no matter where you are.

WALKER: At one point I got a phone call from one of the missing Democrats. They had basically kidnapped themselves, so it was like talking to the hostage and the kidnapper at the same time: "If you ever want to see me again, you'll do exactly as I say!" I wanted to yell back, "Yes, fine. Whatever you want! Just don't hurt, uh, you." It was weird.

ERPENBACH: I heard they got so frustrated that they used a Ouija board to try and contact Richard Nixon for advice.

WALKER: It wasn't a Ouija board, it was a Magic 8-ball. Totally different! One is a flat surface, the other a sphere. The two of them had nothing in common.

ERPENBACH: Tricky Dick gave them some good advice, apparently. Me, all I got was "ask again later." For months! Damn you, Richard Nixon. How much later do I have to wait?

WALKER: I looked closer at the law, and it turned out that we most certainly needed a quorum to pass budgetary bills. But other types of bills *didn't*. So I said, let's pass bills that the Democrats hate!

MICHELLE: As much fun as it was to watch this from afar, it really was politics at its worst. In my view, if Governor Walker had simply allowed the process to play out, then people would have been a lot less upset. As it was, the following months got very, very ugly.

WALKER: Over the next year there were lawsuits, and elections to the state Supreme Court, and recall elections for members of the state legislature—not to mention all the insane protests by unions who were putting their interests above the people of the great state of Wisconsin. The last step by the radical left was to attempt to recall *me* from the office I had just been elected to.

MICHELLE: There had only been two gubernatorial recall elections, both of which were successful. The second and most recent had been the recall of Gray Davis in California and the simultaneous election of Arnold Schwarzenegger.

ARNOLD SCHWARZENEGGER: I'll be back! . . . Unless you mean politics, in which case my career has been terminated.

AXELROD: So it's June 2012 and all eyes are on the Wisconsin recall; it's kind of a bellwether for us. Win or lose, we can also use the state as a litmus test to see what issues grabbed voters' attention.

WALKER: It wasn't "win or lose"; it was a huge loss for the Democrats and their short-sighted union allies. They were soundly defeated.

AXELROD: We thought that since a recall election was such an unusual event, it would tend to attract the more motivated voters—namely, ours.

WALKER: Instead who came out were the regular voters who thought a recall election was a waste of time and an unfair manipulation of the election law. Recalls are for when a governor is corrupt or abuses his power. I won the recall election with more total votes *and* a larger percentage of the total vote.

MICHELLE: It felt like Scott Brown all over again, and that worried us on the campaign. I'm not ashamed to admit that; it was a straight-up defeat a mere four months before the presidential election.

AXELROD: The 2012 general election would define whether progressivism could continue as a viable force in American politics. If we lost then, the argument would become that President Obama had solely been elected due to his race and not because of his ideas.

CLARENCE THOMAS: Personally, I was *appointed* and not *elected,* and I resent the insinuation. And now, back to the silence.

REID: Even if the president were himself reelected, there were still tough times ahead in the Senate. The math was terrible. We had twenty-one seats up for reelection, while the Republicans only had ten. We basically had double the ground to cover.

McCONNELL: We only needed to pick up four seats to take back the Senate and to kill the Obama agenda once and for all. That seemed quite doable, as we had picked up six in the prior election. Plus, the senators up for reelection had gotten their seats in the 2006 anti-Republican wave. Things were looking good, and I was cautiously optimistic—and for the record, that's as optimistic as a Republican can get.

BOEHNER: Other than Ronald Reagan, of course, and look where he is now.

REID: Fortunately we had a little bit of help from our most loyal allies: the Republican primary voters.

RICHARD LUGAR: I had been an Indiana senator for six terms. I was so popular that during my last election the Democrats hadn't even bothered running an opponent against me. I had run for the Republican presidential nomination in 1996. I was also the Republican senator with the most seniority. Literally, no one in the Senate had been a Republican longer than myself. Yet by 2012, I guess I just wasn't enough of a Republican for the GOP base.

RICHARD MOURDOCK: Senator Lugar was a great man and an effective legislator, but he was from another time. I understand why many Republicans dislike the primary process, but Indiana was a very red state, and those states are the ones where we can afford to run candidates who are actual conservatives.

REID: Mourdock beat Senator Lugar by over twenty points in the Republican primary. *Twenty.* Here was a man who was universally respected as perhaps the most knowledgeable foreign policy expert in the Senate, certainly of the Republicans at least.

MARCO RUBIO: That's not true. I can name almost all the countries in Europe and most of them in South America.

REID: I had a very strong positive relationship with Senator Lugar, as did many Democrats. Yet that respect and admiration was now being viewed as a symbol of ideological impurity. On a personal level I was very sad to see my friend go, and I thought the Senate was the worse for it. But on a political level that meant that his seat would now be in play. That sure dried my tears up quickly!

McCONNELL: It was a little unnerving to see Senator Lugar lose the primary, no question.

OLYMPIA SNOWE: That primary threat was why I decided to retire after never having lost an election. Did I know that made it likely that my seat would turn blue? Yes, of course. Did I care? Well, not enough to put up with how toxic Washington had become.

REID: We also got a huge break in Missouri, which was perhaps the biggest Senate swing state of the entire cycle.

AXELROD: Senator Claire McCaskill was easily our most endangered incumbent. Worse, she had some serious scandals that had caused her approval ratings to plummet.

CLAIRE McCASKILL: My husband and I co-owned a private jet with several friends. I admit—and it was public record—that I used this jet to travel between my home state of Missouri and Washington, D.C., as well as within the state. Yes, I used taxpayer money to pay for the flights.

MICHELLE: Politics is about appearances. Remember that story about President Clinton keeping the planes grounded at LAX while he got his hair did for $200?

PRESIDENT BILL CLINTON: Thanks so much for the reminder, Michelle. Great working with you!

MICHELLE: The point is that a Democrat using taxpayer money to pay for her flights on her private jet really wouldn't pass the sniff test in blue New York, let alone Missouri.

McCASKILL: I sent a check as soon as the story broke.

MICHELLE: And then it turned out that she hadn't paid taxes on the thing either.

McCASKILL: Look, I know this sounds hoity-toity and what have you, but here's the truth. Private jets are not the same as regular air travel. You don't really know what the rules and regulations are. It's not like when you get on a commercial plane, where the flight attendant gets up and gives you a demonstration about proper procedures. At least, I think they still have those . . . right?

MICHELLE: I'm not sure . . .

BILL: Maybe?

McCONNELL: I wouldn't know.

REID: They've got to, no?

BOEHNER: I'm pretty sure it's a video now instead of the girl doing the demonstrations. Well, I shouldn't say "girl," that's condescending. Aviation Americans, I think they like to be called nowadays.

McCASKILL: I mean, it's an innocent mistake. You go to a boutique, you pay sales tax on the clothes there. You pay taxes on your houses wherever they happen to be. Easy peasy. But where do you pay taxes on a plane? It's a *plane*. It can go wherever it wants. One minute it's in Virginia, the next it's in Missouri. It just doesn't make any sense, really.

BOEHNER: Cry me a river, Senator.

ROMNEY: I'm with Claire on this one.

McCASKILL: That plane caused me more problems than it was worth. I told my husband to sell the damn thing. I vowed never to step foot on it again, no way and no how.

MICHELLE: That's literally what she told reporters. Again, complaining about the problems that your private jet is causing you—that's not really the choice of words that I would use. They have too many snacks on Air Force One and not enough healthy food. You don't see me complaining, do you? No, because I complained in *private* where no one could see me. They kept giving me excuses and now that I think about it, what sort of trifling nonsense is that? This is Air Force One and I'm the First Lady! . . . Oh, wait. Could Barack have been telling them to ignore what I said? No, that can't be it. Can it? . . . Huh, you know what? I think that *is* it. It *has* to be it! Ooh, he's gonna get it. I'm gonna break every last one of his cigarettes, just you wait.

REID: We knew that Claire was in trouble. But once again, our guardian angels came through. See, the Republicans saw Missouri as a golden pickup opportunity, so they nominated the furthest-right politician they could find.

AXELROD: Suddenly the Senate didn't seem as endangered as we'd feared. Going into the general election, the universal consensus among pollsters was that the same electorate wouldn't turn out again for us a second time. Meaning, single women and minorities, the LGBT community, their numbers would be far lower because "the thrill is gone," so to speak.

MICHELLE: Barack had a hard case to make. Most of the benefits of Obamacare had yet to take hold. Sure, it was next to impossible for the economy to turn around in four years, but many people didn't want to hear so-called excuses.

AXELROD: The best way to turn out our base? Let the Republicans speak for themselves.

MICHELLE: We knew the Romney campaign was scared as well. In August of 2012, Governor Romney announced Congressman Paul Ryan as his running mate.

ROMNEY: My biggest strength as a candidate and as a governor was surely my focus on budgetary concerns and being able to handle state finances in a conservative but fair manner. Congressman Ryan was a perfect complement to that, since his plan was the Republican budgetary blueprint for the House.

AXELROD: Of course we all sat down to read the tea leaves, no pun intended.

SARAH PALIN: Why do *they* get to call them puns, but when we do it, they call it dog whistles? That's just another great example of the lamestream media disrespecting middle America.

AXELROD: "Lamestream" is a pun—a terrible, terrible pun. No one thinks that's a dog whistle.

ROMNEY: Paul Ryan was a pick that would really unite our party.

MICHELLE: It's not hard to find good things to say about Paul Ryan. He is very bright and has a very firm grasp of the issues. He is young, fit, and energetic.

AXELROD: In other words, he's a second-rate Barack. OK, just kidding. No, Ryan was a shrewd choice albeit a telling one. He's pro-life but not a maniac; conservative but not cuckoo. You could put him on camera and not have most Americans recoil with horror.

CHENEY: What are you getting at, son?

AXELROD: The usual line is that you pander to the base in the primaries and then run to the center in the general. Paul Ryan showed that it wasn't just our side who was worried about our voters staying home; Governor Romney wanted those conservatives to turn out so he went with a firm conservative. A severe conservative, you might say.

REID: I've worked with Congressman Ryan; he was a tough negotiator. Ideological in his approach but not as much as some of his colleagues— which doesn't really say a whole lot, if you think about it. The general reaction was that this was a smart, if not particularly risky, decision. I suspect the Republicans learned their lesson about risky decisions in 2008.

PALIN: What are you getting at, Grandpa?

REID: I knew it was just a matter of time before some loose cannon went off and killed the Republicans' momentum. Sure enough, it only took just over a week after the Ryan announcement for the next GOP calamity to hit.

TODD AKIN: When you're going to be a United States senator, you are called upon to have a stance on every issue under the sun. Some are more contentious than others. I do understand that abortion is an issue that many people have strong feelings about, both for and against.

MICHELLE: That man should not use the words *understand* and *abortion* in the same sentence, but that's just my opinion on the matter.

AKIN: I knew of course that the abortion question would come up. How could it not? The Democrats are determined to make it a weapon every chance they get. Rather than trying to protect the unborn, pro-life people are painted as people who just want to oppress women. I could not disagree more, and frankly I resent that accusation.

REID: Wait for it . . .

AKIN: An abortion stops an unborn heart. It doesn't make sense that when a child is nine months in the womb, and can survive on its own, that child isn't a human being. Of course he or she is. So where do you draw the line? Eight months? One? The pro-choice people were playing God, and if you ask me only God should be playing God.

REID: Almost there . . .

AKIN: So whenever the topic of abortion comes up, the pro-choice people always bring up the most extreme situations possible (when they aren't calling *us* "extremists," of course!). "What about if the woman is raped or the victim of incest? Are you going to make her have the baby then?" Well, what difference does it make?

HILLARY RODHAM CLINTON: Oh, no. Leave me out of this one!

AKIN: Of course those circumstances are horrific and terrible. But we need to punish the *assailant,* not the *child*. It isn't that baby's fault that he or she was conceived in a terrible way. You know how they say that when God closes a door, he opens a window? Well, when he opens an assault, he also brings a blessing. Or something like that. I'm not a professional quote maker.

REID: Take us home, Todd!

AKIN: All this is largely beside the point, anyway. The number of abortions that come from rape or incest is a very small percentage of the total. I asked my doctor friend about this, and he told me what I later repeated in an interview: "If it's a legitimate rape, the female body has ways to try to shut that whole thing down."

REID: Bravo. And thank you.

MICHELLE: Maybe Washington is a bubble and doesn't represent America as a whole. Maybe we Democrats are out of touch. It's not hard to make the case that living in the White House isolates you from the rest of the country. But even given all that, I did not know a single person whose jaw didn't drop at those comments.

AXELROD: I didn't believe it at first. I needed to hear the audio for myself; this had to be something taken out of context. I've been around many, many pro-life people and had never heard talk like that.

McCASKILL: I've been married twice and have three wonderful children. But if you asked me what was the happiest day of my life, August 19, 2012, was certainly way up there. Certainly above my daughter Maddie's birth; that one's a real piece of work.

AKIN: Right away the liberal politically correct brigade came out of the woodwork, brandishing their pitchforks in order to attack me.

MICHELLE: No one was being politically correct. They were being scientifically correct, and biologically correct, and anatomically correct. My uterus does not have a stance on school vouchers, and I am willing to bet that no other woman's does either.

BACHMANN: I'll take that bet! I am 100 percent conservative, and that includes every single part of me.

AXELROD: You know, when you deal with the opposing party, you have to understand things from their point of view. They have different values and priorities, so you've got to try and figure out what they want and what they're getting at. Miscommunication isn't the exception, but the norm. So I tried my best to figure out what Todd Akin was getting at, and so help me I was stumped.

ROMNEY: I understand the pro-life position, because I am pro-life. I also understand the pro-choice position, because I am pro-choice. But I didn't understand . . . *that*. Or rather, I understood this was not going to reflect well on our campaign.

MICHELLE: Hand to God, I almost had the White House operator connect me to Mr. Akin so I could ask him what a "legitimate rape" was. That's even forgetting the biology part. I know women who have been assaulted. I don't think any of them have ever questioned the "legitimacy" of their trauma!

AXELROD: Is that a rape that's out of wedlock? I guess that would be illegitimate, so apparently not. OK, still got nothing!

AKIN: Let's just say that some people can get creative in the bedroom and leave it at that. As long as it's in the confines of a Christian marriage, everything is pretty much in play. Even a little butt stuff. I'm a conservative, not a corpse.

McCASKILL: We were jumping up and down with glee so much in our campaign office that one of the interns twisted her ankle, poor thing.

McCONNELL: Todd Akin was blowing the biggest pickup opportunity of the cycle. I was on the phone with him faster than a pregnancy test result. We needed him to step aside to have a candidate who could actually win.

ROMNEY: Comments like that really fed into the narrative that the Republican Party was antiwoman and extreme. I had been trying to fight that impression since I helped create that impression during the primaries.

AXELROD: I can only imagine the pressure Todd Akin felt to step aside . . . Come to think of it, I don't have to imagine it, because Senator Clinton had been feeling it in 2008. We were pushing her to accept the inevitable and endorse as soon as it became clear that we had the nomination in the bag.

HILLARY: Boy, did I ever look forward to those calls. They sure made campaigning even more fun and enjoyable!

AKIN: I didn't feel it appropriate to stand down simply due to one comment. That's how the liberals win: They find something to attack you over and hammer it in until you fold. Well, I'm a fighter. I wasn't just trying to be senator for my ego. No, I was representing many Americans who had historically been left out of the Washington insiders' game.

AXELROD: I'm guessing he means ob-gyns who are really, really bad at their jobs.

MICHELLE: I still want to know what that means, that "the female body has ways to try to shut that whole thing down."

AKIN: I was glad to explain my comments. I'm not the smoothest talker, I'll admit it, but I don't have the luxury of having a teleprompter to carry around.

ROMNEY: He was broadly on my team, so I wished he would just *stop* talking.

McCAIN: I know that feel, Mitt.

AKIN: See, a pregnancy is a miracle from God and baby Jesus. When a man puts his pee-pee inside a woman's bugina and makes an accident, God puts a baby inside of her belly. But sometimes bad men want to put their pee-pee inside the bugina and the woman doesn't want that, and we call that rape.

BACHMANN: Finally, another politician who is willing to tell it like it is.

CHRISTINE O'DONNELL: I'm you, Todd Akin! You tell 'em!

AKIN: Now, I'm not 100 percent sure about what happens next. I'm not a buginacologist. But if the woman doesn't legitimately want the baby in her belly, she sends out a signal to God not to put that soul inside her.

MICHELLE: Jesus freaking Christ.

AKIN: Then the stork knows not to come and leave the child under the leaves in the cabbage patch. If that doesn't work, I think she can leave a tooth under her pillow or find an Easter egg, because both the tooth fairy and the Easter bunny talk to God on the regular.

AXELROD: Don't forget Santa Claus.

AKIN: No, Santa and God aren't on good terms on account of Santa spoiling so many children—and on His son's birthday, no less! The Democrats would know that if they ever bothered to read their Bible but I guess they'd prefer to study the Communist Manifesto.

McCASKILL: After that, my campaign staff and I sat down in my office and tried to think of the craziest things I could say and still get elected. "I think we could learn a lot from Hitler"? We polled that and I still won. We found that declaring myself a Chinese citizen would have made the race a tossup. "It's time to reconsider our opposition to slavery"; that one would have cost me the election.

ROMNEY: I ran the Olympics. I've personally spoken with people from every country on earth. Obviously some nations are more educated than others. Todd Akin was speaking less like an American and more like a . . . well, I'm not going to say it but you can probably guess.

AXELROD: The controversy kind of died down but refused to go away. The Republican Convention started just a few weeks later, at the end of August. Obviously we at the campaign were watching the whole thing with great interest.

MICHELLE: Just as in 2008, the Republicans had to start their festivities late due to bad weather. I don't know if that meant that God was a Democrat or maybe he leaned GOP and knew keeping them off TV would make people like them more.

AXELROD: We were a little worried about Governor Christie's prime-time keynote speech. That was the equivalent speech that President Obama gave back in 2004. Governor Christie is brash, he can be entertaining, and he seemed like the kind of man who would fire up the base while not being a kook.

CHRIS CHRISTIE: I was honored to be given the opportunity to address the convention and speak about the things that mattered to me.

MICHELLE: He talked about his mom and he talked about himself. He didn't even discuss Governor Romney at all.

CHRISTIE: Those were the things that mattered to me.

MICHELLE: I was embarrassed for the Romney campaign, but I was relieved for us.

AXELROD: Governor Christie's appeal was supposed to be a type of antagonism, sticking it to the Left in ways others were too scared to do. But he was apparently more concerned about his national ambitions and his approval ratings back home than about being an attack dog for Governor Romney.

CHRISTIE: Those were the other things that mattered to me, yes.

MICHELLE: Mrs. Romney followed and she was just terrific. I don't know anyone who doesn't like and admire her. The woman has multiple sclerosis and MS is really an awful disease. The fact that she speaks so much about it and is so involved in finding a cure and educating about how to live a full life while managing the disease? I applaud her just as much as everyone else does. What a sad commentary on modern American politics that she and I basically have to be opposed to each other. That's just so *dumb*.

AXELROD: I felt really bad for Ann Romney when an overzealous talking head went after her and said that she had never worked a day in her life. That was reprehensible.

MICHELLE: The low point of the campaign, from our side. We made sure that lady apologized immediately. Give me a break.

AXELROD: I wish the Republicans would be as proactive about attacks on the First Lady, however.

HILLARY: Oh, cry me a river.

AXELROD: So here was the score card for the GOP convention speeches, as we saw it. Ann Romney: great lady, wonderful presentation. Clearly meant what she said and loved her husband, sincere. But we've already seen this show, when Liddy Dole killed it in 1996 for Bob. Minds changed: zero. People aren't voting for a First Lady.

MICHELLE: Then Congressman Ryan came out, gave a perfectly fine speech as well.

AXELROD: Good, solid B+ Republican talk from Ryan. Minds changed: zero. They were blowing opportunity after opportunity. You need home runs to move the undecideds, not these sort of base hits.

MICHELLE: So far so good. The last night we were going to hear from Governor Romney himself, along with some sort of "mystery guest."

AXELROD: We tried to figure out who it could be. First thought was Nancy Reagan because President Reagan was as close to a rock star as the GOP had. But she had spoken at a convention already. So who else? Palin? Why would that be a mystery?

MICHELLE: We sat down and looked through every elected Republican official and none of them warranted this kind of billing.

AXELROD: Look, Governor Romney is an extremely bright man. No question. So we started thinking, Well, what would we do in his position? A good strategy would be to engage us on our core strength, which was young people and social media. It stood to reason that they wanted to keep the name under wraps to get the most Facebook and Twitter reactions possible. Very shrewd, very crafty.

MICHELLE: The Republicans have had issues in the past with appealing to young people. Many of us recall the Bush daughters' talk at the 2004 convention. It was . . . *interesting.*

JENNA BUSH HAGER: In our defense, we were pretty drunk.

BARBARA P. BUSH: She means pretty *and* drunk. We were, like, really pretty and really drunk. What can I say? We take after Dad.

HAGER: Totes!

MICHELLE: OK, so who did the Republicans have that could appeal to young people? Stacey Dash? Rumor had it she was going to endorse the Romney ticket at some point.

AXELROD: That would have been smart. She's beautiful, she's black. They could have done a little riff about the president being "clueless."

MICHELLE: There *definitely* would have been buzz about it on the Internet.

AXELROD: But no. Who did the Republicans pick to get people talking? Who was their big name to seem cool and relevant?

MICHELLE: None other than Dirty Harry himself: Clint Eastwood.

AXELROD: I had only two words: O . . . K . . .

CLINT EASTWOOD: I am as far from being a partisan as you can get. Republican or Democrat, I don't really give a rat's ass about either party. What I look for when I vote is the best man for the job—and I do mean *man,* none of that "Ms. Commander in Chief" shit. It was my sincere conviction that Mitt Romney was as far from being a partisan politician as you could get. The man has proven time and again that he can get the job done.

AXELROD: So we're watching the Eastwood speech, and I had to hand it to the Romney campaign: This was not something that had been expected.

MICHELLE: Everyone knows Clint Eastwood is a straight shooter, literally and figuratively. People love him.

EASTWOOD: I didn't have a script. I most certainly did *not* have any talking points from the campaign. They didn't even bother to try that because they knew where I would have told them to stick their damn talking points.

AXELROD: He needed a script.

MICHELLE: He needed talking points from the campaign.

EASTWOOD: Instead I spoke to an empty chair as if I were addressing the president.

AXELROD: He spoke to an empty chair as if he were having a stroke.

MICHELLE: Why was it an empty chair? A cardboard cutout, I would have understood. That's at least a visual representation. Or maybe even a dummy, you know, calling Barack a "dummy." The gag just didn't land.

ROMNEY: When you're a CEO, you're in charge of the entire firm. When you're running the Olympics, you had better be sure that the ice is at the perfect temperature for the skaters. And when you're the nominee, you have to know that the speaker won't be so . . . baffling.

AXELROD: Romney comes out after that with a speech as good as could be expected. It was polished, it was smart, it was professional—and, in my opinion, it inspired no one. That was the problem with the Romney campaign in a nutshell.

MICHELLE: They got their buzz all right. But I don't think it was the buzz that the Romney/Ryan ticket were hoping for.

AXELROD: We were all ready to counter with a clip of the president replying to a grandfather clock, but we decided to leave well enough alone. Team Romney had blown their chance to use the convention to change the dynamics of the race. We didn't want to be seen as attacking Clint Eastwood anyway.

MICHELLE: Our convention was the following week, in Charlotte. The bar was pretty low. We had a small lead in our eternal polling, and so long as nothing went wrong we would be pulling off a victory. I spoke the first night. I was a bit nervous, of course, but I think I did fairly well.

AXELROD: She was great, and the president was great, and Vice President Biden was great. Everyone did what they were supposed to with no surprises and no slipups—except one. The one surprise, the one thing everyone took away from the convention, was Bill Clinton's speech that Wednesday night.

MICHELLE: *Who the hell is this nigga?* That's what kept going through my head when I was watching Bill Clinton give his keynote speech at the 2004 convention. *Who the hell is he, and where has he been hiding?* We sure didn't see him in the 2008 primaries.

AXELROD: I've had a very long career in politics. I've seen more political speeches than I can count. And as amazing as watching that speech was on television—and I watched it again on tape, just to be sure I wasn't being crazy—it was that much more impressive live. It was almost as good as one of the president's own speeches. That's how good it was.

BOEHNER: I've listened to enough of Bill Clinton's hot air to last a lifetime.

NANCY PELOSI: He nailed it. A+.

McCONNELL: What did I think? I liked his spirit, and he did a good job. If there's one thing senators admire, it's the ability to give long, pointless speeches.

ROMNEY: I got chills, because it felt like I was watching our campaign lose ground in real time.

CHENEY: Eh, I'd give it a B. I've heard better. I mean, come on, it wasn't exactly the "tear down this wall" speech. It's like, what else you got?

BILL: The press liked to pretend that there was animosity between myself and the president. Nothing could be further from the truth. I knew he was the right man doing the best job that he could, and I was more than glad to explain to America the reasons why I felt that way. It turned out that many people agreed with my point of view.

MICHELLE: Did President Clinton steal the spotlight from Barack? I would never say that, because that expression—"steal"—is a dog whistle. So let's change the subject before I get into trouble.

AXELROD: He absolutely rocked the convention. I don't know that the president was all too upset by it. On the one hand, yes, of course he has an ego and someone else is getting more applause than him. On the other hand, the reasons why you should be reelected sound a lot better coming out of someone else's mouth than your own.

MICHELLE: After that convention, we still had a small but sizable lead. More importantly, however, was that we were over 50 percent in the polls. Meaning, even if Governor Romney got every single undecided voter after that point, he would still lose.

AXELROD: We were in the home stretch. We had the four debates coming up in October, and we were getting ready for them. Say what you want about Barack Obama, but this was not a president who didn't know how to hold his own in front of a podium.

MICHELLE: Of course we were waiting for some "October surprise."

AXELROD: Pretty much every campaign has things that they tip the press off to at the last possible minute for maximum possible damage. That's in addition to the regular surprises, of course. In

2012, the October surprise of the campaign came a little earlier than expected.

MICHELLE: We didn't even have to wait a week after the convention for the "surprise" to hit us. And it didn't come from Boston or New York or even our native Chicago. It came from a place that, frankly, I hadn't ever really heard of: Benghazi.

14

WINNER AND STILL CHAMPION, SEPTEMBER–DECEMBER 2012

HILLARY RODHAM CLINTON: The Republicans like to say that I'm paranoid about my enemies. They mock the fact that I outed the "vast right-wing conspiracy" on national television. Well, let me explain something: I wasn't too worried about the Republicans. Them I could handle—and have, for decades. But I'll admit it, I am paranoid. I am, and everyone in the administration is. Every day, we woke up and went to bed thinking about one thing: the possibility of another terrorist attack, maybe even bigger than 9/11.

PRESIDENT GEORGE W. BUSH: That, for me, was the best thing about leaving the White House. I didn't have to worry about another devastating attack like that. Or rather I did worry, but it was out of my hands now.

VICE PRESIDENT DICK CHENEY: That was exactly why I did worry—it was out of President Bush's hands and in the hands of someone hopelessly naive about how the world works and how other countries view us.

MICHELLE OBAMA: Being antiwar is not the same as being antisecurity. Barack took out more terrorists than pretty much any president in history. Peace prize? No, he earned the *rest*-in-peace prize.

HILLARY: Every year as we approach the anniversary of the 9/11 attacks, the so-called chatter from hostile groups increased. This was to be expected, of course. The hard part was figuring out whether someone is actually going to be doing something or if they, you know, are simply celebrating the murder of thousands of innocent people.

MICHELLE: That afternoon we heard that our diplomatic compound in Benghazi, Libya had been stormed.

HILLARY: We were getting very different reports as to what was happening. Nothing was clear except for the fact that it was bad. Later it got worse. There was a second attack at another Benghazi location. This was easily my worst day as secretary of state. The moment I had been dreading had arrived, with four Americans dead.

MICHELLE: Barack was livid. He wanted answers, and he increased security right away.

HILLARY: The media wasn't waiting for answers either—but we didn't have any. If we *had* access to accurate information beforehand, then none of those people would have been killed. Does anyone think that it's easier to get information *after* a compound has been raided? Well, good luck trying to go on television and say, "I don't know." Especially when it comes to the subject of terrorism!

MICHELLE: I asked Barack what had happened and he said that the leading theory was that this was the reaction to some inflammatory video.

HILLARY: I was secretary of state. I was in charge, and that meant I had to take full responsibility—and *that* meant finding someone to go on the Sunday morning shows and talk about this stuff.

SUSAN RICE: Yeah, I did it. Yeah, I looked like a damn fool. Bitch set me up.

MICHELLE: I think some on the right took this to be a sign of Barack's weakness on the international stage. They were trying to make this out to be some sort of Jimmy Carter moment.

CHENEY: I don't think an entire presidency can be regarded as just a "moment."

MITT ROMNEY: It was a tricky position to be in, in terms of campaigning. On the one hand, people were dead and you absolutely don't want to make political hay out of it. On the other hand, we're in the middle of a campaign and everything you say has a political connotation. On the third hand—gosh, by the time I'm done with the hands I'll be a Hindu and not a Mormon—if someone's policies are causing people to be unsafe, that is precisely the most important debate to have. Incompetence in the presidency leads to deaths. And clearly Benghazi did not have to turn out the way that it had.

DAVID AXELROD: The election had to go on. One week later the Romney campaign had a disaster of their own. Now, we knew our job was to portray Governor Romney as elitist and out of touch. Frankly, that wasn't that hard. His father had been a governor of Michigan and a onetime presidential candidate himself. That's as blueblood as it gets.

ROMNEY: That's a lie. My father had dark red Republican blood. It's practically like crude oil, rich and thick.

AXELROD: Governor Romney knew this was a major concern for his campaign, and to his credit he did his best to counter this impression.

ROMNEY: When reporters asked me how many homes I owned, I could honestly answer that I didn't know. If I had given them a number, it would come off terribly. This way, I could tell the truth and still seem normal.

MICHELLE: One of the biggest quotes that came back to haunt Governor Romney was his insistence that "corporations are people, too."

ROMNEY: I meant that in a legal sense. Legally, that's indisputable.

AXELROD: Politically, that's indefensible.

ROMNEY: Let's compromise. Can we agree that maybe they're like— just spitballing here—three-fifths of a person?

MICHELLE: *What?*

ROMNEY: That's not my final number, I'm open to negotiations here.

AXELROD: . . . And then came the release of the tape.

ROMNEY: I was at a donor meeting for some very wealthy contributors to the campaign. In a setting like that, you can be a bit more candid and relaxed, since everyone paid a hefty cover charge to meet you. Plus, these communities are small. If there was a spy there, someone would have noticed.

AXELROD: Except there was a spy.

MICHELLE: And no one noticed.

ROMNEY: I was expressing some of the challenges my campaign and the party as a whole was facing moving forward.

MICHELLE: Here is what he said: "There are 47 percent of the people who will vote for the president no matter what. There are 47 percent who are with him, who are dependent upon government, who believe that they are victims, who believe that government has a responsibility to care for them, who believe that they are entitled to health care, to food, to housing, to you name it."

ROMNEY: That's just a fact.

MICHELLE: Then Governor Romney made a very tenuous connection: "These are people who pay no income tax. Forty-seven percent of Americans pay no income tax. So our message of low taxes doesn't connect."

ROMNEY: It might not be politically correct, but that's the truth.

MICHELLE: Is it? Ronald Reagan was the king of cutting taxes, and he carried forty-four states in 1980. Then, after a gigantic tax cut to the benefit of the wealthy, he got almost 60 percent of the vote in 1984. George H. W. Bush campaigned and won on a "read my lips, no new taxes" pledge. So too did George W. Bush run on cutting taxes. So one of either two things happened in the previous four years: either the American electorate changed completely—in which case as a businessman Governor Romney should adjust to the new market conditions—or he was making excuses for why he couldn't make the sale. I know which choice I found to be more likely.

ROMNEY: The point was that almost half the country relies on the government, and they're automatically going to be for the big-government party.

MICHELLE: The point is, *everyone* in the country relies on the government. The military isn't just for rich people's homes. Public education helps every single student, but the benefits of an educated society are universal.

AXELROD: Here's the problem with Governor Romney's statements. I will grant for the sake of argument that there are plenty of crummy people who want to live on welfare and never work a day in their life. Fine. There is no way that that's 47 percent of America—if it were, we're doomed anyway. Nor is that 47 percent static. Yes, the middle class is shrinking and wealth inequality is increasing. But to say that many of the bottom 47 percent don't make it to the top 53 percent— and vice versa—flies in the face of the aspirations of the American people. Poor people buy into the Republican vision of things, too.

ROMNEY: The part I regret the most about my comments? That they were made public. Only kidding! No, what I regret is the implication that we're a divided, us versus them nation. That's class warfare, and that's been the Democrats' playbook for decades. What I should have said is that there are many people who are beholden to the government and are more interested in their short-term benefit than in the long-term consequences of their choices.

AXELROD: And those people are called "corporate America."

MICHELLE: It fed into the worst stereotypes about the 1 percent and the ultrarich.

HARRY REID: It confirmed who the Republicans worried about and were fighting for—and who they were fighting against.

AXELROD: It was good to go into the October debates with Team Romney on defense.

MICHELLE: Barack had once done an interview where he'd been asked what quality he liked least about himself. He surprised me by saying that there was a "laziness" about him. I didn't know what he meant at first, since he is a very hard worker. But when I thought about it, I got what he was saying. He is a high achiever, but he rarely goes outside his comfort zone. He pushes himself *within* his areas of expertise. This was going to be a bad habit to fall back on going into the debates.

AXELROD: The president wasn't the chosen one anymore; he wasn't the symbol of a new iteration of America like he had been in 2008. There was no George W. Bush to run against, even by proxy. He had to defend his own record.

MICHELLE: A lot of people on the team thought that Governor Romney was just another old rich white Republican just like Senator McCain. I didn't see it that way at all. I thought he was going to be a much smoother debater. When Senator McCain got aggressive, it came across as a bitter old man. When Governor Romney got aggressive, it came across as your boss dressing you down—a very different dynamic.

AXELROD: During the whole debate prep it was kind of . . . well, I think the president just figured that the American people should know his record by now so he didn't really need to defend it. The facts stood on their own.

MICHELLE: And I was like, have you been to Washington? That's not how things operate in this town! Facts are one weapon but hardly the only one and rarely the *best* one.

AXELROD: So we're watching the first debate and Romney came out swinging. You know how he likes to brag about turning around failing companies? Well, we saw that for ourselves. His campaign was failing, he knew it, and he was going to do something about it.

ROMNEY: Darn straight.

MICHELLE: Watching that debate was just awful. It was literally like watching Barack take a beating. Governor Romney kept hitting him again and again, and Barack just stood there taking it.

ROMNEY: President Obama wanted to act like a college professor, so I made sure to do my homework—and then some extra credit besides. It sure did feel good, I'm not going to lie.

AXELROD: The president wouldn't even look up from his podium. Sure, he was responding on the merits but that isn't how debates go. It's political theater, let's be honest. Knowing how to finesse that political theater certainly helped President Obama win the nomination in 2008, and it had been integral to winning the presidency—and now it was being used against him with total corporate efficiency.

ROMNEY: People like to say that I'm kind of stiff and robotic. Well, my critics seemed to forget that the Terminator was a robot, too.

ARNOLD SCHWARZENEGGER: A *Republican* robot. From the future!

MICHELLE: It reminded me of Reagan debating President Carter in 1980, which was absolutely instrumental to the Reagan Revolution that Barack studied so much. Governor Romney wasn't just beating Barack, he was *clowning* him.

AXELROD: Debate ends, everyone is shaking hands on the stage. I'm thinking of what to say to the president. To be honest I hadn't anticipated a blowout. Romney had not been that impressive in the 2008 primary debates, and though he was the best debater in the 2012 Republican primaries, look who was standing onstage next to him.

ROMNEY: I shook the president's hand after it was over and I said, "I'll be back" in an Austrian accent, or at least my best impression of one. He just kind of looked at me in confusion and I knew that I had better leave the jokes to other people. That's fine, they could leave the governing to me. It's what I'm good at, after all. Also, croquet. And polo. And squash.

AXELROD: I didn't need to say anything. The president just waved me off and said, "I know, I know."

PAUL RYAN: The champagne was sure flowing at Romney campaign headquarters that night.

ROMNEY: To be accurate, we didn't actually have champagne. It was a carbonated grape-juice drink, but the effect was the same.

RYAN: Not even a little.

MICHELLE: We weren't just imagining things. All the polls taken right after the debate overwhelmingly called it for Governor Romney.

This was exactly what his campaign needed to change the dynamics. It was very, very scary.

AXELROD: *Especially* since the next debate was the vice presidential one.

MICHELLE: God help us.

RYAN: We had the momentum. I was ready to bring it home. This wasn't just about winning an election. We were having a fundamental debate about what America would look like in five, ten, twenty years.

AXELROD: Paul Ryan has perhaps the best grasp of the issues of anyone that the Republican side had. He knew the numbers inside and out. Plus he's this energetic guy with a great positive energy about him.

MICHELLE: And then there was Joe.

AXELROD: Everyone who works in Washington has their favorite "Bidenism." My favorite was when he called President Obama "the first mainstream African American who is articulate and bright and clean and a nice-looking guy." Boy, did that one ever go over.

MICHELLE: I remember when he complained about "Shylocks" taking advantage of men and women overseas. That's like complaining about "Jemimas" but for Jewish people—except instead of making you pancakes they're absconding with your money in unscrupulous ways.

ROMNEY: What about when he told an African American audience that we were going to put them back in chains? Joe Biden didn't need chains; he needed a muzzle.

CHENEY: The one I liked was when he told that state senator to stand up so the crowd could see him, except the guy was in a wheelchair. Pure class, that man. I left the vice president's office full of farts as a welcoming present for him.

MITCH McCONNELL: That's not to mention all the plagiarism in his speeches back in the day. Though I guess that's the opposite of a gaffe, when you're repeating smart things that someone else had previously written.

RYAN: I wasn't too worried about Joe Biden.

AXELROD: I was very worried about Joe Biden.

MICHELLE: I had confidence in Joe Biden . . . confidence, and a lot of prayers.

AXELROD: Now we're watching the debate, and, so help me, Joe is bringing it home.

MICHELLE: He more than held his own. He started with the Irish-isms, talking about "malarkey." He was entertaining and he was engaging.

VICE PRESIDENT JOE BIDEN: Here's my little secret. Paul Ryan is a great kid. President Obama, tremendously accomplished, a once-in-a-lifetime politician—but still a very young man. What they don't realize is that older people can get away with saying things that they can't. So what they might call a gaffe . . . well, it usually is a gaffe, let's be frank. But that also implies that ol' Joe Biden always speaks his mind and tells the truth. And when you have a politician that people regard as truthful, well, it's a short trip from that to likable and trustworthy. Even if you're black.

AXELROD: Thank you, Mr. Vice President.

BIDEN: Oh, dammit! I was doing so well. Can I get a mulligan? Or maybe a sweet tea? I don't drink alcohol; I guess that's the one thing Governor Romney and I have in common.

AXELROD: It was the *campaign* that got a mulligan. Romney's momentum was halted. So even if our lead shrank a little, as long as both sides maintained the same speed, we were still going to win.

MICHELLE: Now we're ready for the second debate and Barack is not feeling it. He's just not. It's kind of the idea that his actions should speak for themselves. I said, "Well, if that's the case, why write two books?" That got him listening.

AXELROD: The president is a smart man, self-made. And people like that often come off as arrogant and self-assured. Possibly that's somewhat true, as it must be of every president. It's hard for those types to receive input and accept constructive criticism. They know who they are better than you do, so why are you talking? That sort of thing. But I knew Mrs. Obama could get through to him.

MICHELLE: I played that first debate for him on the computer. He was listening to what he was saying and kind of nodding along. Then I turned the sound off. "Watch yourself," I said. "Is that a leader? Is that someone who inspires others? Because *you* do, but that man on the screen doesn't." He got it. Oh boy, did he get it.

AXELROD: Romney was the one who got it in that second debate.

ROMNEY: The president sure had a different demeanor in that second debate. I wish he fought America's enemies as hard as he was fighting against me. Heck, in that case I could even see myself endorsing him. Ha, ha!

AXELROD: One week later, third debate, same thing. Neither candidate delivered a knockout. But our supporters were reassured, and Romney's people were satisfied. That still wasn't good enough for Romney to get any traction.

REID: And that's when the Republican fringe made sure to make themselves heard. They're not quiet, reserved types, that's for sure.

AXELROD: The Indiana Senate race was a long shot for us. The candidates were somewhat close in the polls, but Indiana is a very red state. If I were a gambling man, all my chips would have been put on the GOP. Those Republican voters would grumble but I thought they'd turn out for their man.

RICHARD MOURDOCK: I had won the Republican Senate primary over Senator Lugar because I spoke from the heart and was a strong conservative—which of course included being pro-life. During the debate with my Democratic opponent, I was asked about abortion. It was something that I saw coming and had anticipated—which is more than can be said about how many of these unwed mothers act.

TODD AKIN: This guy's saying what we're all thinking!

MOURDOCK: Then came the gotcha part, asking about exceptions to being pro-life. "What if the woman is raped?" Now, it turned out that the female body does *not* have ways to try to shut that whole thing down. Who knew?

MICHELLE: Everyone. Everyone knew. Helen Keller knew. She knew it so much that it would have been a pic on her Instagram.

MOURDOCK: I didn't want to sound glib and uncaring, which we pro-life Americans are often accused of being. So I said that life is a gift from God, and that even if life begins in the horrible situation of rape, then that is something that God intended to happen. A rape baby is kind of like a present from Jesus, not a punishment.

AKIN: I couldn't have said it better myself!

JEREMIAH WRIGHT: Pardon my French, but these motherfuckers were so rabid that they made me look like Mr. Rogers.

AL SHARPTON: Amen to *that*.

MOURDOCK: The media's reaction was violent and unexpected, not unlike a rape. Yes, I guess you could say I was "raped" by the press.

AXELROD: It got coverage both in Indiana and then throughout the country. Immediately we saw undecided voters shift quickly to Joe Donnelly, our candidate.

MICHELLE: We've all heard of the Reagan Democrats. Why were these GOP candidates so committed to musing about rape on a national stage? Were these supposed to be "Dukakis Republicans" or something? I can't think of any issue that deserves to be handled with greater sensitivity and respect, and the Republicans had *none*.

ROMNEY: What Mr. Mourdock was saying wasn't even that controversial. Obviously if God is in control of the universe, as we all believe he is, then everything that happens is due to his will. But that's not what it sounded like he meant. It sounded like he was telling victims of assault, "Sorry, but that's what God wanted!"

AXELROD: They must have been freaking the hell out at the RNC. Many Republicans went out of their way to publicly denounce him, and these were pro-life politicians to boot. I can only imagine what was going on behind the scenes.

ROMNEY: I called Mr. Mourdock personally to try and get him to apologize, because he obviously upset a lot of people. They were right to be upset, too! I didn't blame them. So I'm having a heated discussion with him and our call gets disconnected. When I redialed and got him back on the line, he started telling me that it was God's will that the call got dropped.

MOURDOCK: That was a joke! It wasn't God's will, it was Sprint's.

ROMNEY: He was very polite, but I've been in corporate America long enough to know when someone is just hearing you out in order to be polite, when they have no real intention of doing what you'd like. It was very frustrating that I was being perceived as some sort of fringe Christian candidate on social issues.

MICHELLE: If Mr. Mourdock wanted to talk religious fundamentalism, he got his wish. Less than a week after his comments, just days before the election, the Eastern Seaboard was hit with a storm of biblical proportions.

CHRIS CHRISTIE: We knew it was coming and we prepared as best we could. The storm was going to be unprecedented in its ferocity. We were going to be as prepared as we could be. I wasn't going to have a Katrina situation on my hands.

MICHELLE: I'm not a meteorologist or a climatologist or an ecologist. I worry about the humidity and my hair, that's as far as that goes. I don't know how much global warming was to blame for this storm. The point was it was looking to be one of the worst weather events in American history.

MICHAEL BLOOMBERG: We shut down as much of New York City as we could. We knew that our infrastructure was going to take a hit, but we didn't know how badly. Some of the subways date back over a hundred years—they weren't designed for this sort of abuse.

MICHELLE: Then all we could do was pray.

CHRISTIE: I felt confident that we had done everything that we could to prepare. I make fun of the press a lot, but they did a great job of warning people about Sandy's dangers and telling them what they needed to do in order to be safe.

AXELROD: Obviously the campaign went into a bit of a holding pattern, because this is the weekend before the Tuesday election.

BLOOMBERG: So Hurricane Sandy comes and goes. There was good news and there was bad news. The bad news is, the lower half of Manhattan lost power. It took me back to 9/11; everyone had that in their minds. Other bad news: the subway system was a complete mess, and we had to try to stabilize it by rerouting trains. But the good news was that there wasn't rioting. We also kept on top of the situation with our seniors and other vulnerable people. And New Yorkers stuck together. It was a mess, but it was a peaceful mess and it was our mess.

CHRISTIE: I said it then and I will say it now: President Obama could not have been more engaged. "How can I help?" he said. "What do you need?"

MICHELLE: People criticize Barack for being a delegator, and he does tend to be above the fray. But the benefit of that approach is that it gives people a sense of control in their own sphere and pride in their work. He can always step in and bat cleanup later. That was the strategy with Sandy. He let the state and local authorities do what was necessary, but he was always one phone call away to be the safety net if they needed one.

CHRISTIE: But let me set the record straight. I never hugged the guy. That was just gravitational attraction pulling him into me. I've usually got three or four schoolkids orbiting me at a time; they're adorable really.

AXELROD: We didn't have to play up the contrast with President Bush and Katrina. The pictures spoke for themselves. All these Republican arguments that the president was incompetent and in over his head—well, the response to the storm showed who had it together and who liked to complain. I don't know who did more for the Obama campaign that year: President Clinton or Governor Christie. And both weren't exactly the president's best friends, either, which made their comments that much more persuasive.

MICHELLE: Coming up on Tuesday, we still didn't know who was going to win the election. It wasn't that it was too close to call. Rather, half the pollsters were calling it for Governor Romney, and the other half for Barack. It was entirely a function of who they predicted would turn out.

ROMNEY: Early in the evening, the networks called Florida for President Obama. Theoretically, we could have won the White House without Florida. But that wasn't likely to happen. That's when I knew we had lost.

RUTH BADER GINSBURG: If I had to adjudicate Florida again it would only be over some Four Loco. That shit was once in a lifetime. Hang this chad, assholes.

NOVEMBER 6, 2012: BARACK OBAMA DEFEATS MITT ROMNEY 332–206 IN THE ELECTORAL COLLEGE TO WIN REELECTION.

AXELROD: Our people turned out again. The numbers were very close to 2008. The Obama coalition wanted to see this journey through and to give the president the opportunity to finish what he'd started. It was a vote of confidence, pure and simple.

MICHELLE: Governor Romney called to concede, and he could not have been more gracious.

ROMNEY: I was glad that it had largely been a clean campaign about the issues and ideas. I was proud that we got as many votes as we did—and I was worried, admittedly, about what four more years of the Obama presidency would do to America. But I had done all that I could, and we simply came up short.

AXELROD: Am I going to sit here and say that God sent Hurricane Sandy as his way of endorsing President Obama for reelection? Am I pointing out that maybe the good Lord knew that the president would rise to the occasion and wanted a chance to demonstrate this? I'll answer yes to both those questions . . . but only because it will really piss off the Republicans.

BUSH: The Bible speaks of the lion lying down with the lamb, not of a hippo hugging a zebra.

REID: The icing on the cake was that, despite the odds, we Democrats ended up *winning* two net Senate seats. That was unbelievable. No one had been predicting that in the beginning of the year.

MOURDOCK: It was God's will that I lost. I couldn't have prevented it.

AKIN: It was a legitimate defeat. We were shut down, plain and simple.

MICHELLE: My faith in America was as strong as ever—just like my personal faith. My only hope was that the Republicans would learn from the defeat of these two . . . can I say "clowns"? I hoped that they would learn from the defeat of these two clowns and move in a more moderate direction. Maybe, I wondered, they could even work together with Barack in his second term.

BIDEN: That's hilarious. Tell us another one!

15

SECOND CHANCES, JANUARY– DECEMBER 2013

MITCH McCONNELL: We started 2013 on a disappointing note, at least in the United States Senate. We had hoped for an expanded roster of Republican senators, if not the majority. We didn't get it.

JOHN BOEHNER: We lost eight seats in the House. Not a huge number, could have been worse.

NANCY PELOSI: Those eight new Democrats put us over two hundred seats. That was a bit of a boost as we looked forward to recapturing the majority. I will point out that we actually received more total votes than the Republican candidates, but thanks to redistricting that didn't translate into more seats.

BOEHNER: Don't hate the player, hate the game.

MICHELLE OBAMA: With the beginning of the second term there wasn't a changing of the guard, of course, but a continuance of the Obama administration. What we did see were some people packing their bags and leaving their posts.

HILLARY RODHAM CLINTON: I had done a job that I was proud of as secretary of state. I had been a loyal supporter of this president, certainly far more than many in the press had expected or probably would have liked. There are fewer headlines for them when there's no intraparty drama.

MICHELLE: Mrs. Clinton left her office with record-high approval ratings, and I was very grateful for all the work that she had done.

ERIC HOLDER: I had my foot out the door as well. Look, I'm a big boy. I knew what I had signed up for. Anyone in my position is going to be under intense scrutiny—as well they should be. Being attorney general is an extremely important role. But things turned when it had gotten personal.

HILLARY: Join the club, buddy.

HOLDER: The Republicans had tried to manufacture a scandal where there wasn't any.

BOEHNER: We'd even had a catchy name for it: "Fast and Furious." It polled well with undecideds. Our other choice was "Guns for Ganja" but that didn't fly.

HOLDER: It had been a highly sensitive Mexican operation where people's lives were in danger, and the Republicans wanted all the information to be made public. It was madness.

BOEHNER: If he hadn't done anything wrong, then he wouldn't have anything to hide.

HOLDER: I had spoken to the president and we dug in our heels.

BOEHNER: So the House had found Attorney General Holder in contempt.

HOLDER: The feeling was mutual and had continued past the 2012 elections, which is why I couldn't wait to get the hell out of Washington. The fun parts? What fun parts? Even the inauguration and all the balls weren't anywhere near the big deal that they had been four years prior.

AGENT ██████████████: I can report that at the end of inauguration night, FLOTUS was heard to yell, "Oh f███, oh f███, oh f███! Thank you, Jesus; thank you for the Twenty-Second Amendment!"

MICHELLE: The very first thing that the new Congress tried to do was to score political points off the Benghazi tragedy.

BOEHNER: We just wanted to get to the bottom of things. No one can deny that this was something that warranted looking into, at the very least to make sure that nothing like it would happen again.

McCONNELL: Humiliating the administration was simply an added bonus.

MICHELLE: When they weren't doing that, they were engaging in a lot of disingenuous posturing over the budget.

BOEHNER: The 2012 election had reminded me a lot of 1996. The American people back then were given a choice: Do you want to re-elect a liberal president, or do you want a conservative Congress? And the voters had said, "Yes, we do!" So 2013 was kind of a stalemate between an emboldened White House and a Tea Party caucus that was starting to chafe. If those Tea Party Republicans hated Washington before they'd arrived, well, living here sure didn't change their impression.

MICHELE BACHMANN: It's still a swamp, except now the blood-suckers are in suits.

MICHELLE: The next major event didn't come out of Washington but out of Florida. That July we were waiting for the verdict in the George Zimmerman/Trayvon Martin trial.

HOLDER: Here were the facts that were not in dispute: First and most important, a young man was dead. Second, he had been in a location where he had every right to be. Third, we knew who had shot and killed him. No one was arguing that George Zimmerman instigated a confrontation that ended up with Trayvon Martin's death. It seemed pretty clear—though it was not my place to say—that Mr. Zimmerman thought that Mr. Martin was trespassing because he didn't look like the other residents. Meaning, he ended up shooting him because he was black.

GEORGE ZIMMERMAN: That's not really fair. I was prepared to kill a child of any race or even gender. Heck, I wouldn't have discriminated against him even if he were in a wheelchair with one of those retard helmets. I'm an American. I shoot everyone *equally.*

MICHELLE: The argument was that Trayvon attacked Zimmerman and therefore Zimmerman had to shoot him. But this all could have been avoided if he had never approached the young man to begin with. Should children be punished for flying off the handle, for acting out? Yes, of course. But not with serious injury. Not with *death.* If a kid puts their hand on the stove, you don't hold it there until the skin falls off. This idea that Trayvon was expected to be more mature than a grown man with a hidden gun? How does that make sense?

HOLDER: So the verdict comes in and we were prepared for the worst. And sure enough, Mr. Zimmerman was acquitted.

MICHELLE: I will never forget the look on that mother's face. It was like a knife in the heart; I couldn't handle it . . . And by "that mother," I mean George Zimmerman, of course. Because he was all smiles. I half expected him to hike up his pants legs and start dancing like James Brown.

HOLDER: As an attorney, I could understand why the verdict was *technically* reached. Florida's Stand Your Ground law allows a person to react with deadly force if they feel threatened. Meaning, if you are afraid, you've got a license to kill. I had thought that sort of thing had been reserved for James Bond, but here we were. Welcome to twenty-first-century America.

DICK CHENEY: I hate it here, can't we go back to the '50s or something?

HOLDER: Civil unrest became a fear. That's the case whenever you have large gatherings of people, even at a sporting event or a concert. Plus, emotions were raw and rightly so. It looked like not only would there be no repercussions for Mr. Zimmerman, but also there wouldn't even be an analysis of what went wrong that got us to this place. No one was really making moves to change the Stand Your Ground law, at least not in Florida. Meaning, this kind of thing could happen again— and again and again and again.

ZIMMERMAN: I was sympathetic to the attorney general's concerns, but Stand Your Ground was irrelevant here. I was on the ground and being punched in the face. I wasn't standing my ground. I wasn't standing my *anything*. What I *under*stood was that my life was in danger and I needed to protect myself.

HOLDER: Fortunately, while there were huge protests, there was no rioting or anything of that nature. Sorry to disappoint those who were expecting another Los Angeles situation, but Americans are better than that—despite what some would like us to believe.

MICHELLE: Barack knew that he needed to say something. At the same time, he didn't want to engage in political posturing over this. "It's not a good idea for teens to be shot dead in the streets" isn't really a partisan position to take.

ZIMMERMAN: Well, it depends on the street and it depends on the kid. They shot Billy the Kid, didn't they? That wasn't a racist thing, was it? . . . I'm asking, because it's possible he was black and they just had white dudes play him in the movies, like when Ben Kingsley was Gandhi.

MICHELLE: So Barack just popped into the regular daily press briefing at the White House and spoke from the cuff. Yes, everyone jokes about the omnipresent teleprompter—no, we don't have one in the bedroom, wise guys!—but this was clearly him being raw and emotional. He wasn't being the president; he was being a man of color and the father of two black children.

HOLDER: President Obama laid out facts that were undeniable, rather than talking points. I think that allowed people to draw conclusions for themselves. Rather than telling them what to think, he told them what he felt and what he had gone through. And he told them to be calm and to not get violent—and that of course went both ways.

MICHELLE: To hear a president, an Ivy League–educated man, an author, a senator, discuss how he'd been followed around at the store was unprecedented. To discuss how it could have been him shot in the street—how a white kid might have had a different outcome to the scenario, one far less deadly—that was touching. He also explicitly rejected this call for a so-called national conversation on race. He had seen firsthand how Democrats won't listen to Republicans, and vice versa. But neighbors can listen to neighbors. When race becomes a nonpolitical issue, then the edge gets taken off the conversation and it becomes about making a system that's better for everyone.

McCONNELL: That of course was the Republicans' goal as well: making a system that was better for everyone. And by everyone, I of course mean the right kind of everyone.

BOEHNER: As fall approached, the House seemed to have had some strong ideas on that subject. The Republican Party has disagreements about many things: immigration, gay rights, education—to name but a few. The one thing we are all united on as Republicans is budgetary discipline, especially when there's a Democrat in the White House.

MICHELLE: I don't think they regarded the presidential election as any kind of referendum on their schemes. They just looked at it as a minor loss in terms of their plans to destroy Barack's biggest legislative achievement: Obamacare. If they couldn't defeat him, they wanted to undo everything that he had brought into being.

BACHMANN: Congress controlled the nation's purse strings. The idea came about that we could defund Obamacare. If we allocated zero dollars to the enforcement of this terribly destructive legislation, then people could feel free to ignore it knowing there would be no repercussions.

MICHELLE: Everyone saw it with their own eyes: The Republicans were encouraging all of America to break the law. This is from the law-and-order party of Nixon and Giuliani! "Laws are binding!" "The Supreme Court is the ultimate arbiter of the Constitution!" . . . except under this president?

HARRY REID: Come September 2013, the federal government was going to be without a budget. Without funding, the government can't spend money and effectively shuts down. I'd been through this once before, with the Newt Gingrich Congress. This time, however, we had the Senate. As usual with the Republicans, I don't think that they thought things through.

BOEHNER: It was a gamble, for sure. When we shut down the government under President Clinton, he came around and offered concessions.

REID: They didn't want surrender; they wanted blackmail. They were insisting that no budget talk can go forward without defunding Obamacare. I was the Senate majority leader. I wasn't about to be given ultimatums by the lower house of Congress, and neither were my colleagues.

MICHELLE: It all started to become a perfect storm of nonsense. You had the spending grind to a halt at the same time as the debt ceiling was being reached at the same time that we were finalizing the healthcare.gov website.

BACHMANN: I was elected to uphold the Constitution, not to help the president to destroy America.

MICHELLE: Sure enough, two opposing things happened on October 1, 2013: The federal government shut down, and healthcare.gov launched.

BOEHNER: We had been saying that Obamacare was not ready for prime time, and that website illustrated how badly this health care scheme was going to operate. It was unstable and virtually no one could make it work. It gave me no small pleasure to see this unfold. If anything, it gave me a great deal of pleasure.

MICHELLE: It was panic at the White House. Complete and utter panic.

BOEHNER: Governments are not good at doing things quickly. A sense of urgency they do not have. Neither do computer programmers, who operate on their own schedule and expect you to be patient while they do their thing. Combine the two and you have nothing short of an embarrassing debacle.

MICHELLE: This wasn't a problem that I could do anything about, certainly. I could have sent all those computer programmers all the healthy meals that they wanted. Heck, I could have sent them all the Popeye's that they wanted—none of it would have mattered. What did I know about setting up a website? I'm still on AOL.

PRESIDENT BILL CLINTON: I've only sent two emails in my life, but only because I wanted free V1agra and to add three inches instantly.

HILLARY: Neither worked.

MICHELLE: It's not as if Barack could do anything either. Affirmative action, taxes, the environment—on those issues he could give a speech, call the parties concerned, *something*. But this nerd stuff? What could he do? Inspire them to nerd harder?

BOEHNER: I've had to deal with those geeks. It's so amazing to watch someone unable to fix your problems while simultaneously making *you* feel like the idiot. They would have made good politicians if they weren't also so damn ugly. . . . Yes, you can quote me on that! Those hellnerds tick me off to no end. If you want to fix a fried PC, the least you can do is get tanned yourself. You know, know your enemy. That's why I always ask for the mulatto setting at the salon.

AL SHARPTON: Everybody wants to be black until the police show up.

MICHELLE: No one was signing up. This was supposed to be a major nationwide site and at one point we had fewer subscribers than the Peaches & Herb Facebook fanpage.

HERB FAME: We are currently back to the sixth Peaches, after the seventh one passed away.

WANDA MAKLE: That's right, I'm Peaches number six *and* number eight. That's two nonconsecutive terms. I'm the Grover Cleveland of funk.

FAME: Woman, you know damn well that Grover Cleveland was the Grover Cleveland of funk. "Ma, Ma, where's my pa?" Bourbon Democrat? Shit, that fat man was the Luther Vandross of his day.

MICHELLE: All Barack could do was to focus on the government shutdown. The American people were blaming the Republicans. Well, what if that changed? What if Barack started to get the blame? He started to examine all the possibilities available.

McCONNELL: We Republicans in the Senate thought the House Republicans were out of their minds, to be blunt. That's not how things work. You can't force a president's hand. Believe me, I would love to as much as anyone. But why would he surrender on his main achievement? We already saw that the Democrats were willing to walk the plank to make sure that Obamacare was passed. Now President Obama was going to win two presidential campaigns and have nothing to show for it? Really?

MICHELLE: Barack's natural inclination is to find some middle ground and to see what works. He's a big picture guy, so he was prepared to negotiate. But then I reminded him what had happened in the 2010 lame duck session. He had caved on one of his major campaign promises, the Bush tax cuts for the wealthy, and for what? He had tried good faith, he had tried compromise, he had tried concessions with the GOP—and they were going to shut down the entire government to force his hand. What do the kids say? "Hell to the no"?

REID: I have to give Senator McConnell credit. The Senate Republicans were ready to sit down and talk. They were ready from the beginning. Sure you had people like Ted Cruz but those were few and far between—in this scenario at least.

McCONNELL: I was waiting for the children to finish with their temper tantrum. They knew where to find me.

BOEHNER: At one point we met with the president and the meeting did not go well.

MICHELLE: The president is the leader of the free world. Why on earth would he be dictated to by someone who is his subordinate, not just in the order of succession, but even within their own branch of government? I think he wanted to see if they would say the same things to his face as they were saying in front of the cameras. Maybe they were playing to the base, who knows?

REID: Nope, they said it and meant it.

BOEHNER: My caucus wasn't budging. It was a very precarious position that we were in. Not only would the consequences of a default have been dire, but so would the political repercussions.

MICHELLE: It wasn't hard for the public at large to see who was holding the gun and who had it against their temple. Support for the GOP was crashing harder than the healthcare.gov site.

JEB BUSH: I would fix it.

CHENEY: I'm surprised that they didn't try to pin that one on us too. "It's not our fault, the evil Republicans are to blame! When things crashed during the Bush years, it was planes and not websites! We have Windows and they had people jumping out of them!"

REID: So the Senate Democrats went ahead with the Senate Republicans and passed a bill that would fund the government—including Obamacare—and take the debt ceiling off the table. What was the goal? A deal that could pass the House.

PELOSI: If you want entertainment, you want a spectacle, then turn to the Republicans. It's a fun circus sideshow, no doubt about it. Heck, they even have an elephant! We can't compete with that. But if you want things done, if you want government to work in a way that actually helps people and solves problems—well, that's why the Democrats are there.

BOEHNER: The vote went forward in the House. All the Democrats voted for it, and most of the Republicans voted against it. We mock the Democrats for not reading the bills, but I'm afraid many of these Tea Party types didn't read the writing on the wall. Or else they were so secure in their districts that they thought that the rest of the government could go to hell. Well, it doesn't work like that.

REID: What a pathetic spectacle.

MICHELLE: We solved that issue only to come into another one, this time from abroad. We knew that Nelson Mandela hadn't been doing well for quite a while, and when he got sick that last time he clearly wasn't long for this world. We were all kind of waiting for the inevitable, going about our day while waiting for that last phone call.

VICE PRESIDENT JOE BIDEN: Nelson Mandela had been an inspiration for people throughout the world. There is no way that President Obama could have been elected without Mandela paving the path for him, absolutely no way. And where would that have left me? Stuck in the Senate, that's where! Ha, ha, ha!

MICHELLE: Here's a fact about politics, about *life*: People in power don't want to surrender that power. In a sense, you can't blame them. It feels nice to be powerful! People smile and nod at you and tell you that your choice of wine was really quite brilliant. Yet there's another aspect to giving up power that we sometimes forget. People in power tend to be not very nice to those who don't have it. And when the have-nots become the haves, a lot of times they get vindictive.

BIDEN: By the 1980s, no one was really defending apartheid anymore, not in this country. The best they could come up with was that it supposedly wasn't our business how South Africa ran their nation. I mean, really? America, the worldwide symbol of decency and fairness and opportunity, we don't have something to say about institutionalized racism that was the worst on earth? Not even a little opinion?

MICHELLE: The white leadership of South Africa saw the writing on the wall. They knew it was the end of the line for their, frankly, evil system. But they were scared of what would happen to them personally. It was Nelson Mandela who promised and provided a peaceful safe transition. There was forgiveness, not vindictiveness—which would certainly have been warranted! That's just another huge reason to admire him.

REID: I think some of my friends on the right thought that as soon as President Obama took office that he'd be demanding quotas and reparations. They were so consumed by race that they couldn't believe a nonwhite president wouldn't be too. And I am certain many Americans agreed, and I am certain many more would have thought that—but for the precedent set by Nelson Mandela. He showed that a black president didn't have to be the president of only black people. A great, great man.

MICHELLE: So on December 5, 2013, we got the news that Mandela had passed. Ninety-five years on this earth, and to have accomplished so much—truly remarkable. I know for a fact that seeing a black U.S. president—and not just black but one generation removed from Africa—was a source of great pride to Mr. Mandela.

We cleared our schedules to be able to fly to RSA in order to extend our sympathies.

PRESIDENT GEORGE W. BUSH: All of us former presidents get together for stuff like this. Maybe if we got together under more pleasant circumstances, then Washington wouldn't be divided as it is.

PRESIDENT JIMMY CARTER: Really? Because I left President Bush three voice-mail messages, and he never even bothered to return any of them.

BUSH: I've been having problems with my cell-phone service ever since I switched to Metro PCS. Sure, the bill is lower every month, but many calls simply don't get through.

CARTER: I also sent at least four emails.

BUSH: I'll have to call Hillary; she's in charge of my email server.

HILLARY: Oops! My bad.

DECEMBER 10, 2013: BARACK OBAMA SPEAKS AT NELSON MANDELA'S MEMORIAL.

OPRAH WINFREY: It was a gala event. Bill Gates was there, Bono, everybody who was everybody. You'd better believe Oprah got herself on that plane; I wasn't about to miss this.

MICHELLE: So Barack goes up to give his speech and I'm sitting there knowing that the whole world is watching. I knew what he was going to say so I kind of looked around at the crowd. Even as First Lady, it's still sometimes surreal to see all these dignitaries—especially when they're all in one place, it's like stepping inside of a newspaper. So I look back at the stage and I notice the sign language guy.

THAMSANQA JANTJIE: Translating the speeches into sign language for the Deaf community was one of the great honors of my life.

MICHELLE: I actually know a very very little bit of sign language. I know "I love you" and I learned the alphabet. But when you give as many speeches as I have and you *watch* as many speeches as I have, you kind of get the gist of the motions. It's kind of like how most people can say something that sounds like it's from another language even if it's not that language's actual words.

BIDEN: Ching chong cling clang! . . . That's my impression of French. Here's Spanish: Nelsono Mandelo es el grande hombre del Southo Africo. See, I've actually studied Spanish.

MICHELLE: I could have sworn that the interpreter wasn't using actual sign language. I waited until Barack said something that I knew the sign for—"love"—and watched closely. But the guy didn't give the sign for love.

JANTJIE: Many people simply don't understand what it's like to be deaf and how sign language actually works.

MICHELLE: The thing is, I *do* know how sign language actually works. It has its own grammar; it's not simply English translated directly.

JANTJIE: Every country has its own sign language. In the United States, it's called AMSLAN, short for American Sign Language. In England it's BSL, British Sign Language. And angels have their own, ANGSLAN, which is what I was using. It's a lot like MOONSLAN, which the moon people use. They all *have* to use sign language because there is no air on the moon and the people living there can't talk normally since sound can't travel in a vacuum.

MICHELLE: Well, it turned out that my suspicions were right. He wasn't doing sign language at all, he was just making random motions with his hands. Then we later found out that the man was mentally ill.

JANTJIE: How? How was I mentally ill? Was I rhyming all the time for no reason or something?

MICHELLE: He had also been institutionalized for a year and a half.

JANTJIE: Nelson Mandela was imprisoned for twenty-seven years. Was he crazy as well? Of course he wasn't. He just told me so himself! . . . What's that, Nelson? . . . You want me to set the orphanage on fire? Do you know how stupid that sounds? It's all the way on the other side of town!

MICHELLE: This isn't to stigmatize those who battle with mental illness. Many Americans suffer from these types of conditions.

CHENEY: Yeah, they're called Democrats.

MICHELLE: But the man had also been charged with rape and housebreaking.

JANTJIE: If it's a crime to get drunk and try to have what Americans refer to as a "booty call" with your ex-girlfriend while she is asleep, then I guess that makes me a criminal!

TODD AKIN: That is not legitimate rape, not by a long shot.

MICHELLE: Not to mention the kidnapping charges.

JANTJIE: It was a young goat. I can see why people would find that confusing; it's the same word as that for a human child.

MICHELLE: The allegations even included attempted murder and what they very kindly refer to as "necklacing."

JANTJIE: This is a game we have in South Africa; even Winnie Mandela liked to play. It's like trick or treat, only instead of giving people candy you put a gasoline-filled tire around their shoulders and then set them on fire.

MICHELLE: I still don't know how he managed to be onstage with Barack. Something really awful could have happened.

JANTJIE: Yes, like Nelson Mandela rising from the grave as a vampire or possibly a zombie . . . What's that, Nelson? "Go stare at the sun"? OK, now you're talking!

16

PACKING THE BAGS, 2014–2016

MICHELLE OBAMA: If the president is from Hawaii, and his presidency was launched in Chicago—well, it ended in Missouri.

ERIC HOLDER: Ferguson is a suburb of St. Louis that's about two-thirds black. On August 9, 2014, there was an altercation between a young man by the name of Michael Brown and a police officer named Darren Wilson. Brown ended up shot in broad daylight, his body lying on the street for the entire neighborhood to see.

MICHELLE: This to me was even more troubling than the George Zimmerman case.

HOLDER: I had to hold my tongue a bit when I was still attorney general. But I would say it is pretty unambiguous that police officers overwhelmingy target young black men, and that their reactions to those situations tend to be much quicker to escalate to violence and are much more prone to end in serious injury or even death.

RUDY GIULIANI: They only target those populations who commit the crimes, like selling loose cigarettes to consenting adults. That's how we cleaned up New York City. Black Americans should be glad that that's who we targeted, because they're also the most likely victims of these thugs.

MICHELLE: The protests began almost immediately. I don't think I had seen tensions with the police that high since the Los Angeles riots.

HOLDER: The difference between Ferguson and the Trayvon Martin case was this: George Zimmerman was a private citizen. His actions might have been a function of the system, but he was only one man. Darren Wilson *was* the system. He represented, to many people, what was wrong in our inner-city communities. Every decade or so civil unrest breaks out because a young black kid is shot by the cops with *no* repercussions, not even getting fired.

MICHELLE: If you were a chef and your undercooked chicken made people sick, you would lose your job. To many people, it didn't matter what was technically legal per se. If, in the course of your job, teenagers die— well, maybe a new line of work might be better for you at the very least.

HOLDER: I could never have said this when I was in office, but poor people with no opportunity and no hope for the future burn things down. America was *started* because of rioting—but when white people riot, it's out of principle, right? The question is: Why do they burn down their own neighborhoods? I would gently suggest that if these young people had the means to travel elsewhere, they wouldn't feel as isolated and as stifled. Things might have been different if there had been more fathers around is the claim. But the same people who complain about the lack of fathers in urban households are the ones clamoring to lock up these young men and throw away the key—and are actually succeeding in doing so.

MICHELLE: The chaos just kept getting worse and worse. Barack went out and spoke about it. He pointed out the undeniable fact that the criminal justice system is not racially impartial.

HOLDER: We have the data. It applies, as the president said, to everything from pulling people over to the drug laws. The war on drugs created a black market—pun intended—for poor black men who had no chance of ever holding down a real job. It's just like a mousetrap; they're lured in by the promise of making money, and then they're caught by the same system that made it so enticing to sell drugs to begin with.

GIULIANI: That's just a load of BS. This is what President Obama wanted, and this is what he got.

HOLDER: No one wanted this—especially black America. That's the whole point of these riots. The people don't want to live the way they do, and they see no chance for it changing. Not when you have half the country telling them they have no right to complain about anything.

MICHELLE: As the midterm elections approached, we had even more situations that were getting out of hand. It seemed like every campaign season was beset by one biblical disaster or another. 2012 saw Hurricane Sandy, and 2014 saw the arrival of Ebola to American shores.

MITCH McCONNELL: When we said that the Obama administration made us sick, we'd only meant it as a figure of speech.

MICHELLE: Ebola is a deadly, deadly disease. It killed quickly and it killed a huge percentage of people who caught it. Worse, it was highly contagious—and medical health professionals were catching it as well. As the disease took them out, they couldn't treat people, and then their would-be patients died. It was horrible. As 2014 progressed, it reached epidemic proportions in West African nations like Guinea and Sierra Leone. Then in September we got our first reported American case in Dallas. People started losing their minds.

JOHN BOEHNER: I blame Hollywood and all those epidemic movies.

MICHELLE: It was a cause for concern, but these types of situations had been a cause for concern for over a decade. After 9/11, plans were drawn up by the government to take care of any biological warfare attacks. We had systems in place, ready to go immediately, in case of an outbreak. And this wasn't even an outbreak but what soon became a handful of cases. Yet people were on television calling for banning all flights from Western Africa.

VICE PRESIDENT DICK CHENEY: I wish this country would just sit down and make up its damn mind. First they want us to import Africans. Then, we're supposed to ban African imports. What's it going to be, America?

MICHELLE: Even though only two people died—which of course is a tragedy but hardly a plague epidemic—the Ebola story fed into American fears.

McCONNELL: That's where we Republicans stepped in!

MICHELLE: I suspected that the best cure for Ebola was an election, and that's exactly what happened. After November, the story faded from the headlines. In politics there's something called the six-year itch. Namely, six years into an administration is almost always devastating for the president's party. We already knew that the midterms would be rough on the incumbent party, but stories of *plague* sure didn't help matters!

PRESIDENT BILL CLINTON: *Almost* always. Sometimes the president's party picks up seats. You know, like under my administration and . . . well, I guess that's it. During the last century, at least.

MICHELLE: On the other hand, if you looked at the elections seat by seat, it didn't seem that bad. We had a shot to mitigate the damage, I thought.

McCONNELL: I was locked in a very close race in my home state of Kentucky against a woman who was half my age. Fortunately, she had half my savvy at politicking or else I would have been in a heap of trouble.

ALISON LUNDERGAN GRIMES: The campaign was going neck and neck until I was asked who I had voted for in the last presidential election. Let's just say that President Obama is not exactly beloved in my state—he didn't even pull 40 percent of the vote in 2012.

McCONNELL: But the question was, did he pull in Mrs. Grimes's vote? And she refused to answer even though everyone knew that she had. Heck, she had even been a delegate for him at the Democratic Convention. Suddenly ol' Mitch McConnell wasn't the only slippery politician in the race.

MICHELLE: Senator McConnell was our biggest target, no question about it. Despite his opponent's gaffe, we still hoped that she could pull it off.

McCONNELL: I was the classic swing race that year. I packed up my office early. Either it was going to be a Republican night, another "shellacking"—in which case I would be moving into Harry Reid's majority leader office—or we would blow our golden opportunity and I would be heading home.

REID: Election night was a bloodbath. Let me put it in perspective:

BLACK MAN, WHITE HOUSE

in 2014, we lost nine seats. In 2008, with Obama's landslide and a national consensus against President Bush and Republicanism, we had only gained *eight* seats.

McCONNELL: We managed to defeat five Democratic incumbents. *Five.* It was sure hard picking out presents for all of them on the way out, but my staff and I managed!

NANCY PELOSI: The House was the same thing. I was hoping for the Speaker's gavel back in my hands. Instead, John Boehner had more Republicans in the House than at any point since the Great Depression. I am hoping and praying that is a coincidence, believe me.

CHRIS CHRISTIE: The governors' races followed the same pro-Republican pattern. We held Florida, which was a supertough one. Governor Rick Scott was running against former governor Charlie Crist, who was now a Democrat.

CHARLIE CRIST: I am considering identifying as a Whig in the next election.

CHRISTIE: Rick Scott wasn't exactly a guy who gave people the warm fuzzies.

RICK SCOTT: The people call me "Skeletor." And by people, I mean those who live in my home. And by those who live in my home, I mean my family and the maid.

CHRISTIE: We took Massachusetts back, Governor Romney's home state—and then we took Illinois, President Obama's home state. And just for good measure we got Arkansas, where Bill Clinton is from.

MICHELLE: We were down to eighteen governors, the lowest number in a generation.

CHRISTIE: Oh, and Maryland! The bluest state! Gee, how could I have forgotten that one?

MICHELLE: I went to talk to Barack and he was oddly calm about it. I think his whole general feeling was, what difference does it make?

HILLARY RODHAM CLINTON: And people say I didn't leave my mark on this administration.

MICHELLE: He had to go out and say something. Barack always said elections had consequences, and the 2014 midterms were certainly consequential. One of the biggest consequences? He felt free to do what he thought was the right thing. In fact, he could do it on his own as president. If the Democrats needed to throw him under the bus for political reasons to save their butts, that was fine.

BOEHNER: We'd gotten word that the president was planning some executive action with regard to immigration after the election. I told the White House both publicly and privately that this would be like waving a red flag in front of a bull.

VICE PRESIDENT JOE BIDEN: "Bull" is right.

MICHELLE: The Republicans—*especially* in the House—had made it perfectly clear that they were going to fight Barack's ideas at every turn. If he was for it, they were against it. Senator McConnell said that his top political priority was to deny Barack reelection. Not to get, say, a balanced budget or even effective government. No, the personal defeat of my husband. As if a huge victory—two years after a big defeat, mind you—was somehow going to chasten the Republicans and make them moderate their approach? Pardon my French, but were these niggas for serious?

HILLARY: They were ready with their subpoenas and their hearings. I had been through all this nonsense before. You get enough people cross-examined by Congress and the appearance is that of a criminal trial. Did anyone doubt they were going to use every tool at their disposal? Was there the slightest possibility that the right-wing press wouldn't take anything they could, whether in context or out of it, and blow it up into something supposedly a hundred times worse than Watergate? Give me a break.

MICHELLE: Conservatives always like to point out that social programs, whether it be welfare or unemployment benefits, can have hidden consequences. The argument goes that if you're paying people who aren't working, then you're giving them a reason not to work and we shouldn't be subsidizing bad behavior. I agree with them! This is absolutely true! Social programs are there to help people based on their needs and have to be structured to make sure that people don't exploit them. Yet the same goes for dealing with a hostile Congress and section of the press. Why reward their bad behavior? It won't lessen it but only encourage it.

McCONNELL: We were prepared to work with the White House on the pressing issue of immigration. Our immigration system was clearly in need of an overhaul.

BOEHNER: And by "the White House" we meant, of course, the next—hopefully Republican—administration.

MICHELLE: The writing was on the wall, and it was written in every language: in English, en español, and everything in between.

BOEHNER: What, like Portuguese?

MICHELLE: Enough was enough. Via executive order, Barack announced that there would be major changes in our deportation policies.

BOEHNER: We warned the president and he did it anyway. It was an unconstitutional power grab that went against the wishes of Congress and the American people.

MICHELLE: It wasn't a power grab at all but a waiving of power. It was exactly like when a police officer stops you for speeding but lets you off without giving you a ticket. Listen, if people have been here for decades, not committing crimes, paying taxes, and being part of their community with their families—were those the people who should be living in fear? Did we want them to be scared to go to school or to call the police? Of course not. If the law dictated that, then clearly something went wrong somewhere along the way. We shouldn't rip apart parents and kids. Our immigration policy should be based on the *conservative* principle of family values.

McCONNELL: I have to say, serving with the president in the Senate and then watching him in the Oval Office—this was a side of him that I'd not seen before. The liberal media always likes to fawn over him and swoon about how he's the coolest guy in the room. Well, that usually applied to his temperament too, from what I'd seen. After 2014, he just seemed to be a bit aggressive and antagonistic.

BOEHNER: It gave me hope that he was turning into a Republican.

MICHELLE: The approach was: What good could Barack do during the last quarter of his presidency? The president had a lot of discretion in his role as head of the executive branch. Where else could we move the country forward? And the answer came back: Cuba.

JOHN KERRY: It wasn't that long ago that the Soviet Union had nuclear missiles in Cuba pointed directly at the United States. It was up to President Kennedy to stare down the USSR and get those nukes taken away—which he did. But what a different world we live in now. President Kennedy is gone, of course. But—despite Putin's machinations in Eastern Europe—so is the Soviet Union. Fidel Castro is eighty-eight years old and handed the presidency to his brother Raul. At eighty-four, the guy's no young man either. The cold war was over, and it was time to start reversing some of those outdated policies.

MICHELLE: Sure, a lot of Cuban Americans in Florida thought this was propping up the regime. But this regime was clearly on its last legs. The idea that Americans should be arrested for going to Cuba didn't really make much sense. Who were they going to be spying for? Boris and Natasha? The funny part was that it was the pope who had been the intermediary that had brokered the deal.

SARAH PALIN: Stop me if you've heard this one before: A Catholic, a Muslim, and a Communist get on the phone together. The Commie says there is no God. The Muslim says there is one God, Allah, and God is great. Then the Catholic says . . . Hold on . . . Wait, was it a Jew? Dang it, it was really funny when I first heard it.

MICHELLE: So Barack ordered a restoration of diplomatic relations with Cuba. Look, if we can talk to North Korea and Iran—albeit secretly—there's no reason we can't talk to Cuba. That's where Gitmo is located, which is so very odd.

MICHELE BACHMANN: A socialist president talking to a communist one. Welcome to Barack Obama's America!

MICHELLE: There were other victories to be had as well. One by one, the Confederate flag started coming down all over the Southern states.

NIKKI HALEY: I am the daughter of immigrants. Our senator Tim Scott is African American. Of course in one sense the Stars and Bars is a symbol of history. But many of those flags came up in light of the civil rights movement, as a gesture of defiance. I am a proud American and a proud Southerner—but why should we have a flag that makes people uncomfortable? Someone posed the question and there really weren't any objections—those people wouldn't be comfortable serving under a female governor of Indian descent anyway. Yeah, why *not* take it down? So we did!

MICHELLE: Amazon, eBay, a bunch of other companies followed suit. Barack said he wanted to be a transformational president—well, this was a big transformation that didn't require passing laws or even any action from Washington. It was people reexamining for themselves what a president meant, what he looked like, and what that said about us.

BIDEN: It was America at its finest.

MICHELLE: Then the Supreme Court tossed us a couple of extra bones.

JOHN ROBERTS: To bring down the entire Affordable Care Act because of some poor legal phrasing seemed to be an enormous overreach of the court's designated role. We are here to uphold the law, and whenever possible defer to Congress and what had been passed. So that's exactly what we did.

RUTH BADER GINSBURG: We also settled the gay marriage debate. Realistically, we couldn't find any reason to deny a couple who were living together and in a committed relationship the legal protections of marriage. This is America. The default is to allow people to do whatever they want—it is the unusual occurrence when an activity is prohibited. We'd had gay marriage in many states by this point, and we simply couldn't find *any* negative consequences, let alone consequences that would make such a legal status socially prohibitive.

MICHELLE: As 2015 progressed, it felt just like 2007 all over. There was Hillary Clinton running for president again. Only this time, instead of opposing her, I was rooting for her. I think she will certainly be the nominee, and I think she will make for a superb president.

HILLARY: I've been waiting for men to get out of my way ever since I've started menopause. It was finally my turn.

MICHELLE: As the 2016 campaign heated up, the president necessarily begins to take a bit of a backseat. It happened with President Bush, and it happened with Barack.

CHENEY: Yeah, they certainly didn't bring up President Bush every chance they got. Never happened, right?

BOEHNER: What would I say was the legacy of the Obama administration? Well, I finally got my dream of becoming Speaker of the House. Thanks, President Obama! I also realized what a pain in the ass that job was. Thanks, Tea Party!

McCONNELL: We have more elected Republican officials than at any point in history, and our party is more conservative than ever. We could not have done that without the president, even if he would have liked it otherwise.

BIDEN: I got a front-row seat to one of the most progressive administrations of my lifetime. Boy, did I feel proud to be a part of this team!

MICHELLE: I will leave it to the historians to determine what the administration did and didn't accomplish, what we could and couldn't have done. Sure, there are moments that I am personally extremely proud of. I think Barack allowed Americans to hope again, after eight years of fear and despair. I think he inspired many young people, who could see concrete proof that even the highest office in the land was within their grasp. I also think the animus and pushback he received was far more intense than either of us had ever suspected or feared—and not only was it *intense,* it was often *effective.* Barack did the best he could with what he had, and that is all that you can expect from any man, whether he is a window washer or the president. At the end of the day, if I had to sum it up, I think Barack was a decent man in an indecent time. It's been real, it's been fun—but it's also been very, very difficult. I know Barack feels the same way.

DONALD TRUMP: Don't worry, everyone. I've got it from here!

HILLARY: Yeah, you're in great hands.

PRESIDENT BARACK OBAMA: Fuck this city, fuck the Republicans, and fuck *all* this shit. I'm going back to Hawaii.

INDEX

Abortion, 258–64, 285–88
Adelson, Sheldon, 232
Affirmative action, 46, 301–2
Affordable Care Act (ACA),
    139–58, 162–65, 170–75
  defunding, 299, 301–2
  Obama's Address to Congress,
    152–57
  Obama signs into law, 172
  Supreme Court reviews,
    237–38, 241–46, 321–22
Afghanistan, 14, 84
AIDS, 41
Akin, Todd, 258–64, 285, 286,
    291, 310
Al Arabiya, 87–88
Alaska, 27, 54, 116, 183
Alexander, Lamar, 103
Algeria, 205
American Express, 51
American Recovery and
    Reinvestment Act of
    2009, 88–89
Anal sex, 8–9
Angle, Sharron, 179–80
Apartheid, 306
Arab Spring, 205–7
Arsenio Hall Show (TV show),
    102
ATF gunwalking scandal, 294–95
Audacity of Hope, The (Obama),
    18–19, 22
Axelrod, David

election of 2008, 25–37, 40,
    43, 44, 45, 50–55, 57–61
  Democratic debates, 28–30
  election night, 61–62
  financial crisis impact,
    58–60
  Iowa caucuses, 33–34
  Obama's "more perfect
    union" speech, 44–46
  Palin as McCain's running
    mate, 54–55, 57–58
  South Carolina primary,
    33–35
  Wright controversy, 41–44
election of 2012, 221–26,
    230–35, 245, 246, 251,
    253, 256–57, 260–71,
    275–91
  debates, 279–86
  Democratic National
    Convention, 270–71
  Hurricane Sandy, 288–90
  Republican National
    Convention, 264–70
  Romney's "47 percent"
    comments, 276–79
  gay marriage, 237–40
  Illinois Senate election of
    Obama, 5–14

Bachmann, Michele
  Cuban policy, 321
  cure for homosexuality, 207, 208

Bachmann, Michele (*cont.*)
  debt ceiling and taxes, 210, 300
  election of 2008, 40–41, 221
  election of 2012, 229, 230,
      260, 263, 296
  flies and mental retardation,
      108
  health care reform, 243, 246,
      299
Bain Capital, 216
Bangladesh, 49
Beck, Glenn, 183
Beer Summit (July 2009),
      119–38
Benghazi attack of 2012, 202,
      272, 274–75, 295, 318
Bennett, Robert, 177
Bentsen, Lloyd, 29
Beyoncé, 79–80
Biden, Jill, 184
Biden, Joseph "Beau," 184–85
Biden, Joseph "Joe"
  Beer Summit (July 2009), 125,
      130, 132–36
  bin Laden killing, 202–6
  bowling, 104
  election of 2008, 27, 33, 38,
      46, 60
    VP selection, 52–54
  election of 2010, 184–85, 186
  election of 2012, 233, 291
    VP debates, 282–84
  first inauguration (2009),
      72–73, 75, 76, 77
  foreign policy, 89, 206
  gay marriage, 239–41
  Giffords shooting, 196–98
  health care reform, 143–44,
      148, 154, 155
  immigration, 317
  legacy of Obama, 323

  Nelson Mandela's memorial,
      305, 308
  presidential appointments,
      113–14
    Hillary as Secretary of State,
        84–87
  rap music, 95
  speaking style of, 133–34
Bin Laden, Osama, 54, 202–6
Birth certificate, 198–201
Blagojevich, Rod, 92–98
Bloomberg, Michael, 217–18, 219,
      288–89
Blue Moon beer, 128–29
Boehner, John, 2, 103, 314
  Bachmann and Republican
      Party, 208
  Benghazi attack of 2012, 202,
      295
  bin Laden killing, 204
  crying of, 69, 195
  debt ceiling and budget, 209,
      210, 213, 299, 300
  election of 2010, 190, 194, 195
  election of 2012, 252, 255, 270,
      293, 295
  Giffords shooting, 196–97
  government shutdown of 2013,
      300, 303–4, 305
  health care reform, 140–41,
      145–49, 152, 153, 171,
      241–42, 301–2
  immigration reform, 317–19
  legacy of Obama, 322–23
  Nobel Prize and Obama, 162
  Operation Fast and Furious,
      294–95
Boston Red Sox, 167, 168
Bouazizi, Mohamed, 205
Bowling, 104
Bradley, Tom, 64–65

"Bradley effect," 65
Braun, Carol Moseley, 5–6, 94
Brotha, 105
Brown, Jerry, 64, 65
Brown, Michael, 311–13
Brown, Scott, 166–70
Brown v. Board of Education, 112
Buckley, William F., 91
Budget sequestration in 2013, 213
Budweiser, 128–29
Burris, Roland, 98–100
Bush, Barbara P., 267
Bush, George H. W., 51, 94, 102
Bush, George W., 291
    approval ratings of, 19
    difference between Barack
        Obama and, 110–11
    dress code at White House, 102
    drinking of, 23
    election of 2000, 10, 49,
        61–62, 67
    election of 2004, 14–15, 19, 51
    Emanuel and, 96, 101
    first inauguration of Obama,
        67–70
    health care, 245
    Iraq war, 14, 83–84, 206
    misstatements of, 105
    Nelson Mandela's memorial,
        307
    Nobel Prize and Obama, 160,
        161
    political change of, 36
    religious right and, 37
    State of the Union speeches,
        153
    tax cuts, 193–94, 209, 277, 303
    terrorism and, 14, 273
Bush, John Ellis "Jeb," 17, 67, 173,
        304
Bush, Laura, 67, 68, 110

Cadillac Records (movie), 79
Cain, Herman, 225–27, 229
California
    gubernatorial election of 1982,
        64–65
    gubernatorial recall election of
        2003, 250
Carter, Jimmy
    election of 1980, 51, 281
    foreign policy, 55
    "malaise" speech, 19
    Nelson Mandela's memorial,
        307
    Nobel Prize, 159–62
Carter, Roslyn, 162
Castle, Michael, 185–88
Castro, Fidel, 320
Cedric the Entertainer, 42–43
Celebrity Apprentice, The (TV
        show), 204
Chao, Elaine, 171
Cheney, Dick, 157, 297
    on Bush, 96
    on Christie, 32
    on Delaware, 197
    on Democrats, 309
    election of 2008, 27, 32, 35, 38,
        39, 40, 54, 61–62
    election of 2012, 216, 257, 270,
        275, 283
    election of 2014, 314
    election of 2016, 322
    first inauguration of Obama,
        67–71
    foreign policy, 206, 207
    gay marriage, 240
    government shutdown of 2013,
        304
    health care, 162–63
    on Hillary Clinton, 202
    humor of, 101, 103, 109

Cheney, Dick (*cont.*)
    Illinois Senate career of
        Obama, 17
    Illinois Senate election of
        Obama, 10, 11
    on JFK, 150
    on LBJ, 195
    on Lewinsky, 27
    Obama's speech at DNC
        (2004), 4
    on Pelosi, 153, 189, 200
    pheasant hunting of, 247
    terrorism, 273
Cheney, Mary, 11–12, 240
Chicago politics, 96–97
Christie, Chris, 32
    election of 2012 and Cain,
        226
    election of 2014, 316–17
    Hurricane Sandy, 288–90
    Republican National
        Convention (2012), 264,
        265
Citizenship conspiracy theories,
    198–201
Civil Rights Act of 1964, 46
Civil unions, 238
Civil War, 34
Cleveland, Grover, 114
Clinton, Bill, 108, 195
    as "America's first black
        president," 69
    on Carter, 161
    election of 1992, 19, 52
    election of 1998, 314
    election of 2008, 34–35, 36,
        52, 77
        Hillary concedes
            nomination, 46–47
        Wright controversy,
            43–44

election of 2012, 217, 219, 228,
    254
    Democratic National
        Convention address,
        270–71
    emails, 301
    gays in the military, 238
    health care reform, 141
    Hillary's Secretary of State
        appointment, 86, 87
    as "man from Hope," 19
    Obama's speech at DNC
        (2004), 1–3, 4
    public relations, 102
    sex and politics, 8–9
Clinton, George, 75–76
Clinton, Hillary
    Benghazi attack, 202, 274–75,
        295, 318
    bin Laden killing, 202–6
    election of 2008, 27–36,
        43–44,
    46–47, 51, 54
        concedes nomination, 46–47
        Democratic debates, 28–30
        Oprah's endorsement,
            22–24
        Wright controversy, 43–44
    election of 2010, 168
    election of 2012, 215–16, 225,
        259, 262, 265, 293–94
    election of 2014, 317
    election of 2016, 322
    first inauguration of Obama,
        72–73, 76–77
    Illinois Senate career of
        Obama, 15–17
    New York Senate career, 16–17,
        18
    Obama's speech at DNC
        (2004), 1–3, 4

Secretary of State, 84–87, 201–7, 273–75, 294
CNBC, 106
Coakley, Martha, 165–70
Colt 45, 126–27
Communism, 10, 55, 206, 263, 320, 321
Cornyn, John, 85
Cosby, Bill, 187
Couric, Katie, 56–57
Crist, Charlie, 172–75, 316
Crowley, James, 120–27, 128–38
Cruise, Tom, 87
Cruz, Ted, 116, 303
Cuba, 320–21

Daily Show, The (TV show), 21, 101
Daley, Richard, 191
Daschle, Tom, 15
Davis, Gray, 250
Death panels, 164
Death penalty, 212
Debt ceiling, 208–13, 300–301, 304–5
Delaware, 53, 132–35, 148, 197
election of 2010, 184–88, 190
Democratic National Convention (2004), 1–4
Democratic National Convention (2012), 270–71
Ditka, Mike, 9, 20
D.L. Hughley Breaks the News (TV show), 63–64
Dodd, Chris, 26, 33
Dole, Elizabeth, 103
Domestic policy, 89–94, 193–96, 318–20. See also Health care
debt ceiling, 208–13, 300–301, 304–5
Domino theory, 206

Drake, 22
Dreams from My Father (Obama), 18
Drudge, Matt, 76–77
Dukakis, Kitty, 29–30
Dukakis, Michael, 25, 29–30
Dukes of Hazzard (TV show), 42
Durbin, Richard, 98

Eastwood, Clint, 267–69
Ebola, 313–14
Ebonics, 16
Edwards, John, 73, 108, 190
election of 2004, 51
election of 2008, 27–30, 32, 33–34
Obama's speech at DNC (2004), 3, 4
sex and politics, 8–9
Egypt, 88, 205, 206–7
Eisenhower, Dwight D., 19
EKIA (Enemy Killed in Action), 203
Election of 1980, 51, 220, 277, 281
Election of 1984, 2, 35, 98, 277
Election of 1988, 2, 29–30
Election of 1992, 19, 52
Election of 1994, 142, 224–25
Election of 1996, 295
Election of 2000, 10, 49, 61–62, 67
Election of 2004, 14–16, 19, 51, 157
Illinois Senate and Obama, 5–14
Obama's DNC speech, 1–4
Election of 2006, 165, 168
Election of 2008, 25–62
Biden as Obama's running mate, 52–54

Election of 2008 (*cont.*)
  Democratic debates, 28–30
  election night, 61–62
  financial crisis of 2007, 58–60
  Hillary concedes nomination,
    46–47
  Iowa caucuses, 32–33
  Nevada primary, 33
  New Hampshire primary, 33
  Obama becomes the nominee,
    25–47
  Obama's "more perfect union"
    speech, 44–46
  Oprah's endorsement of
    Obama, 22–24, 31
  Palin as McCain's running
    mate, 54–58
  South Carolina primary, 33–35
  Wright controversy, 41–44
Election of 2010, 177–92, 193, 221
  Florida and Crist, 172–75
  Massachusetts Senate, 165–70
Election of 2012, 215–91
  Democratic National
    Convention, 270–71
  electoral college results, 290–91
  Hurricane Sandy, 288–90
  Indiana Senate, 285–88
  Iowa caucuses, 226–30
  Missouri and Akin, 258–64
  Missouri and McCaskill,
    253–56
  New Hampshire primary,
    230–31
  presidential debates, 279–82,
    284–85
  Republican candidates, 222–27
  Republican National
    Convention, 264–70
  Romney's "47 percent"
    comment, 276–79

  Ryan as running mate, 256–57
  South Carolina primary, 231, 233
  VP debates, 282–84
Election of 2014, 313–18
Email, 301, 307
Emancipation Proclamation, 4
Emanuel, Rahm
  Beer Summit (July 2009),
    125–29
  Bush's presidency, 67, 83–84
  domestic policy, 89–90
  election of 2010, 165, 166,
    168, 169, 173, 174, 175,
    177–91
  foreign policy, 87–90
  health care reform, 140–44,
    146–49, 152–55, 171–72
  Illinois Senate appointment of
    2008, 92–94, 97–98, 99
  media relations, 87–88, 101–10
  Nobel Prize, 159–62
  Obama's speech at DNC
    (2004), 4
  presidential appointments and
    nominations, 111–12,
    114, 116, 117, 181–82
    Hillary as Secretary of State,
    84–87
  resignation of, 190–92
Erpenbach, Jon, 248–50
Executive orders, 319

Failla, Jimmy, 43
Fame, Herb, 302
Fannie Mae, 59
Faubus, Orval, 1
Ferguson, Missouri, shooting,
    311–13
Fey, Tina, 57–58
Filibusters, 91–92, 170
Financial crisis of 2007, 58–60

First Amendment, 170
First inauguration of Obama, 63–81
   inaugural balls, 74–80
   presidential oath of office, 71–72
Fitzgerald, Peter, 5, 6–7
Florida, 172–75, 316, 320
France, 87
Francis I, Pope, 98, 320
Frank, Barney, 238
Franken, Al, 92
Freddie Mac, 59
Fuck/Marry/Kill, 154

Gaffes, 50
Gates, Henry Louis, Jr., 119–27, 129–38
Gay marriage, 11, 12, 237–41, 241, 322
Gays in the military, 195, 238
Georgia, 134, 197
Gibson, Mel, 37
Giffords, Gabby, 196–98
Gingrich, Newt, 19
   election of 1994, 224–25
   election of 2008, 38, 45
   election of 2010, 221
   election of 2012, 224–25, 228, 231, 232–33
   Speaker of the House, 210
   traditional marriage, 239
Ginsburg, Ruth Bader, 111–13, 243, 244, 290, 322
Giuliani, Rudy, 146, 167, 311, 313
Godfather's Pizza, 225
Goldberg, Whoopi, 102
Gore, Al, 18
Gore, Tipper, 36, 78
Government shutdown of 2013, 302–6

Graham, Stedman, 20
Gravel, Mike, 27, 33
Grayson, Trey, 180
Grimes, Alison Lundergan, 315
Gun control, 196–97

Hager, Jenna Bush, 267
Hagman, Larry, 244
Haiti, 22
Haley, Nikki, 321
Hard Choices (Clinton), 23, 202
"Harry and Louise" (TV ad), 141
Harvard University, 122, 123–24
Harwood, John, 106–8
Hatcher, Richard, 99
Healey, Kerry, 26
Health care, 139–58, 162–65, 170–75
   defunding, 299, 301–2
   Obama's Address to Congress, 152–57
   Obama signs into law, 172
   Supreme Court reviews, 237–38, 241–46, 321–22
Heckling, 154
Hemings, Sally, 46
Hill, Anita, 178
Holder, Eric
   Ferguson, Missouri, shooting, 311–13
   health care reform, 241, 242, 243, 245
   Operation Fast and Furious, 294–95
   Supreme Court, 111, 112, 116–17
   Trayvon Martin shooting, 232, 296–99, 312
Homosexuality, 11, 12, 182, 207–8, 237–40, 241. See also Gay marriage

Hughley, D. L., 63–65, 66, 68, 70–74, 76
Huntsman, Jon, 223–24, 224, 230, 231
Hurricane Katrina, 289–90
Hussein, Saddam, 12–13

Illinois
    Senate appointment of 2008, 92–100
    Senate career of Obama, 15–24
    Senate election of 2004 and Obama, 5–14
Immigration, 317–19
Income taxes, 224, 226, 277
Indiana, 252–53, 285–88
Indigo Girls, 182
Individual mandate, 241–46
Inequality, 219, 278
Invitation to the White House, An (Clinton), 23
Iowa, 32–33, 226–30
Iraq war, 14, 29, 83–84, 87, 206, 207
Israel, 41, 84, 87, 88

Jackson, Jesse
    election of 1984, 2, 35, 98
    election of 2008, 37, 39–40
    Illinois Senate appointment of 2008, 94–99
Jackson, Jesse, Jr., 94–96, 98–99, 100, 160
Jackson, Michael, 97
James, Etta, 79
Jantjie, Thamsanqa, 308–10
Jarrett, Valerie, 74–80, 156
Jay Z, 80
Jefferson, Thomas, 46
Johnson, Lyndon B., 46, 195
Johnson, Nancy, 165

Kagan, Elena, 181–82
Karate Kid, The (movie), 108
Kasich, John, 189
Kennedy, Caroline, 35–36
Kennedy, Edward "Ted," 149–50, 165
Kennedy, John F., 19, 29, 35–36, 106, 150
Kentucky, 180, 315
Kenya, 10, 13, 50, 108
Kerry, John
    Cuba and Soviet Union, 320
    election of 2004, 14–15, 51, 157
        Obama's speech at DNC, 3, 4
Keyes, Alan, 9–13, 22, 76, 99, 180
Keynesian economics, 224–25
King, Gayle, 20–21, 51
King, Larry, 19–20
King, Martin Luther, Jr., 1, 63, 76
Kohl, Herb, 167–68
Kucinich, Dennis, 26, 29, 33, 68, 101
Kutcher, Ashton, 124

LaFollette, Robert, 247
Landrieu, Mary, 163
League of Nations, 247
Leno, Jay, 102–3
Letterman, David, 59–60, 102–5
Lewinsky, Monica, 27
Libya, 207. See also Benghazi attack of 2012
Lieberman, Joe, 53–54, 142–43
Limbaugh, Rush, 10, 202
Living History (Clinton), 18
Lodge, Henry Cabot, 247
Los Angeles riots of 1992, 312

Love, Reggie, 192, 193–94, 196,
      197, 199, 200, 207–8,
      209, 215
Lowden, Susan, 179
Lugar, Richard, 252–53

Ma, Yo-Yo, 123
McCain, Cindy, 47, 51, 128
McCain, John, 85, 155, 262
   election of 2000, 49
   election of 2008, 46–62, 146,
      173
      election night, 61–62
      financial crisis of 2007,
         58–60
      Palin as running mate, 54–58
   gay marriage, 239
   gays in the military ban, 195
   Obama's apology tour, 88–89
McCall, Carl, 85–86
McCarthy, Joe, 247
McCaskill, Claire, 253–56, 260,
      261, 263–64
McConnell, Mitch, 85
   Chicago politics, 96–97, 99
   debt ceiling, 211–13
   domestic policy, 90, 299, 300
   election of 2010, 177–78, 180,
      183, 184, 190
   election of 2012, 252, 253, 254,
      261, 270, 283, 293
   election of 2014, 313–16
   foreign policy, 207, 295
   gay marriage, 239
   government shutdown of 2013,
      303
   health care reform, 139, 140,
      146, 150, 163–64,
      169–72, 242
   immigration, 318, 319
   legacy of Obama, 323

Obama's speech at DNC
      (2004), 4
   Sotomayor nomination, 115,
      117
Makle, Wanda, 302
"Mambo No. 5" (song), 76–77
Mandela, Nelson, 305–9
Marshall, Thurgood, 94
Martin, Trayvon, 231–32,
      296–99, 312
Massachusetts, 25, 316
   Romney's health care, 146, 147,
      149, 151
   Senate election of 2010, 165–70
Medicaid, 163
Medicare, 147, 242–43
Meet the Press (TV show), 239
Mexicans, 16, 21–22, 201, 294
Michigan, 189
Middle East, 84, 205–7
Midterm election of 2010. See
      Election of 2010
Midterm election of 2014. See
      Election of 2014
Miller, Joe, 183
Million Man March, 70
Milwaukee Bucks, 167–68
Missouri, election of 2012,
      253–56, 258–64
"More Perfect Union, A" (speech),
      44–46
Mormonism, 16, 227
Moses, 10
Mourdock, Richard, 252–53,
      285–88, 291
Mubarak, Hosni, 88, 206–7
Murkowski, Lisa, 183

Nebraska, and ACA, 163
Nelson, Ben, 163
Nevada, 33, 178–80

New Deal, 139
New Hampshire, 33, 230–31
New Mexico, 189
New York Senate career of Hillary
    Clinton, 16–17, 18
Nigger, 1, 4
9/11 terrorist attacks, 13–14, 157,
    274
Nixon, Richard, 19, 46, 249,
    250
Nobel Peace Prize, 159–62
Nosuchinsky, Kevin, 119–20
NSA (National Security Agency),
    91
Nutty Professor, The (movie), 131

Oath of office of the President of
    the United States, 71–72
Obama, Barack Hussein, Sr., 13
Obama, Malia, 3
Obama, Michelle
    Beer Summit (July 2009),
        125–29
    birther conspiracy, 198–201
    Bush and Iraq war, 14, 83–84,
        206
    difference between George W.
        and Barack, 110–11
    domestic policy, 89–94,
        193–96, 209, 210, 213,
        299, 300, 318–20
    election of 2008, 25–37,
        39–45, 47, 50–53, 55,
        58–62
        Democratic debates, 28–30
        election night, 61–62
        financial crisis of 2007,
            59–60
        Iowa caucuses, 32–33
        Obama's "more perfect
            union" speech, 44–46

Oprah's endorsement,
    22–24
South Carolina primary,
    33–35
Wright controversy, 41–44
election of 2010, 173, 174, 177,
    178, 180–84, 187–91
election of 2012, 215–23, 230,
    232–35, 246–47, 250,
    251, 254–91, 293–94
    debates, 279–82, 284–85
    Democratic National
        Convention, 270–71
    Hurricane Sandy, 288–90
    Missouri and Akin, 258–64
    Missouri and McCaskill,
        254–56
    Republican candidates,
        222–23, 225, 226
    Republican National
        Convention, 264–70
    Romney's "47 percent"
        comments, 276–79
    Wisconsin gubernatorial
        recall, 247, 248, 250, 251
election of 2014, 313–18
election of 2016, 322
Emanuel's resignation, 191–92
Ferguson, Missouri, shooting,
    311, 312
first inauguration of Obama,
    66–70, 72–75, 80–81
    inaugural balls, 74–80
    presidential oath of office,
        71–72
foreign policy, 87–90, 202,
    204–5, 207, 273, 320–21
gay marriage, 238–39, 240
Giffords shooting, 196–97
government shutdown of 2013,
    302–6

health care reform, 139–54,
156–58, 163–64, 172,
237, 241, 242–45, 301–2,
321–22
Illinois Senate appointment of
2008, 92–93, 96, 97
Illinois Senate career of
Obama, 15–19, 22–24
Illinois Senate election of
Obama, 5–13
legacy of Obama, 323
media relations, 88, 101–10,
198
Nelson Mandela's memorial,
306–10
Nobel Prize, 159–62
Obama's speech at DNC
(2004), 3
Operation Wall Street, 217,
218–19
presidential appointments and
nominations, 83–87
Hillary as Secretary of State,
84–87
Kagan to Supreme Court,
181–82
Sotomayor to Supreme
Court, 113, 114–17
Trayvon Martin shooting,
231–32, 296–99
Obama, Sasha, 3
Obamacare. *See* Health care
Obama Phone, 216
O'Donnell, Christine, 185–88,
195, 263
Office, The (TV show), 133
Ohio, 189
Olde English 800, 126
Operation Fast and Furious,
294–95
Operation Wall Street, 217–19

Oprah Winfrey Show, 21, 22

Palin, Sarah, 320
death panels, 164
election of 2008, 54–58, 60
election of 2010, 183–84
election of 2012, 220, 257, 258
Kenyan flies, 107, 108
on RINOs, 146
Sanders and socialism, 144
special needs child, 104
Paterson, David, 25–26
Patrick, Deval, 25–26, 149, 151
Paul, Rand, 91, 180
Paul, Ron, 199–200, 224, 231,
233
Pawlenty, Tim, 222
Pelosi, Nancy
Bush and Iraq war, 14
debt ceiling, 208, 209, 210
domestic policy, 90
election of 2012, 270, 293
election of 2014, 316
financial crisis of 2007, 59
first inauguration of Obama,
72
government shutdown of 2013,
304–5
health care reform, 139, 141–
43, 145–46, 147, 152–58,
164, 170, 171
as Speaker of the House, 195,
199
Pennsylvania, 177–78, 189, 233
Perot, Ross, 19–20
Perry, Rick, 224, 228–29, 231,
235
PETA (People for the Ethical
Treatment of Animals),
108–9
Pinchback, P. B. S., 25

Plouffe, David, 25
Political donations, 28
Political endorsements, 7
    Oprah's endorsement of
        Obama, 22–24, 31
Political vision, 18
Politicians, types of, 17–18
Powell, Colin, 124
Procter & Gamble, 42
Putin, Vladimir, 86, 320

Quayle, Dan, 29, 92

Racism, 1–2, 64–65, 231–32,
    296, 299
    Obama's "more perfect union"
        speech, 44–46
Rap music, 95
Raven-Symoné, 66
Reagan, Nancy, 66, 110, 161, 266
Reagan, Ronald, 10, 19, 37, 51,
    66, 266, 277, 281
Reagan Democrats, 286–87
Red Stripe, 128–29
Reid, Harry
    debt ceiling, 209–13, 300
    domestic policy, 90–92, 99,
        100, 300
    election of 2004, 15
    election of 2010, 178–80,
        185–87, 189
    election of 2012, 251–53,
        255–59, 285, 291
    election of 2014, 315–16
    financial crisis of 2007, 59
    government shutdown of 2013,
        303–4, 305
    health care reform, 139–45,
        150–51, 157–58, 162,
        163–65, 170, 171, 241,
        242, 243

Illinois Senate career of
    Obama, 16–19
Nelson Mandela's memorial, 306
Nobel Prize and Obama, 162
Religious right, 37–38
"Republican effect," 65
Republican National Committee,
    63
Republican National Convention
    (2012), 264–70
Rhode Island, 148
Rice, Susan, 275
Richardson, Bill, 21–22, 27, 33
RINO (Republican In Name
    Only), 146–47
Risky Business (movie), 87
Roberts, John, 112, 237, 244,
    246, 322
    presidential oath of office,
        71–72
Roe v. Wade, 112
Romney, Ann, 265–66
Romney, Mitt, 38, 187
    election of 2012, 146, 216–20,
        232–35, 237, 246–47,
        260, 261, 262, 270,
        275–91
    debates, 280–81, 282,
        284–85
    "47 percent" comments,
        276–79
    Iowa cauces, 226–30
    New Hampshire, 230–31
    Republican National
        Convention, 264–70
    Ryan as running mate,
        256–57
    South Carolina, 231
    health care reform, 150, 151
    Massachusetts Senate election
        of 2010, 165–66

Roosevelt, Eleanor, 148
Roosevelt, Franklin D., 148
Roosevelt, Theodore, 19–20, 159
Rove, Karl, 32, 49, 65
Rubio, Marco, 174, 253
Russia, 86, 320
Ryan, Jack, 7–8, 9
Ryan, Jeri, 7–8
Ryan, Paul, 18
    debt ceiling, 212
    election of 2012, 256–57, 268,
        281
        VP debates, 282–84

Sanders, Bernie, 143–44
Santorum, Rick, 64, 147, 188
    election of 2012, 220, 224,
        227–31, 233–34
Saturday Night Live (TV show),
    57–58, 101
Scalia, Antonin, 112–13
Schilling, Curt, 167, 169
Schultz, Debbie Wasserman,
    92–93
Schwarzenegger, Arnold, 250, 280
Scott, Rick, 316
Scott, Tim, 321
Sears Tower, 14
Secret Service, 66, 67, 80, 81
Segregation, 1–2, 34
Senate supermajority (2009),
    90–100
Sestak, Joe, 178
Sex and politics, 7–9
Shakespeare, William, 10
Sharpton, Al, 124, 302
    election of 2008, 37–39, 45
        Wright controversy, 41–42
    election of 2012, 227, 286
Shays, Chris, 165
Sign language, 308–10

Slavery, 34, 46
Snapple bottle, 41
Snowe, Olympia, 162, 163, 253
Socialism, 143–44
Social Security, 179
Sotomayor, Sonia, 114–17,
    243–44
Souter, David, 113, 116
South Africa, 305–9
South Carolina, 33–35, 49, 231,
    233
Special Olympics, 104–5
Specter, Arlen, 177–78
Spitzer, Eliot, 25
Stand Your Ground law, 297–98
Stare decisis, 112
Steele, Michael, 63, 73
Stewart, Jon, 21, 63
Supreme Court, 111–17, 181–82
    health care cases, 237–38,
        241–46, 321–22

Taxes, 193–94, 209, 277, 303
Tea Party, 180, 183, 186, 187–88,
    199, 207–8, 209, 221, 229,
    230, 295
Terrorism, 13–14, 84, 273–74
    bin Laden killing, 202–6
Thomas, Clarence, 38, 71, 91, 94,
    117, 146, 177–78, 251
Threesomes, 8–9
Thurmond, Strom, 154
Tide, 42
Truman, Harry, 67–68, 97
Trump, Donald, 49, 185, 204,
    323
    birther conspiracy, 198–201
Tunisia, 205, 206

Vaccination, 41
Vilsack, Tom, 26

Walker, Scott, 247–51
Wall Street, 26, 216–19
Whalen, Lucia, 120–22
White Chicks (movie), 180
White House flies, 106–9
Wilder, Douglas, 26
Wilson, Joe, 154–57, 218
Wilson, Woodrow, 159, 246–47
Winfrey, Oprah, 20–22, 307

endorsement of Obama (2006),
    22–24, 31
Wisconsin gubernatorial recall
    election of 2012, 246–51
Wright, Jeremiah, 37, 41–44, 286

Zimmerman, George, 231–32,
    296–99, 312
Zuccotti Park (New York), 217, 218